"'Paul doesn't care about the marginalized' is a comment rarely on the lips of older church-goers but commonly voiced by younger Christians, even ministers. Works acknowledges but refutes that claim by demonstrating Paul's deep and abiding concern for 'the least of these.' She allows Paul to live in his world, while demonstrating how Paul set in motion principles that would (and still continue to) change the world."

— E. Randolph Richards
author of *Paul Behaving Badly*

"In *The Least of These* Carla Swafford Works offers a clear and robust apologia for the work and writings of Paul. She never lets Paul off the hook. Instead, this book is a wonderful example of charitable reading, extending to Paul both historical understanding and contextual breadth. If you are one of those who loves Jesus but hates Paul, read this book. It will change your outlook."

— Stephen Fowl
Loyola College of Arts & Sciences

The Least of These

Paul and the Marginalized

Carla Swafford Works

WILLIAM B. EERDMANS PUBLISHING COMPANY
GRAND RAPIDS, MICHIGAN

Wm. B. Eerdmans Publishing Co.
4035 Park East Court SE, Grand Rapids, Michigan 49546
www.eerdmans.com

© 2020 Carla Swafford Works
All rights reserved
Published 2020

ISBN 978-0-8028-7446-7

Library of Congress Cataloging-in-Publication Data

Names: Works, Carla Swafford, 1976- author.
Title: The least of these : Paul and the marginalized / Carla Swafford Works.
Description: Grand Rapids : Wm. B. Eerdmans Publishing Co, 2019. |
  Includes bibliographical references and index. | Summary: "The concern expressed for the poor, the oppressed, and the marginalized in the letters of Paul shows that his ideas about ministry and service have been profoundly marked by the self-sacrificial love and humility of Jesus"— Provided by publisher.
Identifiers: LCCN 2019026124 | ISBN 9780802874467 (paperback)
Subjects: LCSH: Bible. Epistles of Paul—Theology. | Marginality, Social—Biblical teaching.
Classification: LCC BS2652 .W67 2019 | DDC 227/.06—dc23
LC record available at https://lccn.loc.gov/2019026124

Unless otherwise noted, Scripture quotations are from New Revised Standard Version Bible, copyright © 1989 National Council of the Churches of Christ in the United States of America. Used by permission. All rights reserved worldwide. http://nrsvbibles.org/

Dedicated to my husband, Nick,
   to our children, Jonathan and Kate.

And to my students who journeyed with me into the world of the text.
   May we all be forever changed by our encounter with the Living Word.

Contents

Foreword by Todd D. Still	xi
Acknowledgments	xiii
Abbreviations	xv
Introduction	1

1. Paul and Poverty — 12

The Poor in the Roman World	12
A Study of the Pauline Congregations	16
Roll Call	19
Conclusions about the Economic Status of Paul's Churches	26
Remembering the Poor and Bearing One Another's Burdens	26
The Collection	27
Remembering the Poor	28
Conclusion	32

2. Paul and Slavery — 34

Slavery in the Roman World	35
Paul and Slavery	40
Philemon	41
1 Corinthians 7:20–24	44
Conclusion	48

CONTENTS

3. Women and the Pauline Mission — 52
- Paul and the Pretense of "Biblical Womanhood" — 53
- 1 Corinthians 11:2–16: Head-Covering and Human Dignity — 55
- Silence and Submission in the Church? — 63
    - 1 Corinthians 14:34–35: A Silencing Text or a Text That Is Silent? — 65
    - 1 Timothy 2: The Real Housewives of Ephesus — 69
- Submission to the Hubs? The Role of Women in the Family — 74
    - 1 Corinthians 7: Bad Housekeeping — 75
    - Ephesians 5: Submission and Sacrificial Love — 78
- Women and the Eschatological Community — 83

4. The Galatian Heirs — 87
- Galatians, Gauls, and Celts: Oh My! — 88
- Three's a Crowd: Paul, the Galatians, and the Teachers — 92
- Descendants of Abraham, Children of God — 94
- The Power of the Promises — 96
    - The Absence of "Land" in Paul's Language — 97
    - Revisiting Land — 99
    - Back to the Future — 101
- Conclusion — 106

5. The Church as the Least of These? — 108
- The Imagery of Infancy in the Writings of Paul's Contemporaries — 111
- Evidence from Daily Life — 115
- Revisiting "Babes in Christ" in 1 Corinthians 3 — 119
- A Multifaceted Metaphor — 123
- The Church as the Least of These? — 124

6. Paul as the Least of These? — 128
- Paul the Persecutor — 130
- Paul's Apostolic Role: A Slave to All? — 134

Slave to All? 1 Corinthians 9:19–23	134
Paul in Chains	147
Conclusion	151

7. Good News for the Least of These — 153

What Is Paul's Gospel?	155
Paul's Revelation and the Urgency of His Mission	161
New Creation and the Witness of the Church	163
What Is at Stake? A Lesson from First Church Corinth	165
Conclusion	172
Bibliography	175
Index of Authors	189
Index of Subjects	191
Index of Citations from Scripture and Other Ancient Sources	197

Foreword

The author of this volume, my friend and fellow *Neutestamentler* Dr. Carla Swafford Works, and I share a good deal in common. Two things merit mention here with special respect to Pauline interpretation. First of all, we both came to the academic study of Paul from an ecclesial context that was by and large appreciative of the apostle, holding him and his (thirteen) letters in high esteem, at times arguably too much so. Thus, far from seeing Paul as a problem to overcome, much less an opponent to conquer, we were taught to perceive Paul as a positive, albeit imperfect, force for God and the good. Additionally, like Carla, I was initially surprised, even as I am continually perplexed, by the decidedly, if not altogether, negative view that many within the church and the academy have of the apostle to the gentiles.[1]

Although few of Paul's critics are as acerbic or overstated as Irish playwright George Bernard Shaw is in the preface to his play *Androcles and the Lion* ("[Paul] does nothing that Jesus would have done, and says nothing that Jesus would have said"), disparagement of Paul remains in vogue for any number of reasons, some of which (as Carla notes) are understandable. "He was prideful," some say, and "patriarchal," others add. Additionally, it is frequently maintained that his views on human sexuality and slavery are hopelessly and dangerously out of touch and simply on the wrong side of history. Then, other critics contend that he perverted Judaism on the one hand and distorted Jesus on the other. Such ridicule and blame are rather a lot for a single individual to bear. Trenchant, relentless, unqualified,

---

1. See further Patrick Gray, *Paul as a Problem in History and Culture: The Apostle and his Critics through the Centuries* (Grand Rapids: Baker Academic, 2016).

wholesale criticism directed at Paul, however, is often not even-handed, fair-minded, or on target.

In her work, Dr. Works does not advocate placing the apostle on a pedestal any more than she suggests simply pillorying Paul. Rather, in *The Least of These: Paul and the Marginalized* she offers a fresh reading of portions of Paul's letters and a reassessment of aspects of his thought. Works accomplishes this necessary and arguably overdue task by demonstrating that the apostle, not unlike his Lord, thought about and cared for vulnerable people. Not only were the oppressed and powerless present in Pauline assemblies and addressed by the apostle in his letters (see chapters 1–3), but also vital elements of Paul's theology, including his ecclesiology and christology, as well as his very conception of ministry, were shaped and animated by selfless, sacrificial service (see chapters 4–7).

The upshot of this clear, courageous, and important book that was fashioned on the anvil of careful research and thoughtful teaching is this: Works graciously challenges both those who think less and those who think more of Paul to reexamine the apostle's life, work, and thought, not least with respect to the least. In so doing, she is able to reconnect further the "last" and the "least" of the apostles (note 1 Corinthians 15:8–9) with Jesus, who insisted in precept and exhibited in practice that the greatest is the one who serves (see esp. Mark 10:41–45).

Todd D. Still
DeLancey Dean and Hinson Professor
Baylor University, Truett Seminary
Waco, Texas

Acknowledgments

When I began my full-time teaching career and naively stood before my large class of over eighty students, I nearly fell through the chasm between Jesus and Paul. Having grown up in a tradition that revered the apostle, I was now faced with the task of inspiring my seminarians to read Paul's letters and to give the apostle a chance. The vast majority of the faces staring back at me had been deeply wounded by interpretations of Pauline texts, as had I. What the church has done in the name of Paul has not always been loving or kind. This book grew out of that classroom. I am indebted to all my students at Wesley Theological Seminary. You have challenged me to be a better teacher and reader and, in the process, a more humble disciple.

I am also deeply indebted to Wesley Theological Seminary, which has granted me sabbatical and resources to further my study. Wesley has been my home for the last decade, and I have been blessed by the encouragement of my colleagues, particularly by Bruce Birch, my former dean and my dear friend. The Wabash Center has also invested resources in the development of parts of this project, and I am grateful. Chapters of this book have been discussed in sections of the Society of Biblical Literature and at the Oxford Institute for Methodist Theological Studies. Those conversations have, I hope, sharpened the work.

Many people have played a particular role in this project. Special thanks are due to Beverly Roberts Gaventa, who has faithfully served as a mentor and who continues to invest in my calling. I am grateful for my editors, James Ernest and Trevor Thompson, and for all those at Eerdmans who have been generous with their talents and resources.

Finally, God has blessed me with friends and family who have encouraged me on this journey. Laura Sweat Holmes has been a valued conversation and writing partner for many years. My parents, siblings, and

ACKNOWLEDGMENTS

in-laws have supported my work by spoiling my children while I attended conferences or traveled for study, and I am indebted to their love, care, and support. My children, Jonathan and Kate, have been constant blessings, and I am grateful to God for them. My husband Nick has been my faithful companion on this entire journey. He read countless drafts, offered critical advice, and rescued me with encouragement. Without his companionship, I would have never fulfilled my calling. I thank God always for him and for our children.

The Feast of Saint Paul of the Cross 2018

Abbreviations

AYB	Anchor Yale Bible
BECNT	Baker Exegetical Commentary on the New Testament
BTB	*Biblical Theology Bulletin*
BTZ	*Berliner Theologische Zeitschrift*
BZNW	*Beihefte zur Zeitschrift für die neutestamentliche Wissenschaft*
HTR	*Harvard Theological Review*
HUT	Hermeneutische Untersuchungen zur Theologie
IBC	Interpretation: A Bible Commentary for Teaching and Preaching
ICC	International Critical Commentary
Int	*Interpretation*
JBL	*Journal of Biblical Literature*
JETS	*Journal of the Evangelical Theological Society*
JR	*Journal of Religion*
JRS	*Journal of Roman Studies*
JSNT	*Journal for the Study of the New Testament*
JSNTSup	Journal for the Study of the New Testament Supplement Series
NIGTC	New International Greek Testament Commentary
NIV	New International Version
NRSV	New Revised Standard Version
NTL	New Testament Library
NovTSup	Supplements to Novum Testamentum
NTS	*New Testament Studies*
NTTS	New Testament Tools and Studies
SANT	Studien zum Alten und Neuen Testament

ABBREVIATIONS

SBLDS	Society of Biblical Literature Dissertation Series
SP	Sacra Pagina
TynBul	Tyndale Bulletin
WBC	Word Biblical Commentary
WUNT	Wissenschaftliche Untersuchungen zum Neuen Testament

Introduction

The apostle Paul does not have a reputation for caring about "the least of these." Most books on Pauline theology focus on the categories of systematic theology with sections on ecclesiology, soteriology, pneumatology, Christology, and eschatology at a minimum. Apart from passing references to the collection for the Jerusalem church, few books on Paul's theology or ethics have any interest in the apostle's concern for the poor, the marginalized, the subjugated, the forgotten, in short, the "least of these."[1]

There is good reason for this. Jesus's teaching is, after all, where we find this concern explicitly stated. In Matt 25, Jesus challenged all would-be disciples to care for the "least"—the hungry, the thirsty, the stranger, the naked, the sick, the imprisoned. The parable itself is not trying to provide exhaustive definitions for the "least" inasmuch as it challenges the disciples to see the "least," for these are the very ones to whom Jesus announces words of blessing (e.g., Matt 5:3–11; 11:2–6; Luke 4:17–21; 6:20–23; 7:18–23). Jesus describes his own mission as preaching "good news to the poor" (Matt 11:5; Luke 4:18–19). The kingdom of heaven is surely good news for the ones upon whom the current empire has trampled, abused, and exploited in its desperate attempts to secure power and to maintain privilege.

---

1. See David Downs's study on the collection and the importance the collection has in Paul's mission and ministry (*The Offering of the Gentiles: Paul's Collection for Jerusalem in Its Chronological, Cultural, and Cultic Contexts*, WUNT 2.248 [Tübingen: Mohr Siebeck, 2008]). In reframing thinking about Paul's concern for poverty, Bruce W. Longenecker's book has made important strides in reclaiming poverty as a critical topic in the study of Paul's letters (*Remember the Poor: Paul, Poverty, and the Greco-Roman World* [Grand Rapids: Eerdmans, 2010]).

INTRODUCTION

It is this portrait of Jesus—the defender of the weak, the champion of the underprivileged, the hero of justice—that so often comes to mind in interpretations of Matt 25:40: "Truly I tell you, just as you did it to one of the least of these my brothers and sisters, you did it to me." Who are "the least of these"? Who are the recipients of cold water or hospitality? Who are the sick or imprisoned? Jesus calls the least *adelphoi*, literally "brothers," though the translation "brothers and sisters" captures its more inclusive use. Debate swirls around Jesus's definition of *adelphoi* here. Does Jesus limit hospitality and acts of mercy only to those who are disciples or those who are in the church? Exactly who are Jesus's brothers and sisters? A parallel word structure appears in Matt 10:42: "And whoever gives to one of the little ones even a drink of cold water in the name of a disciple, truly I say to you, will not lose his reward." There, the previous context includes welcoming Jesus (10:40), a prophet (10:41), and a righteous person (10:41). This parallel has led many to argue that in Matt 25 Jesus intends the acts of mercy to be directed toward believers, or as Donald Hagner puts it, the "Christian treatment of Christians."[2] Regardless of whether the author of Matthew intends to limit the "least" to the disciples or believers, it is clear that in Matthew the mission of the church must be carried outward to all nations (Matt 28:19-20). Thus, even those who are inclined to read Matt 25:31-46 primarily as Christian service to other Christians conclude by extrapolation that nonbelievers could be recipients of mercy.[3] The Gospels present Jesus's ministry as a demonstration of love for *all*—not just those who are considered insiders, who are deemed clean, or who are part of the chosen people. Even if Matt 25:31-46 were removed from the Gospel of Matthew—the only gospel to record this teaching—we would still have multiple portraits of a Jesus who cares for the downtrodden, who heals the sick, who welcomes the stranger, and who feeds the hungry.

Unfortunately, our portraits of Paul tend to look nothing like this Jesus. The missionary is often given credit for spreading the good news and caring about "lost souls," but he is not often viewed as a missionary who cared about the "least." This radical disconnect cannot be blamed on any one factor. Rather, there are multiple interrelated contributors to the perceived gulf between Jesus and Paul. Perhaps chief among them is an unintended consequence of Paul's prime place in Protestant theology. Paul became the champion of particular doctrines—like the doctrine of

---

2. Donald A. Hagner, *Matthew 14-28*, WBC 33A (Word: Dallas, 1995), 745.
3. See Hagner, *Matthew 14-28*, 745.

justification by faith alone. Some even pit this Paul against James, the proponent of works who, like Jesus, cared about the widow and the orphan (Jas 1:27). In efforts to protect Paul from a works-based righteousness, however, sometimes the baby has been thrown out with the bathwater. All acts of loving-kindness, all concern for the poor, all works for "the least" have been sacrificed to protect justification by faith alone, as though faith is only a matter of mental assent with no outward manifestations of action. No doubt, this perceived dichotomy between Paul and James has played a role in creating portraits of Paul that care little for the poor, the stranger, the widow—the "least."

Paul's calloused reputation toward the poor also largely stems from Protestant scholarship that has helped to create a divide between Jesus, teacher of simple truths, and Paul, the defender of doctrine. This line of thinking is best exhibited in the work of William Wrede, whose writings over a hundred years ago have cast long shadows over scholarship connecting Jesus and Paul. It is due to Wrede that Paul is often viewed as a "second founder" of Christianity, who took Christianity on a path different from the one first started by Jesus.[4] According to Wrede, "Jesus never contemplated the Gentile mission."[5] This shift occurred in Paul's mission and had a profound impact on the message. Paul's mission to the gentiles caused him to focus on making the gospel more palatable to non-Jews. For Wrede, the result was a message that did not stress law observance—a gospel steeped in concepts of sin and redemption rather than moral guidance.

> To love our neighbour was probably to Paul, as to all Christians, an established "commandment of the Lord." But it did not mean to him what it meant to Jesus, and in reality is eclipsed by love of associates in church and faith, by love of the "brethren"; and this virtue in the community may have been emphasized in the Jewish Dispersion more than we know. Whether, however, the points of material contact with Jesus in this field be more or less numerous, the special moral atmosphere of the sayings of Jesus, their powerful majestic style, their critical keenness, their stress upon the truth of heart, have never, one may say, been felt by any finely sensitive soul in the moral preaching of Paul.[6]

---

4. William Wrede, *Paul* (London: P. Green, 1907), 180.
5. Wrede, *Paul*, 64.
6. Wrede, *Paul*, 159.

Though Wrede's work was met with much debate, the gulf created between Jesus and Paul has persisted.⁷ The once-assumed position of congruity between the teachings of Jesus and the writings of the apostle is now, in large part, gone. Subsequently, arguing for theological coherence among the New Testament writings has also become a neglected goal in favor of noting the distinctiveness of each book or strand of tradition. Thus, the poor-loving Jesus can stand in contrast with the theologizing Paul.

The apostle's few direct comments on wealth and poverty are often interpreted to refer to spiritual riches rather than economic factors. Even the collection for the poor in Jerusalem is interpreted through this lens. T. E. Schmidt writes regarding the "poor who are saints in Jerusalem" that the title "poor" in this text is not *primarily* an economic designation but a signifier of the longing for the *spiritual* riches of salvation. This is in line with Paul's spiritualization of the terminology of riches, and it may indicate a noneconomic connotation in the reference to Paul's remembering the poor in Galatians 2:10."⁸ Though Schmidt admits that some in the Jerusalem church may have actually been poor, his overall conclusion regarding Paul's concern for poverty is telling: "Neither the appropriate use of riches nor the plight of the economically deprived are dominant concerns for Paul, who usually spiritualizes the vocabulary of riches."⁹ In his appeal for the Corinthians to contribute to the collection in 2 Cor 8:9, Paul arguably makes such an interpretive move: "For you know the grace of our Lord Jesus Christ, that though he was rich, yet for your sake he became poor, so that by his poverty you might become rich." Nonetheless, using Paul's language here as an interpretive key for every mention of wealth of any kind neglects to consider the social and historical contexts of Paul's letters. The apostle himself has experienced poverty and imprisonment, where he would be dependent on others for provisions (e.g., Phil 4:14-18). Plus, he is writing to congregations who are likely living near or slightly above the subsistence

---

7. For an overview of this topic, see John M. G. Barclay, "Jesus and Paul," in *The Dictionary of Paul and His Letters*, ed. Gerald F. Hawthorne, Ralph Martin, and Daniel G. Reid (Downers Grove, IL: InterVarsity, 1993), 492-503. For a recent contribution to the debate see *Jesus and Paul Reconnected: Fresh Pathways into an Old Debate*, ed. Todd D. Still (Grand Rapids: Eerdmans, 2007).

8. T. E. Schmidt, "Riches and Poverty," in *The Dictionary of Paul and His Letters*, 827.

9. Schmidt, "Riches and Poverty," 826.

Introduction

level. Spiritualizing Paul's mention of poverty has kept the apostle on a pedestal removed from the concerns of the poor and needy.

Fortunately, recent studies on Paul and poverty have begun to shatter this perception of the apostle. Sociohistorical studies have highlighted the widespread poverty in the Roman world and have considered the economic constituency of Pauline communities.[10] For example, Bruce Longenecker's *Remember the Poor: Paul, Poverty, and the Greco-Roman World* has argued that the impoverished are integral to Paul's mission.[11] Rather than read the Jerusalem leaders' charge to "remember the poor" (Gal 2:10) only as a reminder to care for the poor among the Jerusalem saints, the concern was that the gentiles, who live in a world with no concept of charity, learn this critical facet of Jewish Scripture, to remember the poor in their midst.[12] Though Longenecker's work is persuasive, Paul's letters are still not considered a primary arena for studying perceptions toward poverty in the Jesus movement. New Testament scholarship tends to gravitate toward the Gospels or James for evidence of charity in the early church.

There is *congruity* between Jesus's teaching and Paul's mission regarding Jesus's concern for the "least of these." To be fair, Paul does not often acknowledge particular sayings of Jesus in his writings. He never recites the parables and mentions teachings or traditions only in passing (e.g., 1 Cor 7:10; 9:14; 11:23; cf. 1 Cor 7:12, 25). It is not the purpose of this book to argue for historical continuity between Jesus's teaching and Paul's

---

10. Wayne Meeks's argument that the Pauline churches made up a cross section of society (*First Urban Christians* [New Haven: Yale University Press, 1983]) has been critiqued by others who point out the minuscule percentage of people who comprised the upper echelon of society (e.g., Steven J. Friesen, "Poverty in Pauline Studies: Beyond the So-Called New Consensus," *JSNT* 26 [2004]: 323-61; Bruce W. Longenecker, "Exposing the Economic Middle: A Revised Economy Scale for the Study of Early Urban Christianity," *JSNT* 31 [2009]: 243-78). Justin J. Meggitt has argued that the Pauline churches did not include the affluent, but rather those living in or near poverty levels (*Paul, Poverty and Survival*, Studies of the New Testament and Its World [Edinburgh: T&T Clark, 1998]). For a discussion of Paul and poverty, see chapter 1.

11. Bruce W. Longenecker, *Remember the Poor: Paul, Poverty, and the Greco-Roman World* (Grand Rapids: Eerdmans, 2010).

12. See also Bruce W. Longenecker, "Good News to the Poor: Jesus, Paul, and Jerusalem," in *Jesus and Paul Reconnected*, 37-65; and "Socio-Economic Profiling of the First Urban Christians," in *After the First Urban Christians: The Social-Scientific Study of Pauline Christianity Twenty-Five Years Later*, ed. Todd D. Still and David G. Horrell (London: T&T Clark, 2009), 36-59.

ministry. We do not have the benefit of knowing which traditions Paul may have received from the risen Christ or from the early church leaders, though he claims to have received some traditions directly from the Lord (e.g., 1 Cor 11:23). This book demonstrates that Paul's mission is congruous with Jesus's concern for the poor, the marginalized, and the powerless. Before laying out this argument, though, it is perhaps necessary to ask the "so-what" question. What is at stake in recovering a portrait of Paul who cares for the least of these?

Saving Paul

Until I began teaching at a theological institution, I was unconcerned about the gulf between Jesus and Paul. I lived and worked quite happily in my Pauline silo, occasionally dabbling in the Gospels for class or various writing projects. I must give credit to my students for inadvertently teaching me that the gulf mattered. These students are training for various kinds of ministry. Because I work in an institution that attracts people from across the theological spectrum—though perhaps more who self-identify as "liberal" or "progressive" Protestant—it became evident early in my Introduction to Epistles class that I had two categories of students: some who hated Paul and some who loved him. Most hated him, but the ones who loved him tended to stem from traditions that were proud of their evangelical roots. These students wanted to study Romans and already had strong opinions about what the letter said. Since, to a large degree, this was also my background, I understood their surprise when others in the class expressed unadulterated hatred of the apostle. The study of Paul was a lightning rod in the class. Even the few who were ambivalent toward the apostle claimed that they would never preach his letters. More and more, I have found that my mission in that class is to save the apostle. For some, Paul needs to be saved from his pedestal, and for others, Paul needs to be saved from Gehenna.

For those who have Paul on a pedestal, it is often hard to think of the former persecutor Saul as a real minister with the same kinds of limitations, fears, and insecurities suffered by the rest of us. For them, Paul is above reproach, flawless in his zealousness, and a model of the church's mission. He is the first (and, perhaps to some, the best) interpreter of Jesus. Because his speech is dripping with theological jargon, his letters have a reputation for being weighty and perplexing. The author of 2 Peter has cause to warn

Introduction

the believers that some things in Paul's letters are "hard to understand, which the ignorant and unstable twist to their own destruction, as they do the other scriptures" (2 Pet 3:16). Nonetheless, for those who see Paul as the ultimate theologian of Christianity, his theological arguments give plenty of room for discussion. There is so much room for debate that the study of Paul's letters tends to gravitate around the theology as though these letters were not addressed to real people in real churches with real problems. At the extreme end of the spectrum, Pedestal Paul is devoid of personality flaws—devoid of personality period. He seems almost divine rather than a human who, God forbid, makes mistakes. He is the representative of the ancient church that is portrayed as flourishing more than struggling. He is zealous and right and simply above reproach. Although at times I confess that I have been quite comfortable with this Paul, I have noticed that the pedestal can be a dangerous place to house the apostle. From the pedestal, one can spiritualize all Paul's language about wealth and poverty, slavery and freedom, male and female, high status and low status. From the ivory tower of this pedestal, the apostle is free to engage discussions of systematic theology without ever acknowledging the plight of others or getting his hands and feet dirty in service.

On the other extreme, some would like to dismiss the apostle Paul from their canons. Indeed, year after year my entering classes of seminarians are full of bright young minds who either hate Paul or attempt to avoid the apostle like a plague. Indeed, this hatred is not limited to students. Several colleagues across the theological disciplines have expressed similar disdain. I cannot really blame them. The Pauline Epistles are a battleground for hot topics—slavery, women in ministry, and homosexuality to name a few.[13] From church culture, my bright-eyed seminarians have discerned that the apostle is a chauvinist, a racist, a sexist, a homophobe, an elitist, or any other hate-filled label that comes to their minds. Their perception of Paul is of an apostle who cares nothing for the "least of these." It is with heavy hearts, fear, and much trepidation that these next church leaders come to my class. They have burning questions—questions that must be addressed before they can even consider reading Paul's letters as anything

---

13. For a study that reframes hot-topic issues through the lens of Paul's narrative theology, see J. R. Daniel Kirk, *Jesus Have I Loved, but Paul? A Narrative Approach to the Problem of Pauline Christianity* (Grand Rapids: Baker, 2011). To consider these topics from the perspective of a classicist, see Sarah Ruden, *Paul among the People: The Apostle Reinterpreted and Reimagined in His Own Time* (New York: Pantheon, 2010).

other than hate-filled church propaganda. Was the apostle a misogynist or a homophobe? Was it fair of preachers in the antebellum South to incorporate Paul's letters into their proslavery arguments? Should the rhetoric of Rom 1 be diminished to debates over homosexuality? When students arrive in my seminary class, instantly I see and feel the tension in the air.

Paul does not help himself either. I imagine that his personality was a bit brusque. It is fascinating that Paul is always finding himself in trouble. His catalogs of hardships are not for the faint of heart—shipwrecks, beatings, starvation, and imprisonment (1 Cor 4:11–13; 2 Cor 4:7–10; 6:4–10; 11:23–27; 12:10). Even the writer of Acts portrays him as the one in the missionary band who gets stoned and left for dead (Acts 14:19). His ministry seems to be met either with eagerness or hostility (see, e.g., Acts 14:4). Isn't it curious that Paul is always the one who gets the others into trouble? He is the perpetrator and instigator. In my mind, Paul's zealousness must have been somewhat abrasive.

So, I cannot blame my students for their displeasure with the apostle. Either they love him or they hate him. But I do wonder whether it is truly fair to the church to send out a group of would-be ministers who have dismissed Paul from their canons. At this point, I can imagine some saying, "Who would dismiss Paul?" Not realizing, of course, that we have all edited our "canon," if not by admission, by practice. Even the Romans-quoting evangelical may not have recently preached from Philemon, let alone read that letter. Yet interpretations of Philemon have played a huge role in the stigmatization of Paul among my students, especially those whose ancestral histories involve enslavement. I do not blame them for being hurt and angry. The enslavement, silencing, marginalization, and ostracism that has been done in the name of Paul's letters should cause the church to question whether this Paul indeed has anything to do with a Jesus who cares for the "least of these."

Does Paul Need to Be Saved?

Surely it takes an incredible amount of hubris to think that one could possibly "save" Paul's reputation. On the other hand, however, it takes an equal amount of hubris to demonize this first-century character when he somehow fails to live up to twenty-first-century expectations or, conversely, when he is quoted as the final authority to silence the voices of others. We are, perhaps, all guilty of abusing this apostle. Some have cast him in

Introduction

their own images to bolster their authority, while others have made him the enemy.

As a teacher, I consider it a challenge to get my students to see Paul in a different light, to read Paul in his first-century context. As a member of the church, I consider it somehow necessary to rescue Paul from the clutches of interpretations that are myopic. As a member of the guild, I can see the effects of critical scholarship trickle down to the pews. The gulf between Jesus and Paul is ever present. All the while, I am painfully aware that my own reading of the apostle comes with the baggage of my experiences and that I do not possess one right way of reading his letters. My own interpretations are constantly evolving. Nevertheless, with each passing year, I find myself in the position of trying to save Paul.

There is more to this apostle than some of our traditions would have us believe. I do not believe that Paul set out to liberate women or to silence them. I do not believe that Paul was aware that his words would one day be used in both abolitionist and proslavery causes. Paul had a mission, and while I may want him to say more about how to live everyday life two thousand years removed from the resurrection, my setting is not Paul's setting. Paul's mission transcends my concerns and, at the same time, informs those concerns.

As I look out at the rows and rows of students peering at me skeptically as we begin our study of Paul, I feel a profound need to apologize to the apostle for the horrific silencing, marginalizing, and enslaving that has been done in his name. While I do not pretend to think that one semester, one class, or one book could forever change perceptions of this complex human being, I at least hope that what I am saying would be allowed to broaden horizons and to provide an opening to take Paul out of the tiny compartments in which we have placed him for our own purposes. Who Paul really is remains a mystery. We cannot interview the apostle, but we can study his letters and try to get a sense of what makes Paul tick.

Does Paul's reputation really need to be saved? Surely someone whose work has endured for two thousand years can handle our insecurities, our questions, and even our criticisms. By writing this book, I do not wish to dismiss the real hurt that some have felt due to harmful interpretations of Paul's letters. Wounds such as these are too deep to be reasoned away. Paul was a fallible human being (like us) who experienced a life-changing call by God that turned his whole world upside down. Seeing the resurrected Lord changed everything he thought he knew about life, about God, and about the world. Paul was not trying to reform the Roman political or social systems of his day, at least not directly. His aims were different and even more urgent. Nonetheless, his ministry was, in many ways, socially and politically radical. It is the contention of this book that Paul needs to be reclaimed as a theologian for the least of these.

An Apostle for the "Least of These"?

As an apostle to the nations, Paul risked his life to take what he considered to be the best news to all people. There is no evidence that he sought out people of any particular status to proclaim his message. It seems that he proclaimed the good news to whomever he met—the powerful and the powerless. In Galatians, Paul acknowledges a commitment in his ministry to remember the poor (Gal 2:10), and his collection for the Jerusalem church spans his gentile mission (1 Cor 16:1-4; 2 Cor 8:1-9:15; Rom 15:25-27). In his farewell address to the church in Ephesus, the writer of Acts places on Paul's lips these words: "In all things I have shown you that by so toiling one must help the weak, remembering the words of the Lord Jesus, how he said, 'It is more blessed to give than to receive'" (Acts 20:35). Although there are good reasons to be critical of Acts's account of Paul's ministry, on this point Paul's letters confirm the apostle's concern to help the weak. If there is a driving question behind this book, it is this: How might we see Paul's theology differently when we consider him as an apostle for the "least of these"?

The first part of the book is devoted to reclaiming the presence of the "least of these" in the Pauline mission, particularly as exhibited in the involvement of the poor, slaves, and women. As chapter 1 will argue, evidence in the Pauline epistles themselves suggests that most of the Pauline communities contained folks who lived at, near, or slightly above the subsistence level. His congregations included a few people of high status but many more who worked for a living—either in trade or as slaves. As someone who also worked with his own hands (1 Cor 4:12; 1 Thess 2:9; cf. 2 Thess 3:8; Acts 18:3; 20:34), he had no problem developing a rapport with those who engaged in what the nobles in Roman society regarded as demeaning labor. The following chapters will consider the implications of Paul's gospel for slaves and for women. Chapter 2 will examine Paul's advice in Philemon and 1 Cor 7:17-24 in light of the evidence of slave life and manumission practices in the first century. The third chapter is devoted to the presence of women in the Pauline mission. Interpretations of Paul's letters have been used to silence women in the church or to limit their ministry functions. This chapter will examine the controversial texts at the heart of these interpretations and read them in light of their first-century contexts.

The second part of the book broadens the theme of the "least" to consider Pauline metaphors and teaching that are inspired by the "least of these." Essentially, this section raises theological implications for Paul's inclusion of the "least" and the role that the "least" plays in his theology and ethics. Chapter 4 will examine Paul's insistence that the Galatians are "children of the promise." The Galatians are a subjugated people, who have been negatively stereotyped by the Romans as "war-mad" barbarians. Paul's gospel, however, grants these outsiders exalted status as God's children. If chapter 4 shows how Paul's gospel exalts a people group who might be considered "least" in the empire, chapter 5 considers how Paul can use a metaphor of least-ness to reframe the churches' thinking about themselves. In 1 Cor 3:1, Paul refers to the Corinthians as "babes in Christ." This metaphor of weakness places the church in the position of the "least" and reminds the Corinthians of their vulnerability and the urgent need to display maturity in Christ. Chapter 7 will examine how Paul sees himself in the role of the "least." Paul tends to gravitate toward imagery of the "least" to portray his ministry: a slave to all, an orphan, a premature infant, impoverished, indebted, a laborer, hungry, naked, and thirsty. This chapter examines the significance of these metaphors in light of Paul's desire to imitate Christ. Finally, the last chapter argues that the "least" is a critical metaphor of Pauline theology because it stems from the Christological paradigm of self-lowering found in Phil 2:5–11. This paradigm has informed Paul's theology and his mission, a mission that has deliberately included and incorporated even the "least of these."

In conclusion, this book is an attempt to reframe thinking on Paul and to reconnect this apostle, in a small way, to the teachings of Jesus. By reviving Paul as a theologian even for the "least of these," it is hoped that my students and colleagues will reexamine this apostle and find in his letters not just theological jargon, but also theology that is attempting to express what God is doing in the real world with real people who have real problems. Paul believed in a God who was rectifying the created order, and the work of that God is good news for the "least of these."

CHAPTER ONE

Paul and Poverty

Paul does not talk about the poor as a category of people. His letters contain no blessing of the poor—even the poor in spirit. There are no parables encouraging believers to give food to the hungry, to give drink to the thirsty, or to give clothes to the naked (see Matt 25:31-46). There is no definition of true religion consisting of the care of widows and orphans (Jas 1:27). Is the apostle then unconcerned with the disenfranchised, the vulnerable, the "least of these"? That is often the assumption. This assumption, though, fails to take into account that poverty was an inescapable reality of the lives of the vast majority of the Roman Empire. Paul even describes himself as being "hungry and thirsty, often without food, cold and naked" (2 Cor 11:27; cf. 1 Cor 4:11). Paul's mission spreads Jesus's good news—Jesus's blessing for the poor—to the largest cities in the Roman world, cities teeming with poverty. This chapter will situate Paul's mission in its socioeconomic context, consider the economic status of the Pauline communities, and examine the implications of Paul's message for the everyday life of the saints.

The Poor in the Roman World

One of the challenges facing any historian is the question of how to define poverty.[1] Poverty can take many forms. It could be a social problem that ostracizes some from resources and privileges others. It could be a problem

---

1. For discussions on defining poverty, see Robin Osborne, "Introduction: Roman Poverty in Context," and Neville Morley, "The Poor in the City of Rome," in *Poverty in the Roman World*, ed. Margaret Atkins and Robin Osborne (Cambridge: Cambridge University Press, 2006), 1–20 (esp. 1–4) and 21–39.

with the structure of an economic system that keeps the poor impoverished even in times of plenty. It could be a temporary hardship that could improve in better times. Poverty in the ancient world tends to be described relative to those who have plenty.[2] In this book, poverty will be given the widest possible definition in an attempt to encompass all these possibilities for material poverty. The term "poverty" describes those whose basic human needs are threatened or, to put it in economic terms, those who live at or near subsistence level.[3] While this definition may seem simple, determining what "subsistence" entailed in the ancient world or how many people could be labeled "poor" is quite complex.

Labeling a distinct people group as "the poor" is problematic. Historians struggle to determine what life was like for the average person in the first-century world. History is, after all, written and preserved by the elite, who comprise a sliver of the population. The wealthy are not concerned about the lives of common people, and whenever they do write about the poor—or more accurately, the non-elite—they write from their own limited perspectives, typically with an agenda that only enhances the gulf between the elite and everyone else. They portray all who do not live a leisurely existence as impoverished.[4] They do not reveal, for instance, whether the nonwealthy could be subdivided into multiple classes. Rather, they are concerned only to demonstrate the luxuries and power of being part of the upper class. The wealthy are the ones who engage in building projects and who fund inscriptions, for instance. It is far more likely for an archaeologist to find remains of well-built mansions or public fountains than it is of shanties and lean-tos inhabited by the poor.

Based on our ancient sources, it seems that there was a stark dichotomy between the elite and everyone else. Historians agree that the wealthy elite comprised a small percentage of the Roman population. The question is how the rest—99 percent of the population—lived. Were the masses destitute? Did they struggle to survive? Was there a difference between the quality of life of urban dwellers and country farmers?

A debate among historians is whether the Roman world consisted of "middle classes"—stratification between the wealthy and the destitute. It is clear that there were elite and non-elite; it is not clear how the non-elite

---

2. Osborne, "Introduction: Roman Poverty in Context," 11.

3. Justin J. Meggitt, *Paul, Poverty and Survival*, Studies of the New Testament and Its World (Edinburgh: T&T Clark, 1998), 4–5.

4. Morley, "Poor in the City of Rome," 26.

might be categorized. In *Paul, Poverty and Survival*, Justin Meggitt has argued that 99 percent of the Roman Empire lived at or near subsistence level. In other words, the Roman Empire consisted of widespread destitution. While Meggitt concedes that some would have had more than others, it is questionable how comfortably any of the non-elite lived. Meggitt argues "that the Empire's economy was essentially pre-industrial in character and incapable of sustaining a mid-range economic group."[5]

It may be unfair to lump all the non-elite into the category of "poor," however. Walter Scheidel has argued that there were *middling groups* between the top 1 percent of the population and the truly destitute. There were, according to Scheidel, classes who would not be deemed wealthy elite, but who would have been "reasonably well cushioned against chronic want" but hardly wealthy enough to live a life of leisure.[6] Neville Morley argues that "many of the most important arenas of social activity—dinners, *collegia*, private bathhouses and gymnasia—required some measure of surplus wealth to gain access."[7] For those with limited resources, access to such privileges might come through a patron-client relationship, which by virtue of the expectation of reciprocity, dictated the exclusion of the poorest members of society. The fact that some among the non-elite had social privileges, though, suggests that not all those hovering near the subsistence level experienced destitution. It would be fair to say that there are classes of people who lived around the subsistence level who were vulnerable, particularly to food shortage, who might have enjoyed certain social privileges, but who have likely experienced some degree of cultural shame due to their circumstances.[8]

Among those who lived around subsistence level, there were always some who were better off than others, but overall access to food was a major concern.[9] Those with access to land had the best chance of securing food. With land, one could not only sustain oneself with food, if the conditions were favorable enough, but land also provided an acceptable security for loans. Even those who did not own land in the countryside could gather

---

5. Meggitt, *Paul, Poverty and Survival*, 7.
6. Walter Scheidel, "Stratification, Deprivation and Quality of life," in *Poverty in the Roman World*, ed. Margaret Atkins and Robin Osborne (Cambridge: Cambridge University Press, 2006), 49.
7. Morley, "Poor in the City of Rome," 34.
8. Morley, "Poor in the City of Rome," 33–36.
9. Meggitt, *Paul, Poverty and Survival*, 60.

food from the land. For those in the country, hunger was episodic rather than epidemic.[10] Those who dwelled in the cities, though, did not have easy access to land. Cities were, by and large, overpopulated. The city of Rome was the first Western city to reach a population of one million. Food was scarce for these urban dwellers. The Roman government provided a grain dole to about one-fifth of the citizen population of the city of Rome, but the grain distribution was only for citizen males. This left women, children, and non-citizens vulnerable.[11] What food source was available to them? Fish came from the Tiber, but the river was also full of the city's untreated sewage.[12] Sickness and disease abounded. Hunger was a real threat and the impetus for some to sell themselves into slavery.

Housing and employment were also concerns in the overcrowded cities. People slept anywhere that was available—in the open air, among the tombs, under stairs, bridges, or theatre awnings, or in taverns.[13] Some constructed lean-tos against other buildings or walls, while others lived outside town in shanties. Those who lived in these shack-like structures lived in constant fear of the officials tearing them down. The cities contained some housing, particularly *insulae*, apartment buildings with multiple floors. The lower floors had larger living quarters, but the upper floors were considerably more subdivided by smaller and smaller rented spaces. Even the roof was a rented space with no more coverage than a lean-to. Though the city of Rome regulated the height of these apartment buildings, the owners would hire construction workers to cram as many floors and rooms into the upper levels as possible. The workmanship was shoddy. The goal was not comfort or safety, but increasing the number of occupants and, thus, the income. The highest floors, with the least desirable living quarters, were rented on a daily basis. Others simply slept in their workshops (*tabernae*), small booths where artisans and their households worked. The non-elite were involved in the kinds of manufacturing jobs available in preindustrial societies. Unskilled workers lived from job to job. Skilled artisans were among the most "wealthy" of the city dwellers but, according to Meggitt, still lived only slightly above subsistence level.[14] It is fair to say that for

---

10. Osborne, "Introduction: Roman Poverty in Context," 4–5.
11. Meggitt, *Paul, Poverty and Survival*, 51–52.
12. Meggitt, *Paul, Poverty and Survival*, 60.
13. Osborne, "Introduction: Roman Poverty in Context," 9; Meggitt, *Paul, Poverty and Survival*, 63.
14. Meggitt, *Paul, Poverty and Survival*, 54, 57, 63–65.

most in the Roman world, daily life lacked luxury. Most had experienced need at some point and had daily reminders of how precarious access to resources could be.

How might this information illuminate our reading of Paul's letters? Even though historians disagree over the presence and size of middling groups, that is, those who were neither wealthy nor destitute, poverty, loosely defined, was prevalent throughout the Roman Empire. Neither Paul nor his churches would have been immune to want. We will have to be cautious in assuming that any in Paul's churches were truly wealthy, but there seem to have been some who had more resources to protect them against deprivation. Considering, though, that Paul was carrying on the teaching of Jesus through the largest cities in the empire, it is of little surprise that Paul would have wanted to preach good news to the poor in cities known to have large quantities of impoverished people.

A Study of the Pauline Congregations

Given the limitations of our knowledge of the life of the average person in the Roman world, situating the Pauline congregations within their socioeconomic status is even more challenging.

Paul's letters provide some insight into the recipients, but not nearly as much as we would hope. There are no accompanying church rolls listing active members and their tithes. Paul does, on occasion, mention someone by name, but he typically reveals little about that person. He would not need to do so since he is writing to people who would already know anyone named in their midst. In this one-sided conversation that is preserved in letter form, Paul does make some assumptions about the recipients. Of course, it is an open question whether his assumptions are correct. Given that he has spent time with most of the people to whom he is writing, with the exception of the Romans, we can at least glean some insight about the churches from his letters. First, though, it is important to situate this study in light of the field.

The debates among historians about whether the Roman Empire could support middling groups are also mirrored in New Testament scholarship. The past few decades have seen an upsurge in studies about the socioeconomic status of Paul's congregations. Wayne Meeks's classic study, *The First Urban Christians*, brought to light the social stratification in the Pauline churches. Using prosopographic evidence, Meeks argues that Paul's congregations included a cross section of society, people from all walks of life. Meeks's evidence assumes that the Roman Empire had middling classes and that 99 percent of the population did not experience abject poverty. His study was groundbreaking in raising the issue of status mobility in the context of the Pauline congregations and in considering the factors that might have attracted members of higher social classes to this early church movement. Since Meeks drew attention to Paul's congregations, more studies have been done that attempt to place Paul's congregations within the evidence that we have for the economy of the Roman world.

Before Meeks argued that the church contained members from the upper classes, the old consensus was that most of Paul's congregations constituted the poor and destitute.[15] This consensus still has supporters. Justin Meggitt's work, for instance, falls into this category. As represented by Meeks's study, a so-called new consensus has emerged, though, that considers Paul's congregations as comprising people of higher social status and wealth. At the extreme end of this consensus are those who would even categorize the early believers as wealthy.[16] Those whose work might fall into the category of the old consensus have rightly criticized the new consensus for assuming that the Pauline congregations would have contained those from the upper echelons of society.

Perhaps there are elements of truth on both sides of the debate. Bruce Longenecker has argued that the new consensus has often been misrepresented as claiming that the believers were wealthy and that there were no destitute in Paul's churches.[17] Yet those affiliated with the old consensus might be criticized for not recognizing that some in the churches had more of a surplus than others. The Pauline congregations likely consisted of economic stratifications living near subsistence level, with some who had moderately more of a surplus than others and some whose existence was more dire. In other words, contra seeing the Roman world in a bifurcation of the wealthy elite and the impoverished, there were classes of people, middling groups, in Paul's churches who did not come from the elite in society. Longenecker builds upon the work of Steven Friesen, who

---

15. For an excellent overview of the socioeconomic study of Paul's letters, see Bruce Longenecker, "Socio-Economic Profiling of the First Urban Christians," in *After the First Urban Christians: The Social-Scientific Study of Pauline Christianity Twenty-Five Years Later*, ed. Todd D. Still and David G. Horrell (New York: T&T Clark, 2009), 36–59.

16. For an overview, see Longenecker, "Socio-Economic Profiling," 36–59.

17. Longenecker, "Socio-Economic Profiling," 39–45.

classified the Roman world into poverty scales.[18] Longenecker adjusts the percentages of each "economic scale" (ES) based upon his own study of the evidence of poverty in the Roman world. The adjusted chart is as follows:[19]

Economic Scale	Description	Includes	Percentages of the Population
ES1	Imperial Elites	Imperial dynasty, Roman senatorial families, a few retainers, local royalty, a few freedpersons	0.04
ES2	Regional or provincial elites	Equestrian families, provincial officials, some retainers, some decurial families, some freedpersons, some retired military officers	1
ES3	Municipal elites	Most decurial families, wealthy men and women who did not hold office, some freedpersons, some retainers, some veterans, some merchants	1.76
ES4	Moderate surplus	Some merchants, some traders, some freedpersons, some artisans (especially those who employ others), military veterans	17

---

18. Steven J. Friesen, "Poverty in Pauline Studies: Beyond the So-Called New Consensus," *JSNT* 26 (2004): 323–61.

19. This is Friesen's chart reproduced with Longenecker's adjusted percentages. See Longenecker, "Socio-Economic Profiling," 44. Friesen later revised his scale: Walter Scheidel and Steven J. Friesen, "The Size of the Economy and the Distribution of Income in the Roman Empire," *JRS* 99 (2009): 61–91.

Paul and Poverty

Economic Scale	Description	Includes	Percentages of the Population
ES5	Stable near subsistence level (with reasonable hope of remaining above the minimum level to sustain life)	Many merchants and traders, regular wage earners, artisans, large-shop owners, freedpersons, some farm families	25
ES6	At subsistence level (and often below minimum level to sustain life)	Small-farm families, laborers (skilled and unskilled), artisans (esp. those employed by others), wage earners, most merchants and traders, small-shop/tavern owners	30
ES7	Below subsistence level	Some farm families, unattached widows, orphans, beggars, disabled, unskilled day laborers, prisoners	25

This chart indicates the presence of middling groups. Longenecker's revisions to Friesen's earlier work decrease the percentages of those in ES6–ES7. Friesen had a combined total of 68 percent of the population living at or below subsistence level (40 percent in ES6 and 28 percent in ES7). This decrease allows for a significant increase in those who were stable economically or who lived with some moderate surplus. Friesen's percentages for those categories are as follows: ES4 at 7 percent and ES5 at 22 percent. Longenecker's revisions significantly increase the size of the middling groups from Friesen's proposed 29 percent of the population to 42 percent of the population. In Longenecker's model, more than half the population still lived at or often below the subsistence level. How might the Pauline churches reflect the economic stratification of the larger society?

Roll Call

Who attends the Pauline house churches? We have a few names, particularly with the churches in Corinth and Rome, since the apostle writes to the Romans from Corinth and includes names in the final greetings (Rom 16). A long list of Roman believers are named, but since Paul reveals little about the church in the letter, it is hard to glean much about the church's socioeconomic status. Fortunately, more information about First Church Corinth is available. This is mainly due to the fact that two long letters to this church have been preserved in our canon, and in them Paul is giving advice on specific problems that reveal something about the believers' social situation. Based on the evidence in the letters and Acts, at least sixteen individuals are affiliated with the Corinthian congregation, and it is clear that some of these represent whole households, as is specifically the case with Stephanus (1 Cor 16:15). Knowing a name does not necessarily mean that we know anything about the person's social status, however. Sometimes the details that Paul provides about a parishioner are vague, such as the reference to Erastus in Rom 16:23 as a "steward" of the city. Therefore, we have to look for other clues in these letters rather than relying explicitly on names or the rare mention of status. In some cases, Paul's instructions to the churches assume a certain social situation. For instance, in the Thessalonian correspondence, it does not make sense for Paul to tell the Thessalonians to work with their own hands if they were in fact relying on their day-to-day labor to support themselves (1 Thess 4:9–12; 2 Thess 3:6–12). This section will highlight the rationale for proposing that Paul's churches consist of what might be called *middling groups*—those of higher social status (who may still not be part of the elite) as well as those whose economic status may be even closer to the subsistence level—and those who may be destitute.

First, it is important to note that no evidence exists that the Pauline congregations attracted those from the upper echelons of society (ES1–3)—those who were truly wealthy and powerful. Often 1 Cor 1:26 is cited as an indication that some in the congregation enjoyed noble status: "Consider your own call, brothers and sisters: not many of you were wise by human standards, not many were powerful, not many were of noble birth." This verse, which could be a rhetorical flourish, does more to highlight the majority than it does to suggest that any are truly powerful. In fact, it could be inferred that the vast majority of the Corinthians, and particularly the "know-it-alls" who were boasting in wisdom, were not truly rich and powerful in their world; rather they exerted power only in the church. Nevertheless, Paul's letters indicate that some enjoyed more social standing or resources than others—even if they were not part of the highest economic strata.

The individual who has perhaps received the most attention in New Testament scholarship as a representative of higher social status among the Pauline Christians is Erastus. Paul names him as a "city treasurer" or "steward" (*ho oikonomos tēs poleōs*) in Rom 16:23. The title given is rather vague, but it has most often been interpreted as a city official. Plus, archaeological evidence confirms that someone named Erastus was an aedile during the middle of the first century. An inscription in a sidewalk bears his name. An aedile is not necessarily the same as a city treasurer, though. Plus, Meggitt argues that the name Erastus is far more common than has often been considered.[20] It is questionable whether the Erastus whose name is preserved in the pavement and who would clearly be of the civic elite is the same Erastus who is a companion of Paul. Nonetheless, it is significant that Paul mentions any such title with his name in Rom 16:23. Furthermore, his name is mentioned alongside the name of Gaius, who can host the "whole church" of Corinth in his home. It seems that Paul is highlighting wealthier figures in Corinth who may have connections to Rome or whose presence in a list of greetings might lend some respectability to Paul's letter to a church in the heart of the empire.

Because the early church did not have the legal right to assemble publicly, the churches were a network of cell groups meeting in members' homes. It is not insignificant that those who host churches have a living space, even if that space is modest. Gaius stands out among those who serve as hosts. Paul does not say much about Gaius, but what he does reveal indicates that Gaius may have enjoyed some status within the community. In 1 Corinthians, the apostle mentions that he personally baptized Gaius (1 Cor 1:14) along with Crispus, who may be the former synagogue leader (Acts 18:8). He also notes in Rom 16:23 that Gaius's home is large enough to host the whole Corinthian congregation. How many people might be part of this church? At least sixteen individuals are associated with the Corinthian saints, and some are heads of households. Accounting for spouses and household members, there could easily have been fifty to one hundred Corinthian believers and possibly more. Even if the church is on the small end of that spectrum, Gaius's home could not be a tiny one-room apartment.

Paul identifies others as hosts: for example, Nympha (Col 4:15), Philemon, and Prisca and Aquila (Rom 16:3–5; 1 Cor 16:19; cf. 2 Tim 4:19; Acts 18:1–27). Unlike Gaius, nothing indicates that they host a "whole" church,

---

20. Meggitt, *Paul, Poverty and Survival*, 139.

meaning all the believers in town. Philemon hosts a gathering that includes other leaders, Apphia and Archippus, who may possibly be part of Philemon's household. He also has at least one slave, Onesimus. Paul's letter implies that Onesimus has been away from his master for some time and claims that this slave is not integral to the operation of Philemon's household (v. 11). Perhaps Philemon has other servants who do the work that Onesimus would have done. In any case, Philemon is the paterfamilias of his household, who has the power to decide Onesimus's fate. He also has the ability to offer hospitality to Paul (v. 22) and to host a house church. These markers indicate some status.

Some women mentioned in relation to Paul's churches appear to be heads of their households or important enough figures within the community that they serve the community in the role of benefactor. Nympha and Prisca were mentioned above as hosts of house churches. Likewise, Lydia offers hospitality to Paul when she and her household become the first converts in Macedonia (Acts 16). Phoebe is called a patron of Paul and a deacon of the church in Cenchreae in Rom 16:1-2. She has the means to travel and to offer some support for Paul's mission. Chloe is mentioned in 1 Corinthians. Those from her household are the ones who report to Paul some of the problems occurring in the Corinthian church, though it is not clear that Chloe is part of the church. She is mentioned as the head of the household from which the reports came. Presumably, though, the Corinthians know her, since Paul does not bother to say anymore about her.

Others are mentioned in Paul's letters who have status in their community, but who may not necessarily have much wealth. For instance, Paul refers to Stephanus in 1 Corinthians as a head of his household (1 Cor 16:15-16). It seems that he is part of the delegation that brought the Corinthians' letter to Paul (1 Cor 16:17). Paul gives him some authority in the community, because members of his household were the first converts in Achaia (1 Cor 16:15). Paul urges the church to listen to them and to work alongside them for the sake of the gospel (1 Cor 16:16). Furthermore, if the Crispus of 1 Cor 1:14 is the same as the one in Acts 18, and there is little reason to doubt this, then he is a former synagogue leader (Acts 18:8). He as well as Sosthenes (1 Cor 1:1; Acts 18:17) would have been respected in the Jewish community before their involvement with the church.

Paul's instructions regarding the collection in 1 Cor 16:1-4 may also provide some evidence regarding the status of most of the believers in First Church Corinth. Paul advises them to set aside each week whatever extra they earn and to save it for when he comes. Nothing indicates that there would be large amounts each week. As Bruce Longenecker argues, this advice makes more sense if the believers were able to give only a little each time.[21] Over time, those small offerings accumulate to a respectable sum. This advice also seems to be directed at those who are living above or near subsistence level. Those living below subsistence level would not have any extra to set aside. There must have been a few households in the Corinthian church who could join in this weekly practice.

Labor may also be an indicator of status. Those who live near subsistence level typically work with their own hands. In 1 Thess 4:11-12, Paul tells the church "to aspire to live quietly, to mind your own affairs, and to work with your hands, as we directed you, so that you may behave properly toward outsiders and be dependent on no one." This advice assumes that some in the community are living at another's expense. The social elite considered labor to be demeaning.[22] It appears that some in the church would rather be clients of wealthy patrons than resort to demeaning labor to support themselves and their families. According to Bruce Winter, Paul's advice here is indicative of the social etiquette surrounding the patron-client relationship. If some are serving as benefactors in the community, then that would indicate a fairly significant social status. Acts mentions benefactors who are, in some way, supporting the community. Jason, for instance, has hosted Paul as well as a church in his home (Acts 17:6-9). If others are relying upon the benefaction of wealthy patrons, then they are clients who are obligated to show honor and loyalty to their benefactors. In many ways, accepting gifts from a patron makes one indebted, not just monetarily, but socially, politically, and publicly. Clients were expected to be present at the morning greeting at the home of their wealthy patron. The larger the gathering of clients, the more status, honor, and power was associated with the patron. In return for their loyalty each morning, the patron

---

21. Longenecker, "Socio-Economic Profiling," 48.
22. Ronald F. Hock argues that the wealthy view labor as demeaning, *The Social Context of Paul's Ministry: Tentmaking and Apostleship* (Philadelphia: Fortress, 1980), 66-67. Hock, "Paul's Tentmaking and the Problem of His Social Class," *JBL* 97 (1978): 555-64, esp. 560-62, 564; and "Paul and Greco-Roman Education," in *Paul in the Greco-Roman World: A Handbook*, ed. J. Paul Sampley (Harrisburg, PA: Trinity Press International, 2003), 198-227. Hock also argues that Paul views labor from the perspective of the wealthy. This thesis has been challenged by Todd D. Still, "Did Paul Loathe Manual Labor? Revisiting the Work of Ronald F. Hock on the Apostle's Tentmaking and Social Class," *JBL* 125 (2006): 781-95.

offered money and food to those gathered. The benefactor who managed to spread his or her wealth to support many clients could, therefore, gather quite a following of clientele who would be duty bound to show fidelity in return. This would not only give them the appearance of power, but would also grant them some political leverage. Since the poor had no means to reciprocate loyalty with their assets or social networks, benefactors did not establish a patron-client relationship with the poor.[23]

Paul's instructions for the Thessalonian believers to lead a quiet life and to mind their own business would be a stark contrast to this life in the public sphere where one's very presence is used to support the ambitions of another. Continual reliance upon the patron only feeds the cycle of honor that is due. Breaking free from this dependency can incur the patron's enmity. Winter reads Paul's advice as a way to navigate the tensions between the duties of a client to show respect and honor and the ability of the client to be less dependent upon his wealthy patron. A client might reasonably win the respect of outsiders (1 Thess 4:12) by making no further demands of the patron than what was his right—for example, the demand of daily food.[24] This, Winter argues, would keep clients from meddling in the affairs of others and help them to mind their own business.[25] The advice to work with one's own hands and to be dependent upon no one would enable believers to share goods with one another, to become Christian benefactors as it were.[26] The believers could set about doing good (2 Thess 3:6-15). Those who refuse to work with their own hands are not only called "idle" in 2 Thess 3:6-15, but they are taking support away from others who need it and failing to contribute to the good of the whole.

How does the evidence in the Thessalonian correspondence relate to the issue of the socioeconomic status of the Pauline churches? Enough people in the church are duty bound in a patron-client relationship for Paul to find it necessary to address this situation. If Paul also wrote 2 Thessalonians, then he has addressed it in two letters. The lowest on the socioeco-

---

23. Bruce W. Winter, *Seek the Welfare of the City: Christians as Benefactors and Citizens* (Grand Rapids: Eerdmans, 1994), 45-47.

24. Winter, *Seek the Welfare of the City*, 47, 49, 51.

25. This advice may have worked for a time, but, as Winter argues, by the time 2 Thessalonians is written, a famine had occurred, and the letter must address again the realities that some had returned to dependency on a patron for food (*Seek the Welfare of the City*, 50).

26. Winter, *Seek the Welfare of the City*, 57.

nomic spectrum are not among clientele. Although giving is not supposed to be motivated by self-interest (Aristotle, *Nicomachean Ethics* 1385a35–1385b3), clients are expected to show proper gratitude in return with their political support, their loyalty, and their service.[27] The "idle" Thessalonians are people who are electing not to work with their own hands, as Paul does, likely due to the social stigma surrounding labor as it relates to class. They would rather have the honor associated with being a client of a powerful patron and not have to work to support themselves. Most in the Roman world do not have the luxury of electing not to work. While there may be a few wealthy patrons in Thessalonica, the evidence that Winter highlights suggests that many of the Thessalonian believers can support themselves and, through their labor, become Christian benefactors who support those in the community who are actually destitute, those who have always worked and yet struggle to live near subsistence level.

The Corinthian correspondence also indicates status differences among members of the congregation. In First Church Corinth, a division exists between those who have homes and those who have nothing. Gerd Theissen famously related divisions in the community to the divisions in socioeconomic status.[28] It is clear that some of the abuses of the Lord's Table are related to resources. In 1 Cor 11:17–22, some have food and drink, and others go hungry. Some have homes, while others have nothing. Though it has been debated how wealthy those with houses truly are, it is significant that hunger is a dividing factor in the church. Some do not have resources to bring to this church potluck. Plus, it appears that no one is sharing with the hungry whenever they do arrive for worship. Paul accuses those who have too much food and drink of humiliating their brothers and sisters and despising the church of God (1 Cor 11:22). His advice to welcome one another is rooted in the way in which Jesus has welcomed all in love (11:23–26). Rather than preserve the social distinctions of their world, the gathering of believers should model Christ's willingness to set aside his status for the sake of another's well-being (Phil 2:5–11). Welcoming one another (11:33) implies receiving even those who have nothing, as though showing hospitality to a friend. If hospitality were practiced in the church,

---

27. See, e.g., Isocrates, *To Demonicus* 29; Aristotle, *Nicomachean Ethics* 1163b12–15; Seneca, *On Benefits* 2.22.1; 2.24.2; 2.25.3; 4.20.2; 4.24.2; *Letters* 81.27; Cicero, *On Duties* 1.47–48.

28. Gerd Theissen, *The Social Setting of Pauline Christianity: Essays on Corinth*, ed. and trans. John H. Schütz (Philadelphia: Fortress, 1982).

then there would not be hunger or drunkenness at the church potluck. In other words, there would not be some who have food and drink in excess and others who have need. While this may seem basic to a twenty-first-century Western culture, hospitality in the first century was a duty incumbent upon those who were trying to maintain some social status. It was offered only to those who could reciprocate in kind. An assembly where even the poor are dining and eating like those who have status would not be a common sight in the first-century world. Yet this visual would display Christ's love for all. A table that does anything else is not proclaiming "Christ's death until he comes" (11:26).

Conclusions about the Economic Status of Paul's Churches

The Pauline churches represent a cross section of ES4–ES7 in Longenecker's revision of the economic scale. Longenecker argues that the rhetoric of Paul's letters largely assumes ES5, though at times ES6. If this is correct, then the majority in Paul's churches are living slightly above the subsistence level. While some are living at moderate surplus and can host gatherings, most do not. Then, others "have nothing" (1 Cor 11:22). Paul's gospel is attracting people whose economic status reflects the vast majority of the Roman population. The members of these churches are not immune to want, and they have found good news in the apostle's message.

Remembering the Poor and Bearing One Another's Burdens

Though Paul's ministry encompassed the poor, the apostle has not received much credit for teaching his churches to care for the poor in their midst. When considering the role of charity in Paul's mission, a natural place to begin is the collection. Although most in the Pauline faith communities will never meet the believers in Jerusalem or even travel to that area of the Roman Empire, Paul invites them to participate in a collection for the poor in that city. This project spans Paul's mission and binds the churches together in one life-giving project. In many ways, this offering of the gentiles is a realization of Paul's vision at the end of the letter to the Romans: people from every nation coming together to praise God (Rom 15:7–13). *The collection is a larger-scale project of what Paul would have the believers do every day: remember the poor in their midst and bear one another's burdens.*

The Collection

The collection for the Jerusalem saints is an effort that encompasses the northeastern Mediterranean world as Paul knew it. The campaign is as massive as Paul's mission. Churches throughout Galatia, Macedonia, Achaia, Mysia, and Lydia are affiliated with this offering. Plus, there is potential for more church involvement since Paul traveled through other regions and towns as well (e.g., Ptolemais, Tyre, and Caesarea on the way to Jerusalem, Acts 21:7–8). He also made requests for the participation of churches whom he had not yet visited, as evidenced in the letter to the Romans. While scholars have not reached a consensus on the purpose of the collection, it is clear that this project was dear to Paul and his mission. He was willing to risk the dangers of undertaking such a collection in an empire that had allowed the Jews to participate in the temple tax but that might, understandably, be skeptical whether non-Jews should be sending large sums of money to a former capital city vanquished by Rome.

The apostle was willing to sacrifice his life to bring the collection to Jerusalem. The author of Acts portrays his resolve in a way that calls to mind Jesus's own determination to go to Jerusalem (cf. Acts 19:21 with Luke 9:51). Paul had more than enough warning of what would occur when he arrived in the city. Though told by the Holy Spirit through Agabus that the Jerusalem authorities would bind him (Acts 21:7–14), Paul would not be dissuaded from his mission: "For I am ready not only to be imprisoned but even to die at Jerusalem for the name of the Lord Jesus" (Acts 21:13). In Rom 15:31, he indicates his intentions to deliver the offering to Jerusalem, acknowledges that he may need to be rescued, and requests prayer that he might be able to fulfill his mission.

This relief effort for the poor embodied for Paul God's work among the nations. In Rom 15:26–27, Paul uses language of indebtedness as he urges the gentile believers to contribute to the needs of the Jerusalem saints. Paul insists that the gospel is God's power for salvation to the Jew first and then to the gentile (Rom 1:16–17). It is, after all, through a Jew that God revealed Godself to the nations. Furthermore, Jewish believers have commissioned Paul to be an apostle to the nations.

The collection is presented under the umbrella of God's grace (2 Cor 8:1; 2 Cor 9:8–15). Everything that the Corinthians have is a gift from God (see 1 Cor 1:30). The apostle uses Christ's own willingness to give of himself as the epitome of generosity (2 Cor 8:9): "For you know the generous act of our Lord Jesus Christ, that though he was rich, yet for your sakes he became poor, so that by his poverty you might become rich." Furthermore, he recalls the Lord's provision of manna for the Israelites in their wilderness wanderings in his recitation of Exod 16:18: "The one who had much did not have too much, and the one who had little did not have too little" (2 Cor 8:15). The words that Paul uses to describe this collection suggest that Paul sees it as service (*diakoneō* and *leitourgeō*, Rom 15:25-27; *diakonia* and *leitourgia*, 2 Cor 9:12; *diakoneō*, 2 Cor 8:20; *diakonia*, 2 Cor 8:4; 9:1, 13), a binding partnership (*koinōnia*, Rom 15:26; 2 Cor 8:4), a gift (1 Cor 16:3; 2 Cor 8:4, 6, 7, 19), a collection (*logeia*, 1 Cor 16:1, 2), and a blessing (*eulogia*, 2 Cor 9:5). Perhaps, most telling, Paul portrays the collection as the proof of the Corinthians' love (2 Cor 8:24).

The collection promises more than spiritual rewards. In 2 Cor 8:10-15, Paul instructs the church to give according to their means. This advice comes immediately after he has given Christ's example of becoming impoverished for the sake of the world. Perhaps to allay any misunderstanding, he clarifies that he is not asking the believers to burden themselves but to give as they are able from their abundance (2 Cor 8:13-14). What is often overlooked, or read in terms of spiritual blessing, is the notion that the roles may one day be reversed. The Corinthians may find themselves in need, and Paul expects that the Jerusalem church would reciprocate in kind: "It is a question of a fair balance between your present abundance and their need, so that their abundance may be for your need, in order that there may be a fair balance" (2 Cor 8:13b-14).[29] Paul even cites Scripture in support of this exchange (Exod 16:18). A sense of interdependence connects these believers, even though they are miles apart. They are not just unified spiritually, but the collection demonstrates that they also have a responsibility to one another.

Remembering the Poor

Is the collection the only way that the believers are invited to "remember the poor"? No. Remembering the poor and bearing one another's burdens are central to the message that Paul preaches. In Gal 2, when Paul is recounting his trip to Jerusalem with Barnabas and Titus, he says that

---

29. See also Meggitt, *Paul, Poverty and Survival*, 161; David J. Downs, *Alms: Charity, Reward, and Atonement in Early Christianity* (Waco: Baylor University Press, 2016), 154.

James, Peter, and John—pillars of the church—recognized his mission to the nations and charged him also to remember the poor, "which is the very thing I was eager to do" (Gal 2:10). Unfortunately, this verse has often been interpreted as a brief reference to the collection for the Jerusalem saints, although he does not mention the offering in this context. When the verse is read in such a manner, we struggle to understand why the apostle would even recount this exchange in a letter that seemingly has more pressing issues to address—issues of life and death from the apostle's perspective.

What happens when we consider Paul's concern to remember the poor not as tangential to his argument in Galatians, but as a core piece of his mission there? This question was raised by Bruce Longenecker in his groundbreaking book, *Remember the Poor: Paul, Poverty, and the Greco-Roman World*. Longenecker challenges the traditional reading of Gal 2:10, which sees the Jerusalem leaders' charge to remember the poor as the impetus for Paul's massive collection for the Jerusalem saints. Instead, he argues that this stipulation lies at the very heart of the gospel, a gospel that embodies care for the vulnerable.[30] Longenecker's reading of Galatians through this lens results in a more coherent argument that counters the "gospel" of the opposing teachers. These other teachers are promoting a message that requires law observance—particularly circumcision and food laws—and this message appears to be linked with the authority of the Jerusalem church. Paul reminds the believers at the beginning of his letter that the Jerusalem pillars have commissioned him for the mission to the nations with only one stipulation—the remembrance of the poor. These Jerusalem leaders did not demand circumcision or kosher practices. They could have made other demands, but they did not. They wanted the mission to the nations to reflect Christ's sacrificial love for the vulnerable. Remembering the poor is not limited to a collection for impoverished Jerusalem saints whom the Galatians would never meet. Remembering the poor is a way of life—a way modeled by the cross and encouraged by the law (cf. Gal 5:14).

One of the reasons that the Jerusalem leaders may have raised this particular stipulation is a concern that acts of charity may not be as common among the nations. Gentiles were not known for their charity toward the poor. While beggars existed everywhere and almsgiving must have been part of everyday life, there were few efforts to address the quality of life of those who were living in abject poverty. Longenecker argues, "The Jerusalem leaders were anxious that the good news preached by Paul and

---

30. Longenecker, *Remember the Poor*, 211.

Barnabas, a good news free from the requirement of circumcision, should nonetheless continue to look like a Jewish good news in relation to one of Judaism's most socially distinctive features: that is, its care for the poor."[31] In Jewish faith and practice, the law demanded care for the most vulnerable in society, even if the prophetic witness indicates that the law was not always followed by Jewish leaders. Those outside Judaism were not completely without charity, though. As Longenecker points out, the Galatians, who cared for Paul when he was ill, ignored normal superstitions about strangers—particularly ones who were sick. Paul says that they would have even plucked out their eyes for him (Gal 4:15). So the Galatians, who are desperate to exhibit their faith in a tangible way, have already demonstrated a willingness to love another sacrificially. Paul's appeal to their care for him highlights for the Galatians how faith is demonstrated in acts of love.[32]

For Paul, Christ's love embodies the fulfillment of loving one's neighbor. In Gal 5:14, Paul cites Lev 19:18 as the summation of the whole law: "You shall love your neighbor as yourself."[33] He exhorts the Galatians: "Bear one another's burdens, and in this way you will fulfill the law of Christ" (Gal 6:2). Loving one another as Christ has loved is a manifestation of the Spirit's work. Longenecker reads the closing exhortations to bear one another's burdens (6:2) and to do good (6:9-10) as echoes of the reference to remembering the poor in 2:10. The letter then is bookended by cruciform morality that cares for the vulnerable in their midst.[34]

There would have been plenty in the Pauline churches who felt vulnerable or who lacked resources. Since most in the Pauline churches were living near subsistence level, it is most likely that any of them could experience need at any given time. There would have been years of plenty and years of want in this agriculturally based empire. The exhortation of support was not just urging the wealthy to give to the poor.[35] Rather, the believers were invited to practice acts of mercy toward one another and the poor in their midst. There was a sense of mutualism in giving and receiving, and these acts of reciprocity helped bind the believers together.[36] Just

---

31. Longenecker, *Remember the Poor*, 60-107, 199, quoting 203.
32. Longenecker, *Remember the Poor*, 207-19.
33. See Rom 13:8-10.
34. Longenecker, *Remember the Poor*, 216.
35. See also Downs, *Alms*, 143-75.
36. Downs prefers the term "almsgiving," which he uses as a term that can expect reciprocity. Meggitt uses the term "mutualism" to describe this interchange.

as Paul uses familial language to describe the believers as members of a new household, bearing one another's burdens and loving one's neighbor as oneself also contributes to community building.

With Paul's ministry associated with "remembering the poor," the Pauline church-planting movement looks much more like the portrait of Jesus in the Gospels and the teachings in James. Remembering the poor is a fundamental aspect of Jewish faith and practice. It is not surprising that the Jesus movement would also carry on this tradition. Perhaps the surprise is that Paul's letters grew to be interpreted otherwise.

Since the post-Reformation readings of Pauline letters have focused on faith rather than works, is there any evidence that the early church read these letters differently? In his thought-provoking book, *Alms: Charity, Reward, and Atonement in Early Christianity*, David Downs argues that the early church from its beginning until the mid-fourth century had a contingent who not only practiced caring for the poor, but who also viewed almsgiving as a means of atonement. Though Downs is careful to articulate that Paul does not teach that sin can be redeemed through almsgiving, he does demonstrate that Paul encourages "meritorious almsgiving in the sense that care for the poor will be recognized and rewarded by God, both in the present and in the future (1 Tim 6:17–19; Phil 4:14–19; Gal 4:12–15; 2 Cor 9:6–12)."[37] The tradition of storing up treasure in the afterlife by giving alms is present both in the Gospels and the Pauline tradition, as 1 Tim 6:17–19 demonstrates: "As for those who in the present age are rich, command them not to be haughty, or to set their hopes on the uncertainty of riches, but rather on God who richly provides us with everything for our enjoyment. They are to do good, to be rich in good works, generous, and ready to share, thus storing up for themselves the treasure of a good foundation for the future, so that they may take hold of the life that really is life." Finally, in 2 Cor 9:6–16, as Paul is concluding his discussion of the collection, he makes his final appeal to encourage the Corinthians' generosity. He never claims that God will give them all the material goods that they want. There is no prosperity gospel here. Part of the rationale for giving to the Jerusalem church is that, should the Corinthians find themselves in need, the Jerusalem believers might come to their aid. Rather, the apostle promises that God will "increase the harvest of your righteousness" (2 Cor 9:10). God is the one who provides every blessing (9:8), and God has given the believers the ability to share their resources. Paul frames the collection

37. Downs, *Alms*, 173.

as supplying the needs of the saints, but also as thanksgiving to God (2 Cor 9:12) and a manifestation of their confession of the gospel by "your sharing with them [i.e., the Jerusalem church] and with all others" (2 Cor 9:13). As demonstrated by the addition of "all" in 2 Cor 9:13, the concern to care for the needs of others is not limited to the Jerusalem saints; it is indeed part of following in the footsteps of Christ.

As seen in 2 Cor 8–9, the rationale for giving is established in what God has done in Christ. Imitating Christ looks like remembering the vulnerable, standing in solidarity with the weak, bearing one another's burdens, and doing good with the resources that one has. It should not be forgotten that Paul scolded the Corinthians for allowing some to go hungry as they gathered for the Lord's Table (1 Cor 11:17-34). He corrected them by reminding them of Christ's willing sacrifice of himself for the sake of the world. A worship service where some are starving and in need while others have enough to be full and drunk can hardly be called a remembrance of Christ's love. Rather, Paul accuses the Corinthians of despising God's church and humiliating those who have nothing (1 Cor 11:22).

Conclusion

When Paul's mission is examined in its context, the apostle's ministry mirrors that of Jesus. His message attracts those who need good news in the age of empire—people who were living near subsistence level. In the agriculturally based Roman Empire, there would have had been times of plenty and times of want. Paul calls the believers to care for one another, to bear one another's burdens, and to remember the poor. By taking a collection for the impoverished Jerusalem saints, Paul demonstrates that this early church movement is bound to one another in love. The believers must not only think of themselves as part of the same household, but also act as though they are part of the same household, caring for one another and helping one another survive. These acts of mutual care extend even to believers whom they might never meet in the far reaches of the Roman Empire.

FURTHER READING

Downs, David J. *Alms: Charity, Reward, and Atonement in Early Christianity*. Waco: Baylor University Press, 2016. Downs demonstrates that from the church's inception until the mid-third century, a strand of Christianity promoted and practiced meritorious almsgiving as a means of atonement. This book is thought-provoking and carefully researched.

Longenecker, Bruce W. *Remember the Poor: Paul, Poverty, and the Greco-Roman World*. Grand Rapids: Eerdmans, 2010. This book examines the poor in the Greco-Roman world and reconsiders Paul's mission in light of that research. Longenecker reclaims Paul's reference to remembering the poor in Gal 2:10 as a central part of the Pauline mission rather than merely a reference to the collection for the Jerusalem saints.

Meeks, Wayne. *The First Urban Christians: The Social World of the Apostle Paul*. New Haven: Yale University Press, 1983. This now classic study is a must read for those who are interested in thinking about the socioeconomic life of the Pauline churches. Though the field has evolved, this study has made a major impact on the field.

Meggitt, Justin J. *Paul, Poverty and Survival*. Edinburgh: T&T Clark, 1998. Meggitt's study challenged the assumptions created by the new consensus and caused scholarship to revisit the reality of poverty in the early church movement. Though his work has been debated and criticized, this book is a force to be reckoned with.

Still, Todd, and David G. Horrell, eds. *After the First Urban Christians: The Social-Scientific Study of Pauline Christianity Twenty-Five Years Later*. New York: T&T Clark, 2009. In light of the legacy created by Wayne Meeks's *First Urban Christians*, this collection of essays continues and assesses the social-scientific approach to Pauline studies.

CHAPTER TWO

Paul and Slavery

I can do nothing to rescue the Bible—let alone the Pauline Letters—from its use in proslavery arguments. The biblical text—including Paul's letters—has been used to support both sides of the slavery debate. The giants of the faith do not rise up against this institution. Abraham not only had slaves. Genesis says that God blessed him with more (Gen 24:35). Jesus does not lead a rebellion against slavery—nor does Paul or any of the disciples. They lived in a world that neither questioned the institution nor thought to structure society differently.[1] For the centuries spanning the biblical canon, slavery was a fixture of everyday life. And while there are commands for the just treatment of slaves, I am not convinced that those who preserved these texts dared to imagine daily life without this institution—especially when their world was dominated by foreign powers that owed no allegiance to a God who would allow his own son to come in the form of a slave (Phil 2:7). Slavery is incompatible with a gospel of abundant life, and yet in Paul's world slavery was engrained in "this present evil age" (to borrow language from Gal 1:4).

It is not the goal of this chapter to claim that Paul was an abolitionist, though I myself am on that side of the debate. Paul does not attack systemic slavery. He does, however, preach a gospel that has ramifications that he himself may not have been prepared to negotiate. Furthermore, he may have been content to allow the gospel to create chaos in his society because he believed that Jesus would return within his lifetime. Why spend all his time launching a full-scale attack on the Roman slavery system when there were no clear steps—no protocol—for success? As hard as it may be

---

1. See also Dale B. Martin, *Slavery as Salvation: The Metaphor of Slavery in Pauline Christianity* (New Haven: Yale University Press, 1990), 42.

Paul and Slavery

for modern readers to grasp, even freeing all the slaves would not have ensured that all had freedom or even a chance at life abundant. Rather, the early church's tactic of spreading the gospel to the largest cities in the Roman Empire produced disruption in the social hierarchies. The powerful were humbled. The lowly were raised. And all were dining together at the same table, praising God with one voice. At least, that is the vision that Paul urges the church to exhibit—even though his letters demonstrate the real struggle to do so (see Rom 15:1–13; 1 Cor 11:17–34).

How does the church live into the baptismal confession of neither slave nor free, male nor female, Jew nor gentile (see Gal 3:28; 1 Cor 12:13)? The apostle's passion for the gentile mission would indicate that these qualifiers are not merely rhetorical flourish. After all, Paul was imprisoned and willing to die for his conviction that God was working among the nations. This chapter will offer a glimpse of slavery in the Roman world and then consider some of the evidence from Paul's letters in light of this information.

Slavery in the Roman World

When thinking about slavery in the Roman world, I am reminded of a song from the musical *Les Misérables*, which brings to life Victor Hugo's masterpiece about the years leading up to the French Revolution. The song, "Look Down," is sung by Javert, the representative of the law who is intent on keeping watch on Jean Valjean, a man who had been arrested for stealing a loaf of bread to feed his sister's child. Valjean served nineteen years for this crime. The song succinctly makes the audience aware of this history as Valjean is about to leave prison. He is not really free, though. He is no longer working in a chain gang, but he is on parole. The stigma of being a "slave to the law" haunts him until he breaks parole, leaves behind his identity as prisoner number 24601, and reinvents his life with the help of a bishop and by the grace of God. Javert never quits hunting him. The song ends: "Look down, look down, you'll always be a slave. Look down, look down, you're standing in your grave."[2] As it turns out, the song, sung in the first act, prepares the audience for the reality that the once-imprisoned Valjean "will always be a slave," even when he is "free." His former identity haunts him. Though Valjean was a prisoner, treated like a slave, there are

---

2. Alain Albert Boubill, Claude Michel Schönberg, Herbert Kretzmer, and Jean Marc Natel (Warner/Chappel Music, Inc.).

35

parallels between the stigma of prison and the realities of slavery in the ancient world.

As Orlando Patterson has well argued, slavery is a means of social death.[3] Slavery alienates one from forming social bonds beyond those managed by a slaveholder. As a social construct, slavery involves the complete domination of an individual or a whole group of people. Although some slaves were certainly treated more humanely than others and held positions of power, socially, most slaves were among the "least" in society, whether they were part of a wealthy family or confined to work in a chain gang. Attached to the institution was a social shame that followed a person even after manumission. Freed slaves were never really free. They were always indebted to their masters.

The Roman world had slaves in abundance. By some estimates, slaves comprised anywhere from 15 to 33 percent of the population.[4] Though masters created death certificates for their slaves to avoid further taxation,[5] there are no means to determine how many slaves existed in the Roman Empire. Slaves were constantly being brought into the Roman Empire.[6] As Mitzi Smith has observed, "Romans rarely enslaved other Romans."[7] There were captured people from all parts of the conquered world. If one had the ability to walk around the streets of first-century Rome, it would have been difficult to discern who was a slave and who was a free person, especially among the urban poor.[8]

Every household did not own slaves, but slaves were everywhere in every job imaginable—even in positions of power. The land in this preindustrial society was often worked by slaves, and manufacturing required cheap labor. Many families were too poor to afford them, but the rich flaunted

---

3. Orlando Patterson, *Slavery and Social Death: A Comparative Study* (Cambridge: Harvard University Press, 1982), 1–34.

4. J. Albert Harrill, "Paul and Slavery," in *Paul in the Greco-Roman World: A Handbook*, vol. 2, edited by J. Paul Sampley (London: Bloomsbury T&T Clark, 2016), 306–7. See also the lengthy treatment of manumission practices in J. Albert Harrill, *The Manumission of Slaves in Early Christianity*, HUT 32 (Tübingen: Mohr Siebeck, 1995).

5. Jennifer A. Glancy, *Slavery in Early Christianity* (Oxford: Oxford University Press, 2002), 42.

6. Harrill, "Paul and Slavery," 306–7.

7. Mitzi J. Smith, "Slavery in the Early Church," in *True to Our Native Land: An African American New Testament Commentary*, ed. Brian K. Blount (Minneapolis: Fortress Press, 2007), 12.

8. Martin, *Slavery as Salvation*, 22.

their wealth with slaves who were left in charge of frivolous tasks—such as a slave whose work was devoted to baking pastries. The more specialized the service, the more wealthy the household.[9] Slaves within a wealthy household had ranks or degrees of authority related to their service, education, or skill set. Unlike modern slavery, which often prohibited the education of slaves, Romans prized educated servants.[10] For example, slaves could be engineers, doctors, managers, teachers, or philosophers.[11] Some slaves, due to their household and management positions, had more power than free persons—especially when the slave was representing a powerful master.[12] The more skilled among them could gain not only power, but also become quite wealthy.

Slaves, particularly those in skilled positions, accrued assets, called a *peculium*. The assets could include money, goods, land, tools, or resources—including other slaves.[13] Though everything technically belonged to the master, the slave could use the assets however he or she wished. This gave slaves the opportunity to purchase their freedom—even though the price of freedom for educated and managerial servants could be high. Martin lists an example of a slave doctor who had to pay 50,000 sesterces for his freedom. Compared to his other honors—for example, 30,000 for statues in the temple of Heracles and 37,000 to the public for paving streets—his freedom came at quite a price.[14]

Nonetheless, manumission was part of the slavery system. With the possibility of freedom dangling before slaves, Romans believed that manumission practices would promote better service and obedience. By the time of Augustus, the number of freedpersons had grown so large that the emperor created laws to govern the amount being set free. According to Augustan law, the slave of a Roman citizen had to be at least thirty before formal manumission could occur.[15] There was no guarantee, however, that

---

9. Glancy, *Slavery in Early Christianity*, 44.

10. Harrill, "Paul and Slavery," 312.

11. See Martin, *Slavery as Salvation*, 8, 22; Harrill, "Paul and Slavery," 312–13; Glancy, *Slavery in Early Christianity*, 40.

12. Martin, *Slavery as Salvation*, 22; Glancy, *Slavery in Early Christianity*, 43; Smith, "Slavery in the Early Church," 14.

13. Harrill, "Paul and Slavery," 312.

14. Martin, *Slavery as Salvation*, 7–8.

15. Harrill, "Paul and Slavery," 309. According to A. A. Rupprecht, slaves could expect to be manumitted by the age of thirty, but this is unlikely ("Slave, Slavery," in

manumission occurred at that age. Many scholars assume that slaves were freed after six years of service, but this number is based on a remark by Cicero, who talks about prisoners of war being manumitted after six years (*Eighth Philippic* 32). J. Albert Harrill notes that the reference to six years should be interpreted as mere rhetoric regarding the Roman state being politically enslaved (from the perspective of a Roman senator) under Julius Caesar's power from 49 BCE to 43 BCE.[16] Cicero himself did not practice manumission after six years of a slave's service. Thus, it is questionable whether this practice was followed throughout the empire. In reality, although Augustus created laws to govern manumission, relatively few slaves had the opportunity to purchase their freedom.

Manumission did not equate to the freedom to start a new life apart from the former owner. Even when slaves were manumitted, they still were connected to their former master by their social status. In some parts of the empire, the contract for manumission required the slave to remain in the master's service until the master's death. Even as freedpersons, Romans believed, slaves owed their master loyalty. The master-slave relationship transformed to one of a patron-client. This meant that even with freedom, the slave was socially and likely financially indebted to the former master. Plus, many slaves, particularly those who were educated or who had business experience, were worth more to their former masters once freed. The more successful the freedperson, the more social honor and, perhaps, the more wealth potential there was for the master, whose former slave could work for him as a client.[17]

Manumission did not necessarily entail the conferral of rights. According to Martin, a slave of a Roman citizen could be granted citizenship upon manumission.[18] Not all slaves had this opportunity, however, especially during the early empire. There were degrees of manumission under Roman law, ranging from a full citizen to a Junian Latin. Like slaves, Junian Latins were not allowed to have a legally recognized marriage, to receive an inheritance, to create a will, or to enter into Roman contracts.[19] Thus, being free did not involve the freedom to start one's own house-

---

Dictionary of Paul and His Letters, ed. Gerald F. Hawthorne, Ralph Martin, and Daniel G. Reid [Downers Grove, IL: InterVarsity, 1993], 881-82).

16. Harrill, "Paul and Slavery," 309.
17. Harrill, "Paul and Slavery," 308-10; Smith, "Slavery in the Early Church," 15.
18. Martin, *Slavery as Salvation*, 32.
19. Harrill, "Paul and Slavery," 309.

hold—at least not a household recognized under Roman law. Though there is evidence of slave families who lived together (as slaves and after being freed),[20] slave families did not enjoy the legal status of citizens. Slave couples did not have the legal right to a marriage. Though slaves had children, they were not legally allowed to claim those children as their own.[21] Only full citizens could enter into contracts of marriage, receive an inheritance, or create a will. Only a small portion of the freed slaves would have been able to secure full citizenship.[22] Without the right to claim paternity, they could not establish a legal household where an inheritance is passed to the next generation.

Nonetheless, the hope of a better life was the basis of a common theme in first-century culture of the "slave who made good."[23] In literature from the time period, this slave was able to use servitude to save enough money to make the freeborn wary and even a bit jealous. The wealthy mocked those who used slavery to gain social status, and they maintained a disdain for servitude and the labor associated with slaves. Stories abounded romanticizing the struggle of people who escaped slavery and gained honor.[24] As someone who grew up in one of the poorest states in the United States, I cannot help but see the parallel with the so-called American dream—if you just work hard enough you can have the big house with the white picket fence, the perfect marriage and 2.5 children. The marginalized and the poor know that the "American dream" serves those in power very well. It is true that some Roman slaves were able to use their slavery to climb the social ladder and find honor in their culture, but many more worked tirelessly for a dream that never came true. Most never saw freedom.[25]

The cruelty of Roman slavery should not be overlooked, even if manumission was a possibility for a select few. Both male and female slaves were subject to rape and physical violence.[26] Some slaves were forced to serve as prostitutes. Slaves who worked the mines and mills died in large

---

20. See Dale Martin, "Slave Families and Slaves in Families," in *Early Christian Families in Context: An Interdisciplinary Dialogue*, ed. David Balch and Carolyn Osiek (Grand Rapids: Eerdmans, 2003), 207-30.

21. Glancy, *Slavery in Early Christianity*, 11.

22. Harrill, "Paul and Slavery," 310.

23. Martin, *Slavery as Salvation*, 35.

24. Martin, *Slavery as Salvation*, 30-49.

25. Harrill, "Paul and Slavery," 310; Smith, "Slavery in the Early Church," 14-15.

26. Harrill, "Paul and Slavery," 310; Glancy, *Slavery in Early Christianity*, 50-57.

numbers due to the working conditions.[27] Runaways could be killed or subject to torture.[28] Torture was a standard practice when slaves had to testify for court. The torture might consist of beating with a whip, burning with boiling pitch, hot metal, or torches, or even racking, which involved being strapped to a device intended to separate the body limb by limb. For owners who did not want to get their own hands dirty in beating slaves, they could hire torturers. Advertisements have been found for such services as flogging and crucifixion, both for a surprisingly low rate.[29] Slaves—no matter their position—were, after all, considered property rather than human beings.

Paul and Slavery

Slaves and former slaves were among the communities to whom Paul ministered.[30] For example, Andronicus and Urbanus, listed among the names in Rom 16, are common slave names in the literature and inscriptions of the first century.[31] Plus, the letter to Philemon concerns Onesimus, a slave who has been separated from his master—either by running away or by being away for what might be considered too long. Though it is impossible to know how many slaves were members of the Pauline churches, slavery was such a part of everyday life that it is of little wonder that Paul's letters—which are frequently forced to consider how the gospel impinges upon daily matters—would bear glimpses of what the gospel of abundant life might mean for those who were not treated as though they were entitled to happiness or to basic human dignity. It is worth considering two passages in particular that have been used on both sides of the debate about Paul's attitude toward slavery—the letter to Philemon and 1 Cor 7:20-24.

---

27. Harrill, "Paul and Slavery," 310-11.
28. Sarah Ruden, *Paul among the People: The Apostle Reinterpreted and Reimagined in His Own Time* (New York: Pantheon, 2010), 152.
29. Harrill, "Paul and Slavery," 311.
30. Contra Glancy, who argues that the purity standards, especially those set forth in 1 Cor 5-7, would present an obstacle to most slaves participating in the Pauline communities (*Slavery in Early Christianity*, 49-50).
31. Rupprecht, "Slave, Slavery," 882.

Philemon

It is a wonder that this brief letter made it into the canon. It circulated early in the collection of Paul's letters. The letter is addressed to the slaveholder Philemon, Apphia, Archippus, and the church that meets in Philemon's house, though Paul primarily is speaking to Philemon. The apostle is still in prison (vv. 9–10, 13) and is making plans for after his release, when he hopes to stay in Philemon's home (v. 22). The letter concerns Onesimus, a slave of Philemon's household, who is with Paul and has been with Paul for a while. The apostle writes to urge Philemon to welcome Onesimus back.[32]

There are roughly two broad ways in which Onesimus's predicament has been interpreted. Either Onesimus has run away from Philemon's household, or he was sent by Philemon to help Paul and has stayed away longer than what, Paul fears, Philemon might consider reasonable. In both cases, Onesimus could expect severe treatment from his master. Paul's letter attempts to mollify any potential anger on Philemon's part. In building the case to receive Onesimus warmly upon his arrival, Paul makes a play on the name "Onesimus," which means useless. He writes that "useless" has become "useful" to him and the mission (v. 11). Apparently, Onesimus, who has become a believer, has proven quite useful in the mission, and Paul sees great potential for his work for the gospel. Whether Onesimus is a runaway or was dispatched by Philemon for Paul's sake, Paul urges the master to welcome Onesimus back, not as one might receive a slave, but as one might receive a brother (v. 16).

Paul's vague reference to being welcomed "as" a brother has been interpreted both to support slavery and to argue against it. Though Paul must have assumed that Philemon would understand his instructions and even reminds Philemon of this master's own indebtedness to the apostle, the legal status of Onesimus is not at all clear. Is Paul asking Philemon to release Onesimus? Or is he asking Philemon not to punish him like a runaway? In the first-century context, either option is demanding much of Philemon. Whatever Paul is asking, he seems to believe that Philemon will comply, since he praises Philemon's obedience and shares his plans to

---

32. For an overview of the history of interpretation of this letter, see Demetrius K. Williams, "'No Longer as a Slave': Reading the Interpretation History of Paul's Epistle to Philemon," in *Onesimus Our Brother: Reading Religion, Race, and Culture in Philemon*, ed. Matthew V. Johnson, James A. Noel, and Demetrius K. Williams (Minneapolis: Fortress Press, 2012), 11–46.

visit the household upon his release (vv. 21-22). Furthermore, by addressing more than Philemon—the greetings include Apphia, Archippus, and the church that meets in Philemon's house—Paul has expanded this matter from one between Paul, Onesimus, and Philemon to a matter that now concerns the whole church.[33]

It is not insignificant that Paul treats this situation as a church matter. Whatever Onesimus's status under Roman law—and at the time Paul is writing, he would still be a slave—Paul grants this slave the same title that he has used to describe Philemon: "brother." The same characteristics he has used to depict Philemon in the beginning of the letter—"beloved" and a coworker—he also uses to characterize his relationship to Onesimus, who has been working for the gospel and whom Paul describes as "my own heart" (v. 12). Whatever social status Philemon enjoys in Roman society, his social status does not undermine his family of faith. There is no longer slave or free in Christ (Gal 3:28).[34]

Paul's appeal to welcome Onesimus interweaves language of indebtedness and proposes status upheaval. Onesimus's status is raised from that of a slave to that of a beloved brother.[35] Meanwhile, Paul and Philemon, who have social capital in this situation, are both described in ways that emphasize lowliness. No reference to Paul as apostle appears at the beginning of this letter—only Paul as prisoner of Christ Jesus. Though Paul is a presbyter (ambassador or elder), and thus someone of standing, he emphasizes his chains (v. 9). Paul has the social capital to make such demands of Philemon because, as the apostle reminds this master, Philemon is indebted to him (v. 19). Plus, Paul offers to pay whatever Onesimus might owe Philemon. As Lloyd Lewis notes, "Now Paul demonstrates that he and Onesimus are interchangeable. Paul assumes the debts of Onesimus to Philemon as his

---

33. Lloyd A. Lewis, "Philemon," in *True to Our Native Land: An African American New Testament Commentary*, ed. Brian K. Blount (Minneapolis: Fortress, 2007), 440.

34. Lewis reads Paul's instructions in this letter through the lenses of the familial language of the family of God and the baptismal equality presented in Gal 3:28 in "The Philemon-Paul-Onesimus Triangle," in *Stony the Road We Trod: African American Biblical Interpretation*, ed. Cain Hope Felder (Minneapolis: Fortress, 1991), 232-46.

35. See also Lewis, "Philemon," 442. Mitzi J. Smith argues that the fictive status as brother would not eliminate the oppressor-oppressed relationship ("Utility, Fraternity, and Reconciliation: Ancient Slavery as a Context for the Return of Onesimus," in *Onesimus Our Brother: Reading Religion, Race, and Culture in Philemon*, ed. Matthew V. Johnson, James A. Noel, and Demetrius K. Williams (Minneapolis: Fortress Press, 2012), 51.

own (v. 19)."³⁶ Paul urges Philemon to receive Onesimus, just as he would receive Paul (v. 17).

By asking Philemon to act in such a manner, Paul is asking that Philemon lower himself socially, treat this slave as a beloved brother, and welcome this slave as he would welcome someone to whom he owes his very life (v. 17-19). And as though the letter is not asking a lot of Philemon to begin with, Paul plans to visit. Philemon is indebted to Paul. Paul's visit will ensure that Philemon complies, just as Paul praises him for doing (vv. 21-22).

What is at stake in this letter? Unfortunately, our pressing questions about Onesimus's legal status remain unanswered. But some consistent patterns emerge in Paul's letter. First, those who have status must be willing to relinquish it for the sake of the gospel. Onesimus has been working with Paul and for the mission. He has proven quite useful. Whether he can be classified as a runaway slave or a slave who has been away too long does not really matter. Paul treats Philemon as though Philemon has the legal right to punish Onesimus, and Paul is holding Philemon to a much higher standard than Roman law. Second, Paul does not honor the line between individual matters and community matters. What one does with one's body or one's household has implications for the health and well-being of the community (see, e.g., 1 Cor 5:1-13; 6:12-20). Paul includes the entire church in this matter. He does not simply address Philemon, who is the one with the legal authority to decide how to treat his slave. Rather, Paul has made it clear that they are all brothers and sisters in Christ. Their loyalty is to Christ.

If Paul's instructions imply the freedom of Onesimus, why doesn't Paul ask Philemon to free all his slaves? Since Philemon's household could function well enough without Onesimus (who was "useless" to Philemon) and he is wealthy enough to have a guest room, then it is likely that Philemon had other slaves. Others in the church likely had slaves, too. What are the implications of this letter for discussions of Paul's views on slavery?

Though this may be a good question, in many ways, it is the wrong question. Legally freeing Onesimus would not have made him any less dependent upon his former master. As noted in the previous section, freedpersons were still socially bound—still dependent—upon their master's households. Freeing Onesimus would not give him the freedom to go on mission with Paul or serve the community. He would be free to serve Philemon without the social stigma of slavery. But he would forever be

36. Lewis, "Philemon," 442-43.

attached to Philemon's household. He would still be in a position of trying to appease his former master. Sarah Ruden notes instances where even a freedperson requires someone to intercede when the former master is angry.[37] In my context, we are fond of saying that freedom is not free. In the Roman world, freedom—at least for a slave—does not really exist.

Though "freedom" does not mean that the slave becomes an equal to the master, *brotherhood* would. Paul claims Onesimus as a son and places himself in the patriarchal role to Philemon by reminding Philemon that he owes Paul his very life. As Ruden beautifully articulates, "A slave was a *filius neminis*, a son of no one. No man could claim him as a child, and no slave could make a claim on any man as his father."[38] Paul equalizes the position of Onesimus and Philemon. They are *brothers*. Yet, true to form, Paul does not stay in the patriarchal spot. He simultaneously lowers himself. Though an elder, he is but a prisoner. Though a freeborn citizen, he is in chains. Though Philemon is indebted to him, he now becomes indebted to Philemon. He is a brother alongside the others. Brothers inherit equally.[39] Brothers are the future of the household.

It is absolutely true that Paul does not tackle the slavery system. Even manumission maintains a social hierarchy that privileges the masters. He does, however, let the gospel create social upheaval in the households that claim Christ as Lord. In the bonds of brotherhood, all can claim an inheritance. In the bonds of brotherhood, all are indebted to one another's well-being. Beyond the church, it was not common to fabricate relationships of brotherhood. The stakes are simply too high. Brotherhood would make Onesimus not just a slave, but, as Ruden argues, a *human being*.[40]

1 Corinthians 7:20–24

These verses have presented a quandary for many interpreters. They are housed in a passage that is devoted to marriage. Paul is answering the Corinthians' questions (finally), and apparently the believers have wondered about marriage, divorce, and singleness in light of the belief that Christ might return any day. In the midst of Paul's long response, he mentions

---

37. Ruden, *Paul among the People*, 158–59.
38. Ruden, *Paul among the People*, 165.
39. Ruden, *Paul among the People*, 164.
40. Ruden, *Paul among the People*, 158, 164.

circumcision and slavery. It is as though he has the baptismal confession in his head: in Christ, there is neither slave nor free, Jew nor Greek, male and female. Most of 1 Cor 7 is devoted to issues that may have arisen due to differing interpretations of being neither male nor female in Christ. The Corinthians are wondering how to live out that confession in daily life. Furthermore, if Christ's return is imminent, should believers marry off their sons and daughters to secure their future? In the midst of these pressing questions, Paul mentions the other facets of this confession—how it might affect slaves, the circumcised, and the uncircumcised (1 Cor 7:17-24).

A quick comparison of some modern translations of 1 Cor 7:21 reveals just how convoluted the Greek is.

> KJV: Art thou called being a servant? Care not for it: but if thou mayest be made free, use it rather.

> NRSV: Were you a slave when called? Do not be concerned about it. Even if you can gain your freedom, make use of your present condition now more than ever.

> NIV: Were you a slave when you were called? Don't let it trouble you—although if you can gain your freedom, do so.

> NJB: So, if when you were called, you were a slave, do not think it matters—even if you have a chance of freedom, you should prefer to make full use of your condition as a slave.

In these examples of popular translations, the meaning of the verse seems to change considerably from one translation to the next. The King James Version and the New International Version both urge the slave to take advantage of gaining freedom if that is possible. On the contrary, the New Revised Standard Version and the New Jerusalem Bible tell the slave to be content as a servant and somehow use that position for the sake of the gospel. Is Paul telling slaves to take advantage of gaining their freedom or to take advantage of their position as slaves? Given that some of our popular Bible translations are not clear and consistent, it is not surprising that this passage was used on both sides of the argument about Paul's attitude toward slavery.

This critical verse is bracketed by pleas to remain in the state in which one was called by God. In fact, this appeal transitions from the topic of circumcision to the issue of slavery. That each one should lead the life in which the Lord has called him or her is the overall refrain of the paragraph.

> 1 Cor 7:17 (NRSV): However that may be, let each of you lead the life that the Lord has assigned, to which God called you. This is my rule in all the churches.
> 7:18–19: Topic of circumcision or uncircumcision
> 1 Cor 7:20 (NRSV): Let each of you remain in the condition in which you were called.
> 7:21–23: Topic of slaves
> 1 Cor 7:24 (NRSV): In whatever condition you were called, brothers and sisters, there remain with God.

Furthermore, the mention of God serves as a framing device and the theological underpinning (1 Cor 7:17, 24). God is the one who calls each person regardless of his or her station in life (vv. 17 and 24). God calls just as we are—circumcised or uncircumcised, slave or free.

Based on the overall focus of the paragraph, then, how do we interpret verse 21? As we have seen, the modern translations are torn between allowing an exception to the overall rule (of remaining in the position that one had when God calls) or making even slaves abide by the rule. A literal translation of verse 21 would look something like this: "A slave you were called, do not let it be a concern to you, but if also you are able to become free, rather do so." Given the rhythm of the paragraph, a less wooden translation would be: "Were you a slave when you were called? Do not let that be a concern to you, but if you are able to become free, all the more do so." It is the last half of this verse that has caused the most variance in translation. The NRSV reads, "Even if you can gain your freedom, make use of your present condition now more than ever." There is no reference to "your present condition" in Greek. The New Jerusalem Bible also adds to the sentiment: "you should prefer to make full use of your condition as a slave." The Greek is sparse here. The immediate reference of "rather do so" is the conditional clause "if you are able to become free."

If we look in the larger context, Paul is fond of giving rules and guidelines and then allowing an exception. For instance, he would prefer for the unmarried to remain single like he is, because they could devote themselves to the mission without being bogged down with "worldly troubles" (7:28; cf. 7:32), but he provides an exception for those who cannot control themselves and burn with desire (7:8–9, 36–38). In 7:10, Paul commands that the wife should not separate from her husband, but he immediately provides a caveat that if she does leave him, she should remain single or be reconciled with her husband (v. 11). (Notably, there is no such caveat regarding a husband divorcing his wife!) He urges those who are married to unbelievers to remain in their marriages and not to seek a divorce (7:13). The exception is if the unbelieving partner wants to separate, then the believer should allow it (7:15).

Thus, when read in light of the context, Paul is consistent in telling all to remain in the state in which they were called—married or single, slave or free, circumcised and uncircumcised. God called them as they were. God shows no partiality. Nonetheless, life is messy. Jesus may be coming back any day (as Paul firmly believes, 7:29–31), but the church has to face the messiness of what it means to live a life worthy of the gospel in whatever position they find themselves. That means that none of these guidelines are hard and fast rules. Paul provides exception after exception—for marriage and singleness and even slavery. Furthermore, if the letter to Philemon is any indication, then it would make more sense to read 7:21 as an exception to the general rule. A freedperson may not be able to enjoy complete freedom from their former master, but he or she would have a bit more freedom than when a slave. A freedperson could devote more time in service to the gospel than in service to a master. If Paul is concerned that marriage would steal one away from devotion to the gospel, he would not deny that slavery presents an even greater obstacle to that devotion.

What do we make of the odd line, "Do not become slaves of humans" (7:23)? Dale Martin has argued that some may have sold themselves into slavery to advance themselves socially. This was a risky venture, but for the impoverished, slavery offered a chance to survive. It also offered the ability to acquire skills and training. Attaching oneself to a respectable family meant that even after purchasing one's freedom, that former slave would always be affiliated with the powerful household. Having a patron had benefits. Wealthy patrons had power in the local courts. They had access to other benefactors and access to resources. Martin contends, "As surprising as it may sound to modern ears, slavery was arguably the most important channel through which outsiders entered the mainstream of Roman power structures."[41] As noted earlier, being a slave did not necessarily place one as the least in society. Since powerful people had slaves manage their businesses and estates on their behalf, some slaves were placed in positions of

---

41. Martin, *Slavery as Salvation*, 23, 30–49, quoting 32.

power.[42] While it may sound odd that Paul felt the need to tell the Corinthians not to become enslaved, this advice is in keeping with the general theme of the chapter. Paul wanted believers to prioritize their service to the gospel rather than try to secure a future for themselves, especially in light of Christ's imminent return.

Conclusion

Paul did not directly fight slavery. The institution itself was not in question in Paul's day. This does not mean that Paul or the early churches were calloused to the conditions of the least among them. Evidence shows that some churches provided funds to manumit Christian slaves.[43] Though Paul did not take up the topic of slavery directly, some important lessons emerge from his letter to Philemon and his direct advice to slaves in 1 Cor 7.

The gospel disrupts the social order. The baptismal formula of Gal 3:28 (cf. 1 Cor 12:13) suggests that all are not only welcome but that all are also present in the church—slave and free. When Paul admonishes the believers to love one another and bear one another's burdens, slaves are not immune from receiving love and care. The letter to Philemon may be directed at the slaveholder, but it is addressed to the whole church that meets in Philemon's house. Paul makes Onesimus's plight a matter for the church. This move alone suggests that Paul did not see this slave as Philemon's property. Rather, Onesimus is a beloved member of the community, and his welfare is presented as a concern for all.

All are not only wanted, but all are also considered beneficial in the ministry. Onesimus, whose name means "useless," has become "useful" to the mission. In 1 Cor 7, it is clear that Paul is prioritizing the ministry of the gospel above all else—even a secure future for members of the church. Slaves, too, are part of that ministry. It is because of this priority that Paul advises them to seek their freedom if possible. But he also is concerned that free persons would not place themselves into slavery voluntarily. Slavery—like marriage (!)—is presented as an obstacle to one's full devotion to the mission.

The gospel demands embracing slaves not as property, but as humans and, even more than that, as brothers and sisters. The familial language

---

42. Martin, *Slavery as Salvation*, 22.
43. Martin, *Slavery as Salvation*, 8.

that describes the relationships in the church has perhaps been too quickly overlooked as a powerful means of resistance.

In the church, slaves and masters were siblings. Slaves who could never dream of an inheritance were now heirs of the promises of God. Slaves who could never claim anyone as father were now children of God. In the letter to Philemon, Paul took on multiple roles simultaneously—prisoner, elder, father, and brother. The mission took this one who was in the powerful position of a respected elder and humbled him as a prisoner, a slave of the state. He is asking Philemon to humble himself by relinquishing his role as master and welcoming Onesimus—not as a slave who has shamed his master, but as a beloved brother who is integral to the mission of the church.

In the epilogue of the musical *Les Misérables*, in the wake of the French Revolution, the oppressed imagine a different world. Earlier the plight of the masses had been captured in the words of the song, "Do You Hear the People Sing?":

> Do you hear the people sing?
> Singing the songs of angry men?
> It is the music of the people
> Who will not be slaves again!
> When the beating of your heart
> Echoes the beating of the drums
> There is a life about to start
> When tomorrow comes!

The anticipation of another world—of freedom—spurs on the revolution. At the end of the musical, the tune returns, and the words of "angry men" are expressed in hope for the "wretched of the earth":

> They will live again in freedom
> In the garden of the Lord
> We will walk behind the ploughshare;
> We will put away the sword.
> The chain will be broken
> And all men will have their reward.[44]

---

44. Alain Albert Boubill, Claude Michel Schönberg, Herbert Kretzmer, and Jean Marc Natel.

The hope is for life abundant that is available to all. This is exactly what Paul's gospel is offering: abundant life that only God can provide. For Paul, though, he believes that God is breaking down barriers *in the present*. The power of God's salvation does not wait for life "beyond the barricade." Though God's kingdom will not come to fruition until Christ comes again, God's reign has already begun. God is disrupting the social orders that degrade most and elevate a few. God sees *all* as beloved children. If the church had even tried to live into this calling to bear witness to this other world, this reign of God where all are free and all can experience life abundant, the French Revolution might not have been necessary. Oh how very different history might be if the believers followed Paul's advice to treat those beside them as beloved siblings.

FURTHER READING

Glancy, Jennifer A. *Slavery in Early Christianity.* Oxford: Oxford University Press, 2002. Glancy examines the evidence of slave life in the first-century churches. Though I disagree with the conclusion that the purity practices of the Pauline churches would have marginalized or prohibited slave participation, the book is well researched and thought-provoking.

Harrill, J. Albert. *Slaves in the New Testament: Literary, Social, and Moral Dimensions.* Minneapolis: Fortress, 2006. Harrill has written multiple works on slavery in the Roman world. This book is an excellent resource for those interested in studying the topic in light of the New Testament.

Joshell, Sandra R. *Slavery in the Roman World.* Cambridge Introduction to Roman Civilization. Cambridge: Cambridge University Press, 2010. This account of slavery appeals to an array of resources—literature, law, and art—to give the reader a glimpse of life for slaves in the Roman world.

Lewis, Lloyd A. "An African American Appraisal of the Philemon-Paul-Onesimus Triangle." Pages 232-46 in *Stony the Road We Trod: African American Biblical Interpretation*, ed. Cain Hope Felder. Minneapolis: Fortress, 1991. This classic article deftly addresses the issues that have plagued the interpretation of the letter to Philemon and reframes the interpretation through the lens of the undisputed letters of Paul, particularly through Galatians.

Martin, Dale B. *Slavery as Salvation: The Metaphor of Slavery in Pauline Christianity*. New Haven: Yale University Press, 1990. Martin reads Paul's letters, particularly the prominence of the metaphor of slavery, through the lenses of the evidence of slave life in the first-century world.

CHAPTER THREE

Women and the Pauline Mission

This message was scrawled on a yellow Post-it Note by a seminary student in my course, Women and the Letters of Paul:

> I'm struggling with the Bible as a whole when it contains so many contradictions, harmful statements, etc. . . . This class is forcing me to figure out where the Bible fits in my faith (having been used to harm so many) when it didn't play a huge role in my church or faith early on.[1]

This note, like all the notes collected at the beginning of that class, was unsigned. The assignment was simple: Write on a Post-it Note (or two or three) your questions, concerns, or obstacles in the study of Paul's letters, particularly regarding the role of women in Paul's ministry. Having such a checkered past with the apostle myself, raised in a Southern Baptist church that did not support women in ministry, I was anticipating some challenging questions and obstacles, or "speed bumps," as my colleague Sharon Ringe calls them.[2] "How can I (a woman) defend my call to ministry when these texts are used to delegitimize it?" reads another note. Other students raised similar questions, but the pain of a history of (mis)interpretation had left its mark: "Why the heck are these letters—highly contextualized letters written by some dude who never even knew Jesus—even 'sacred Scripture' / 'the Word of God' anyways? What makes Paul so damn special?" Another student recounts an experience from her teen years, when a young man

---

1. A student in my class, Women and the Letters of Paul, Wesley Theological Seminary, Washington, DC, September 2016.
2. Frederick C. Tiffany and Sharon H. Ringe, *Biblical Interpretation: A Roadmap* (Nashville: Abingdon, 1996), 56.

convinced his college-aged girlfriend, a woman whom my student had looked up to, that the calling to ministry that she was experiencing had to be from Satan, not Jesus. The student writes that she has "hated" (with the word underscored) 1 Tim 2 ever since.

It is perhaps important to note that my seminary context is United Methodist, a denomination where women are affirmed as church leaders. Some of my students come from churches or denominations that would never fully support a female pastor, but all the students in this seminary class have expressed some call to ministry. The vast majority are women. Some of them are also grappling with Pauline texts that have been used in the debates over homosexuality. Others are haunted by Pauline passages used to justify enslavement and wondering whether they should listen to an apostle whose writings have been associated with such a grave injustice. One thing is clear: Multiple layers of woundedness are in this classroom, but a willingness to struggle with the text is also there.

Some of my students are simply trying to redeem the text for the sake of their future ministry. Given the topic of the class, which is also the topic of this chapter, the pressing question for my female students has become, *how* can they redeem Pauline texts whose interpretation has been used to thwart their God-given calling, to silence them into submission, or even to threaten them to stay in abusive relationships? Isn't this the apostle who declares that women should be silent in the church and learn from their husbands at home (1 Cor 14:34–35)? Before we quench the Holy Spirit in the name of biblical literacy, perhaps it is time for us to reconsider Paul's words on women in light of their historical context.

Paul and the Pretense of "Biblical Womanhood"

One thing is certain: Paul's letters are still at the forefront of debates about women's roles in ministry and at home. For example, the Council on Biblical Manhood and Womanhood formed in 1987, largely in response to the rise of feminism within the ranks of the evangelical church, and hoped to set the record straight on the roles that men and, particularly, women should play in the life of their family and church. In 1987, the Council composed and adopted the Danvers Statement of Biblical Manhood and Womanhood. This statement relies heavily on the Pauline tradition—more specifically, Ephesians, 1 Timothy, and Titus, letters that much of critical scholarship doubts were written by the apostle. According to "Affirmation 4" of the statement, the fall introduced distortions into the relationship between men and women, and this distortion is to blame for why women resist limitations in their leadership roles in church or try to use their gifts for ministries that are not "appropriate." The statement relies heavily on the household codes and urges women to be model wives, submitting to husbands who are required to love them.

The biblical texts upon which the Danvers Statement relies are limited in scope and culturally bound. The household codes of Ephesians and Colossians (and 1 Peter) assume the power distinctions between male and female (as well as slave and master and children and parents). Regardless of whether these letters are Pauline, they appear to represent a later development in the life of the church, a time when the believers realized that Christ's return might not occur within their lifetime. This meant that the church started thinking about how to preserve traditions and teachings for the next generation. Church leadership offices were beginning to form, and Christians were urged to appear like respectable citizens within their society with households that exhibited model behaviors. Since the early Christians did not have the legal right of assembly in a public space, these model households would help the church exist under the radar of an ever-suspicious Roman Empire. It also meant that believers had to learn how to live faithfully in whatever social position they happened to find themselves. If already married upon coming to the faith, what does that marriage look like in light of submission to the Crucified One? The household codes provided much-needed instruction in light of such questions.

The full witness of Paul's letters provides a much more complex view of "womanhood" than the household codes alone. The women in Paul's churches are not wallflowers, but participants. They are leaders, patrons, servants, prophets, and apostles. In its creation of "biblical womanhood," the Danvers Statement does not take into account any of the women who are serving in leadership in Paul's churches. There is no mention of Junia (Rom 16:7), Phoebe (Rom 16:1-2), Prisca (Rom 16:3-5), Euodia (Phil 4:2-3), Syntyche (Phil 4:2-3), or Nympha (Col 4:15). In fact, it is easy to see that some texts from the Pauline tradition have trumped others in the creation of this statement. Nonetheless, the Danvers Statement on "biblical womanhood" raises an interesting hermeneutical dilemma: Can we discern from Paul's letters what he thought about the role of women? How concerned is Paul about "manhood" and "womanhood"?

The apostle is writing letters to real churches with real problems. He does not sit down and write a treatise on women. The only place where he takes up the topic of the household in his undisputed letters is in 1 Cor 7, and there it seems that he is forced to take a stand and offer advice only due to the Corinthians' letter asking him about marriage and singleness in a community awaiting Christ's return. All his advice is focused on the proclamation of the gospel. He advises the Corinthians *not* to marry and to avoid being consumed by household matters, but he offers concessions for those who feel that they must marry. Ironically, if 1 Cor 7 were taken into account in the Danvers Statement, single Christian women who are going about the mission of the gospel would be the model for "biblical womanhood." Single women are not submitting to husbands, but only to Christ. If the early church followed Paul's advice in 1 Cor 7, the church would be taking on an enormous responsibility to care for all the women who did not marry so that they could participate in the ministry of the gospel.

We cannot interview the women in Paul's churches. We do not have the privilege of hearing their voices at all in the biblical witness. Paul's letters offer us glimpses into the lives of the communities, but those glimpses are always filtered through Paul's lenses, through the lenses of the folks reporting issues to Paul, and through our own lenses as readers. With one passage telling women to be silent in church and another passage telling them what to wear whenever they pray and prophesy before the community, it is not difficult to see why my students—and church tradition—have found the witness on women to be messy and problematic. This chapter will examine a few of the passages at the center of the storm, in the hope of recovering some insights about the presence and role of women in the Pauline mission.

1 Corinthians 11:2–16: Head-Covering and Human Dignity

While 1 Cor 11:2–16 may not win an award for being the simplest to understand, it would also be a shame for this text to be completely dismissed in the life of the church. The lectionary overlooks it, although scholarship, particularly feminist scholarship, has invested countless hours in its struggle to understand this text. In *Encountering God in Tyrannical Texts: Reflections on Paul, Women, and the Authority of Scripture*, Francis Taylor Gench devotes a large percentage of her book to grappling with this text.[3] And

---

3. Francis Taylor Gench, *Encountering God in Tyrannical Texts: Reflections on Paul, Women, and the Authority of Scripture* (Louisville: Westminster John Knox, 2015).

for good reason. It is convoluted. Scholars cannot decide whether women are casting their veils aside or letting their hair down. Paul's words are not precise either. He is talking about covering the head (*katakaluptomai*), but never employs the typical word for a veil (*krēdemnon*). In 1 Cor 11:10, the apostle declares that women are to have "authority" over their heads whenever they get up to pray and prophesy in the assembly. What does it mean for women to have authority over their own heads? Notably this passage has *no concern for whether women are allowed to pray and prophesy before a mixed assembly*. It is simply a given that women are engaged in this worship leadership. (For some of my readers, this point needs to sink in. Ironically, Affirmation 6 of the Danvers Statement actually cites 1 Cor 11:2–16 as proof that "some governing and teaching roles within the church are restricted to men"!) The entire passage is about how women appear before the congregation *whenever* they engage in worship leadership.

Why is head-covering such a big issue? Our interpretations of head-covering have focused on gender. *Women* wear veils. It is common to interpret 1 Cor 11:2–16 in light of the baptismal formula in Gal 3:28, which appears to erase the male-female dichotomy in Christ. Reading in this light, interpreters suggest that when the baptismal formula is repeated in 1 Cor 12:13, Paul omits the male-female pair because it is an issue at Corinth. The issue in 1 Cor 11:2–16, according to this framework, is that women have tried to live into the equality presented by the baptismal formula. In other words, they are enjoying their newfound freedom in Christ. Their action of unveiling would make them, in at least one respect, more like their male counterparts, as though it is the first-century equivalent of bra-burning. Read in this light, the veil becomes a symbol of all things feminine. Thus, Paul's advice to cover the head would reintroduce gender norms back into the community.

If the women are using this baptismal formula to claim their freedom in Christ and therefore to present themselves unveiled, however, Paul does not address their rationale. In fact, if freedom is the underlying problem disturbing worship, he will later tell the same church, "where the Spirit of the Lord is, there is freedom" (2 Cor 3:17). If the women are boasting of freedom in Christ, it seems odd that Paul would be so careless in a following letter. What if gender distinctions are not assumed to be the heart of the problem in 1 Cor 11:2–16?

Frequently, this text is dismissed as another place where Paul misses the mark when it comes to women. Forcing women to wear veils and urging men to go coverless reinforces gender distinctions and, according to some, denigrates women. I do not think that Paul, or any first-century male, could imagine a world where women and men were considered equal. (Indeed, as a female living in the twenty-first century, I still wonder what that world would look like.) Focusing solely on the male-female dichotomy, while tempting, given that the instructions are different based on gender, will produce an interpretation that ends where it began—with Paul reinforcing gender distinctions in his advice. Paul does this. Period. Even if "head" is taken to mean "source" in verse 3, women come from men and men come from women (1 Cor 11:12). The genders are not the same, even if interdependent (1 Cor 11:11). Frankly, an ancient writer appealing to gender distinctions is not newsworthy. And the fact that we get stuck there says more about our own context than Paul's. A closer look at this text reveals that there is more than meets the eye in this head-covering headline.

Before we consider Paul's advice regarding veiling, it is perhaps important to pause and ask how this topic came to Paul's attention. Paul has written 1 Corinthians in direct response to questions raised by the church in a letter (7:1) and to matters made known to him by Chloe's people (1:11). We know that the church has asked for Paul's advice on particular matters because Paul refers to their letter in 1 Cor 7:1: "Now concerning the matters about which you wrote." Several other topics after 7:1 begin with Paul writing, "now concerning," as though to address yet another topic raised by the Corinthians, such as whether to consume idol food (8:1), the use of spiritual gifts in the assembly (12:1), and the logistics of the collection (16:1). The topic of head-covering in worship, however, does not begin with the phrase "now concerning," suggesting that this topic was *not* included among the official questions sent by the church. Rather, it seems that this issue was not among the church's list of approved questions to ask the apostle. Paul must have learned about the problem from Chloe's people.

Why might it be significant that Chloe's people are the source for whatever is happening in worship in regard to women's heads? Perhaps this issue has ramifications for those who are not of the wealthiest classes of women in the community. It is quite possible that Chloe's people are slaves of Chloe's household, since the phrase "those of Chloe" is a typical way to address servants of a household. Whoever they are, whether slaves, freedpersons, or family, their primary identity is with Chloe's house. They are not heads of the household themselves. They seem to be Paul's source for matters that might be of interest to those who are not in power. In fact, it appears that Chloe's people share information that some in the church would rather not have Paul know. They have told Paul about the inequities at the Lord's Table where those who have homes and food are getting full and drunk before the working class even arrive for worship (11:17–34). The church did not volunteer that some were hiring prostitutes (6:12–20) or suing one another in court (6:1–11). Somehow, the topic of the man sleeping with his stepmom also did not make the church's official list of questions to Paul, likely since the man was of high enough social status that most in the church were not in a position, due to social etiquette, to reproach him. Perhaps Chloe's people help represent the voices of those who do not find themselves in positions of power—those who have nothing and those who are not deemed wise by the rest of the world. Maybe they are among those in their society who cannot legally bring a lawsuit, since slaves and freedpersons cannot legally sue masters or former masters. Perhaps, as slaves, they stand in solidarity with other slaves in the church who may be forced into prostitution. When Paul's response to the Corinthians arrived, the church had to listen to its dirty laundry being aired (*for six chapters!*) before the apostle finally got to the church's official questions in chapter 7! The issue of head-covering in worship does not appear to be a concern to those in power, but it is an issue voiced to Paul on behalf of those who are most vulnerable in the congregation.

What happens when we read this passage in light of what the veil symbolizes in the first century, especially with regard to social status? Surrounding the instructions of 1 Cor 11:2–16 are topics where the church is divided between the haves and the have-nots. As Gerd Theissen famously argued, the tensions in the Corinthian congregation cannot be divorced from economic status.[4] As stated above, according to 1 Cor 11:17–34, there are real divisions at the Lord's Table between those who have plenty and those who have nothing. Perhaps less obvious to twenty-first-century readers, though, are the social distinctions surrounding the issue of eating idol food (1 Cor 8:1–11:1). In 1 Cor 8:1–13, some in the congregation are eating food that has been sacrificed to idols at the local temple. For these congregants to be present at the temple indicates that they have been invited to a banquet. Receiving such an invitation was an indicator of status. Patronage was the social fabric that secured a household's honorable status in society. Dinner parties helped form and establish alliances within a larger network of benefaction. Those who received an invitation were not in a position to offend the host of the party and, thereby, risk bringing shame upon their household. Nor were

---

4. Gerd Theissen, *The Social Setting of Pauline Christianity: Essays on Corinth*, ed. and trans. John H. Schütz (Philadelphia: Fortress, 1982).

they in a position to refuse whatever they had been served at the party. However, they were at least among the invited guests, even if they were in some way indebted to the host. The host would not be issuing an invitation to those who had no means to reciprocate the host's generosity. In other words, the "have-nots" of society might not ever be special guests at a banquet. Those who never received such invitations were not deemed important enough in the social network to be included. They were not calloused to the rituals of the banquets because they were not used to being present. The dilemma of whether to consume idol food at a banquet, therefore, is a situation that does not present itself to all in First Church Corinth. Rather, the witness of those of higher social status, who appear to be honoring other gods through their idol-food consumption, is a threat to those in the church who are not used to going through the motions of honoring the god or goddess of the local temple. The issue of idol-food consumption is, thus, more than a matter of fleeing idolatry. It is a matter of considering the needs of the one for whom Christ died, and socioeconomic realities are at play.

Since it is the case that First Church Corinth is divided along socioeconomic lines as well as over practical, ethical, and theological matters, why do discussions of 11:2-16 focus solely on gender without considering that not all women at the assembly would be treated equally? In other words, how might veiling be related to social honor?

The text itself introduces honor and shame into the argument. In 1 Cor 11:5, Paul says that it is shameful for a woman to pray or prophesy with an unveiled head. In fact, he says that for a woman to pray unveiled is the same as having her head shaved, though in verse 6, it seems that having a shaved head might be preferable to letting down one's hair. There is something implied here about a woman's hair. *A respectable woman's hair should not be visible in public.* For this reason, a Roman wife wears a veil in public. More than an indication of gender, it is a sign of modesty, decency, and respect. Roman wives were to be veiled as a symbol of their status in society.[5] To be a freeborn citizen wife would be the highest honor that the Corinthian culture could grant to a female. In *Paul among the People*, Sarah Ruden, a classicist, argues that wearing veils was closely linked to entitlement. Roman wives enjoyed the privilege of wearing veils.[6] Many studies have

---

5. Bruce Winter, *After Paul Left Corinth: The Influence of Secular Ethics and Social Change* (Grand Rapids: Eerdmans, 2001), 121-41.

6. Sarah Ruden, *Paul among the People: The Apostle Reinterpreted and Reimagined in His Own Time* (New York: Pantheon, 2010), 86-87.

shown that, although women were not considered equal to men in Greco-Roman society, Roman wives exerted power and influence within their households. The household was largely theirs to manage.[7] Many Roman wives held positions of authority, even beyond their households, as patrons and benefactors.[8]

It has been argued that some women of higher status—especially those who are hosting the house churches—might remove their veils in the comfort of their own homes. Winter contends that the women who are appearing unveiled before the Corinthian assembly are wives who, perhaps in the intimacy of their own household, have removed their veils to try to appear more like the "new" Roman wife in upper-class society, who "claims for herself the indulgence in sexuality of a woman of pleasure."[9] Removal of the veil, then, would be a deliberate decision on the part of some wives who might be drawing attention to their "secular status" when praying and prophesying and who did not desire to appear married. We know that women served as hosts of the house churches: for example, Prisca (Rom 16:3-4), Nympha (Col 4:15), or Lydia (Acts 16:14-15). It is possible that they, as Winter suggests, are leading the assembly since they might typically feel comfortable in their own home. However, it is hard to imagine that the wives are removing their veils to be like "new" Roman wives who are attempting to attract richer sexual partners, as Winter suggests.[10] First of all, this assembly does not appear to be full of wealthy men, and second, the wives in this church appear to have a reputation for withholding sex rather than being sexually promiscuous (7:1-6). Nothing in 1 Cor 7 indicates that married women are refusing the most obvious sign of their marriage status—wearing the veil. Furthermore, Paul chastises men for visiting prostitutes (6:12-20). Even if women are not intentionally behaving like the "new" Roman wives, could they be removing the veil in a more intimate sphere, as they would at their own homes?

How "intimate" is the gathering of First Church Corinth? Even if the "whole church" can gather in Gaius's home (Rom 16:23), it seems unlikely that the whole church gathers each time. In fact, the inclusion of the qualifier "whole" seems to indicate that the church most often meets in house-

---

7. Carolyn Osiek and Margaret Y. MacDonald, *A Woman's Place: House Churches in Earliest Christianity* (Minneapolis: Fortress, 2006), 154-57.

8. Osiek and MacDonald, *A Woman's Place*, 157-59.

9. Winter, *After Paul Left Corinth*, 123; cf. 129.

10. Winter, *After Paul Left Corinth*, 121-31.

holds and gathers occasionally as a whole body. Furthermore, the church seems to comprise those of varying social levels, and Paul has to teach them to love one another. Nothing indicates that the "haves" are considerate or even cognizant of the needs of the "have-nots." This congregation seems to preserve social distinctions even in the smallest assemblies rather than treat all the church members as beloved family (see, e.g., 1 Cor 11:17–34). Given the church's propensity to be entrenched in its social status, and based upon all that a veil symbolizes, it seems unlikely that the wives were electing to remove their veils.

What might the lack of head-covering convey? Losing status as a Roman wife was directly linked to losing the right to wear a veil. If accused of adultery, Roman women were no longer allowed to wear the floor-length stola or veil.[11] Hair was viewed as erotic, a feature suitable for a lover to see. With her head exposed, the wife was publicly disgraced as an adulteress. Paul likens being unveiled to the shame of a shaved head, the sign of an adulteress (11:5–6).[12] It was customary, however, for prostitutes to have exposed locks. The temple prostitutes would appear before cultic assemblies with their hair down. To help modern-day readers understand the scandal, Richard Hays likens the situation of 1 Cor 11:2–16 to a woman coming to church topless.[13] This would be unthinkably scandalous. Surely, Paul does not want the Corinthians' worship services in any way resembling the temple down the street.

Having a bare head suggested sexual availability, but the veil offered protection. There were few benefits of being a female in the ancient world. If being a woman was one's lot in life, then the most-respected females of the ancient world were those who had the right to wear a veil in public. The veil protected them from objectification. It was a symbol of modesty and propriety.

Not every woman in First Church Corinth had the privilege of veiling. Slaves could not legally marry or, by custom or law, present themselves publicly as though having the same status as Roman freeborn wives. Ruden argues that the prostitutes or former prostitutes in the church would not have had the right to cover themselves.[14] While Ruden notes that most

---

11. Ruden, *Paul among the People*, 87.
12. Winter, *After Paul Left Corinth*, 133.
13. Richard B. Hays, *First Corinthians*, IBC (Louisville: Westminster John Knox, 1997), 186.
14. Ruden, *Paul among the People*, 86–87.

prostitutes were slaves, the realities of slavery meant that even those slave women who were not deemed prostitutes were always vulnerable to sexual attack. By virtue of being slaves, they were considered sexually available to their masters. If some women are praying and prophesying with head uncovered, might they be women who are not normally allowed by custom or by law to cover themselves? What if these women are not libertarians basking in their freedom in Christ and burning their veils? What if they are not women who have the legal privilege of marrying? What if they are slave women or freedwomen who are using their freedom in Christ to pray and prophesy before the assembly? Whenever they get up to pray, they are appearing as they normally would, with heads uncovered, hair visible, because that is the way their culture *requires* them to be seen—as sexual prey. What if Paul is arguing that *all* women have authority over their own heads no matter who they are or whom they "belong to"? After all, every woman in this assembly has been bought with a price, and now they are Christ's (6:19–20).

Paul's advice here—for *all* women to pray and prophesy with a covering—would be countercultural. It would grant status to women who, outside the church, could never hope to be treated with the respect granted a Roman wife. It seems that the Corinthians had made some headway (pun intended) by allowing women to have a voice in the assembly, but they were still allowing the distinctions of elitism and servitude to be present. Removing the veil was not a suitable equalizer. On the other hand, for all to be veiled, for all to be protected from objectification, for all to be treated with the utmost honor that the first century could offer to women, leveled the playing field. Donning the veil treated all women with human dignity and respect. Ruden concludes, "If the women complied—and later church tradition suggests they did—you could have looked at a congregation and not necessarily been able to tell who was an honored wife and mother and who had been forced, or maybe was still being forced, to service twenty or thirty men a day. This had never happened in any public gathering before."[15]

It is true that 1 Cor 11:2–16 does not erase gender distinctions, but we twenty-first-century readers could get so focused on wanting Paul to create equality between the genders that we neglect to consider the implications of the church becoming a safe haven for those whom society has abused, discarded, and neglected. Perhaps churches today who are drawing im-

---

15. Ruden, *Paul among the People*, 88.

plications from this passage should not be trying to apply first-century gender hierarchies to a twenty-first-century world, but rather asking how the church might elevate the status of all who walk through its doors. How might all who enter be given the privileges, honor, and status that our culture affords only to a select few? How might the church be changed if one were to look at the pews on Sunday and not be able to tell by appearance who was on welfare and who worked on Wall Street? What are the ramifications for the church to be a safe haven, a beacon of human dignity and respect to the least in our society? Furthermore, how can the church provide a welcome space for all not just to be present, but also to lead in worship. Read in its context, this passage offers many challenges for the church today.

Silence and Submission in the Church?

Any female who expresses a desire to minister in a context that does not ordain women is already well aware of the "clobber" texts. In 1 Cor 14:34-35, Paul commands women to be silent in the assembly and to ask their husbands at home if they have questions: "For it is shameful for a woman to speak in church" (14:35). The situation for women only grows more dire in 1 Tim 2:11-12: "Let a woman learn in silence with full submission. I permit no woman to teach or to have authority over a man; she is to keep silent." In many churches, the interpretation of these passages has successfully silenced the rest of the Pauline witness regarding women in church leadership. Indeed, the committee responsible for amending the 2000 Baptist Faith and Message, the official statement of faith of the Southern Baptist Convention, decided that the Baptist Faith and Message of 1998 and of 1963 was too vague regarding the gender of church leadership and voted to change the statement to read: "While both men and women are gifted for service in the church, the office of pastor is limited to men as qualified by Scripture" ("The Church," 2000 Baptist Faith and Message). The Scripture cited in support of this statement includes the instructions for women, bishops, and deacons in 1 Tim 2:9-3:15. The instructions to husbands and wives in the household codes of Eph 5:22-32 are also cited, even though those texts refer to household dynamics and do not mention church leadership offices. Oddly, 1 Cor 14:34-35 is absent from the list of supporting texts regarding male-only church leadership, even though that passage seems to silence women in worship.

Not surprisingly, the 2000 Baptist Faith and Message Statement ignores texts where women are clearly taking leadership roles, for example: the Corinthian women leading worship by praying and prophesying (1 Cor 11:2-16); Euodia and Syntyche, who are called Paul's "coworkers" who have struggled alongside him in the work of the gospel (Phil 4:2-3); Phoebe, the deacon of the church at Cenchrea, who has been a benefactor (*prostatis*) of Paul and who has been commissioned by the apostle to deliver the letter to the Roman believers (Rom 16:1-2); Prisca, who is a coworker who has risked her life for the gospel and who hosts a church in her home (Rom 16:3-4; 1 Cor 16:19; cf. Acts 18:2-3); Mary, who is praised for working hard among the Roman believers (Rom 16:6); Junia, a fellow prisoner whom Paul names as preeminent among the apostles (Rom 16:7); or the other laborers in Rome: Tryphaena, Tryphosa (16:12), Rufus's mother (16:13), Julia, and Nereus's sister (16:15). These are just the women named in Paul's undisputed letters. We could also include Nympha, who hosts the church of Colossae (Col 4:15), or any of the women from Acts, like Lydia (Acts 16), who are critical to the church's mission. Of course, none of these women are called "pastor," but "pastor" is not a title that Paul uses for leadership. The 2000 Baptist Faith and Message's qualification that only men can hold the "office of pastor" rests on the prohibition of women to have authority over men in 1 Tim 2:11-12 and perhaps on the qualification in the same letter that an overseer be a "one-woman" man (3:3).

How much weight should any one passage in Paul's letters carry when it comes to disqualifying an entire gender from church leadership? Are the commands in 1 Timothy intended to be a prohibition against women serving in leadership roles in all churches or simply where Timothy is serving? If the commands apply to all churches across time, why do the other letters have so many examples of women serving in leadership positions? Similarly, if the commands in 1 Cor 14:34-35 intended to silence all women, then why were some women allowed to pray and prophesy before the assembly if they would only cover their heads (1 Cor 11:2-16)?

Paul did not silence every woman in every church, nor did he intend to silence all women across time. The apostle clearly had women as coworkers. He even called Junia an "apostle" (Rom 16:7). Of course, various English translators have translated Junia as Junias, a male name, to fit their own theology that prohibits women from such leadership roles.[16]

---

16. For a translation history of this text, see Eldon Epp, *Junia: The First Woman Apostle* (Minneapolis: Fortress, 2005), 65-69.

Nevertheless, since no evidence supports the name being masculine, we are forced to consider that Paul referred to a woman as an "apostle"! If Paul allowed women to be leaders and to speak in church, how do we interpret 1 Cor 14:34-35 and 1 Tim 2:11-12? Or, to phrase this another way, *since* Paul served with women as coworkers—at least one even as an apostle (Rom 16:7), the same leadership title he uses for himself—to interpret these texts as a universal mandate for all women of all time would contradict what Paul actually practices. It is better to ask how each of these texts functions within its context.

1 Corinthians 14:34-35: A Silencing Text or a Text That Is Silent?

In contrast to 1 Cor 11:2-16 where women are praying and prophesying in worship, Paul's commands regarding women in 1 Cor 14:34-35 appear to silence women in church. The command is not said just once, but reiterated several times: "Women *should be silent* (*sigaō*) in the churches. For they are *not permitted to speak*, but *should be subordinate* (*hypotassō*), as the law also says. If there is anything they desire to know, let them ask their husbands at home. For it is *shameful for a woman to speak* in church" (NRSV; italics added for emphasis). To be sure, some of the language echoes the context. For example, the spirits of the prophets, in 1 Cor 14:32, are also to be subordinate (*hypotassō*) to the prophets. The one who speaks in tongues must be silent (*sigaō*, 14:28) if no interpreter is present. One prophet must be quiet (*sigaō*, 14:30) while the next one is prophesying. Notably, *all* are permitted to prophesy, one by one (14:31), until verses 34-35 add some restrictions to women. What is going on here? Is Paul contradicting himself? Are these verses added by a later scribe? Is Paul addressing a particular situation that would be known to First Church Corinth but that mystifies us?

The manuscript tradition places the silencing of women in one of two places: either as verses 34-35 or after verse 40. All ancient manuscripts contain the instructions, but the earliest manuscripts couch the instruction in the midst of the advice regarding prophets, as verses 34-35. Thus, the note on women interrupting in worship interrupts Paul's train of thought regarding prophets, with verse 37 returning to instructions about prophecy in worship. Perhaps realizing the interruption to the flow of argument, other ancient scribes understandably elect to move the commands about women to the end of the section (after v. 40), before Paul picks up a new topic in 15:1. Since all our ancient manuscripts are still a couple hundred years (at best) removed from the first century, some scholars have wondered whether verses 34–35 were in Paul's original letter. It is common for notes written in the margin of a document to be inserted in the text when copied by scribes. Material added to the body of a text is called an interpolation. One family of manuscripts inserts the marginal note in one location while another set of manuscripts chooses another (at the end of the chapter). Then subsequent manuscripts preserve the text as copied. If these verses represent a marginal note, the note would have been added early, since we do not have any manuscripts that omit the text.

Those who argue that the verses are part of the original letter have attempted to explain the text in its context by trying to remove the apparent contradiction between the approval of women's public prayer and prophecy in 1 Cor 11:5 and the limitation of women's speech in 1 Cor 14:34. One popular view is to claim that Paul is citing a Corinthian slogan that silences women—a position that he quickly rebuts in verse 36, "Or did the word of God originate with you only?"[17] After all, Paul appears to cite the Corinthians elsewhere (1 Cor 6:12; 10:23), but in each of these cases, it is difficult to discern whether he is quoting anyone, since no quotation marks appear in the Greek text. As noted above, however, much of the language in these verses is language that is repeated in the context. This would suggest that the verses are either Pauline or written by someone who is deliberately echoing instructions in the context.

If Paul wrote these verses, then he must be appealing to a particular dilemma that is occurring in the context of worship. The verses should not be interpreted as a general prohibition to all women to be silent in church, since women are clearly taking leadership roles in worship according to 1 Cor 11:5. The speech of the women must be particularly disruptive while the prophets are speaking. Thiselton argues that Paul is forbidding speech that interrupts the prophetic activity by publicly "sifting or weighing the words of prophets, especially by asking probing questions about the prophet's theology or even the prophet's lifestyle in public."[18] Since husbands are mentioned in these instructions, Thiselton suggests that publicly testing or questioning the prophet would become particularly sensitive if

---

17. D. W. Odell-Scott, "Let the Women Speak in Church: An Egalitarian Interpretation of 1 Cor 14:33b-36," *BTB* 13 (1983): 90-93. For an excellent overview, see Anthony C. Thiselton, *The First Epistle to the Corinthians*, NIGTC (Grand Rapids: Eerdmans, 2000), 1151.

18. Thiselton, *First Epistle to the Corinthians*, 1158.

Women and the Pauline Mission

a wife were questioning her own husband before the assembly. Indeed, in first-century culture, for a wife to challenge her husband publicly would be unthinkably shameful. If the instructions in 1 Cor 7:1-6 are any indication, then there does seem to be some friction between husbands and wives within this assembly. Thiselton's reading attempts to be generous to Paul and to women in worship leadership.

What if we are being too generous? What if Paul intended to silence women in leadership? Antoinette Wire makes this argument by reading the letter through the lens of the Corinthian women prophets. These women are abstaining from sexual relations with their husbands and refusing to don veils since the church is meeting in private homes. They are highlighting the teaching of new creation in Christ where there is neither male nor female. Wire notes that Paul does not emphasize the erasure of distinctions between male and female when he cites the baptismal formula in this letter (12:12-13), because of how these female prophets are using this teaching in Corinth. Wire's rereading of 1 Corinthians traces many of the divisions to the work of the women prophets. Thus, the silencing in 1 Cor 14:34-35 is the key piece of advice that would solve many of the problems in Corinth. From Wire's perspective, Paul has been carefully crafting his argument to get to this point.[19] Wire's reading assumes that women in leadership are the root cause of many of the divisions in the community. Thus, Paul's advice is directed at this specific group. Her rereading of the letter necessarily highlights certain issues—like sexual abstinence in marriage and wearing veils, while spending less time on others, such as the divisions at the Lord's Table. Yet it seems that in Wire's reading, all the problems in Corinth are somehow traced back to these women who refuse to cover their heads. It is noteworthy that this reconstruction grants the women prophets an inordinate amount of influence in the early church community, even if Paul is attempting to curtail their influence.

If 1 Cor 14:34-35 were part of the original letter and later scribes moved the instructions to the end of the section, then we do not have much evidence of what is going on that would compel Paul to write these words. Both Thiselton and Wire, for instance, whose readings are quite different, are attempting to offer reconstructions that make sense of the silencing. The clues in the text suggest that married women, who already enjoy some status in society, are somehow disrupting the worship service with their

---

19. Antoinette Clark Wire, *The Corinthian Women Prophets: A Reconstruction through Paul's Rhetoric* (Minneapolis: Fortress, 1990), 153-55, 184-86.

questions. Since Paul tells even the prophets to shut up when another receives a revelation (v. 32), it is not inconceivable that the apostle would tell any faction in the church to be quiet and to stop disrupting worship. This entire section of the letter is devoted to the orderly use of gifts during worship to edify the community. If there are privileged women who are talking during the service—which, we must bear in mind, is in someone's house without the benefit of a sound system and a projector screen—it would be disruptive and would most likely prevent others from hearing what the prophets are saying. If, as Thiselton suggests, the women are correcting or questioning their own husbands, then the shame brought upon the husbands would be significant. It is perhaps worth noting, however, that this is an assembly where women are present. This may not be surprising to a twenty-first-century church, but as Sarah Ruden points out, it was odd for women to be present at a first-century assembly containing men. Ruden writes, "There was no approved public forum for *any* kind of women's self-expression, not even in the arts and religion. They had ritual functions. Some were priestesses. All citizen women took part in public ceremonies from time to time, on special occasions. They watched, or made the motions and spoke the traditional words (if any). It was not on offer to do anything else."[20] Not only are women present in First Church Corinth, but they have voice. The issue in 1 Cor 14:34–35 seems to be an abuse of that privilege. Nonetheless, the presence of women in an assembly with men and the ability for women to speak at all (1 Cor 11:5) would be radical for the time.[21]

On the other hand, the verses—due to their variations of placement in the manuscript tradition—could represent a later addition, an interpolation. Though the verses echo some of the language in the surrounding context, they also contain oddities if written by Paul. For example, verse 34 cites the law as a rationale for silence and subordination. It is not common for Paul to cite the law as the primary reason why the church should abstain from certain behavior. The verses sound remarkably like the household codes of Colossians or Ephesians, with their commands for women to be subject to their husbands, or the Pastoral Epistles, with their prohibition of women having any authority over men (1 Tim 2:11–12). Although nothing is said about the situation in 1 Cor 14, the prohibition to speak is clear. Plus, it is considered shameful for the women to speak in the assembly (v. 35).

20. Ruden, *Paul among the People*, 78–80, quoting 80.
21. Ruden, *Paul among the People*, 81.

Women and the Pauline Mission

In 1 Cor 11, it is only shameful for a woman to prophesy with her head uncovered—not to prophesy period. If a later scribe added these verses to the margins of 1 Corinthians, it was likely done to place this text in concert with the restrictions of the later letters, which were written during a time when the church knew that the return of Christ was not as imminent as once believed. Rather than live the life of a single so that one could avoid the time-consuming tasks of running a household and, thus, have more time to evangelize, as Paul does (1 Cor 7), now believers were expected to create households—respectable households—with women who were model wives and men who were model husbands. The church needed to survive to the next generation, and the only way to do that was to make some accommodations to their environment.

While I tend to lean toward these verses as a non-Pauline interpolation, if Paul did write them and include them as part of his instructions to First Church Corinth, then they must be interpreted in concert with 1 Cor 11:5. Clearly, women are praying and prophesying in the assembly, and there is no prohibition of this activity based solely on gender. Whichever side the reader takes in the inclusion of these verses, stripping them out of their context to make them a mandate for all women to be silent in church across time is to use the commands in a way that Paul never intended. This would contradict Paul's own practices, which allowed women to serve in leadership capacities.

1 Timothy 2: The Real Housewives of Ephesus

By the time that 1 Timothy is written, a fundamental shift has occurred in the early churches. Households, which had been convenient meeting places for the church's urgent mission, have now become the key to maintaining the church's teaching and doctrine. Gone is the advice to remain single (1 Cor 7:25–38) or for married men to live as though they do not have wives (1 Cor 7:29). Rather than praising virgins and unmarried women for focusing on the work of the Lord (1 Cor 7:34), now younger women are told to marry, bear children, and manage their households even if their husbands have died (1 Tim 5:14). The unmarried women who are widows, who were an asset to the mission according to 1 Cor 7, have now become a burden to the church (1 Tim 5:16). There appear to be too many unmarried women for the church to support. Now, the believers must decide who is "really" (*ontōs*) a widow and who should remarry (1 Tim 5:5, 9-15). Those younger than sixty (!) need not apply (1 Tim 5:9).

The Pastoral Epistles, as a whole, preserve some negative stereotypes about women, stereotypes that are largely representative of the wider culture. The younger women are characterized as gossips and busybodies with little control, if any, over the desires of the flesh (1 Tim 5:11-13). The older women must be told to be reverent and not to create scandal or slander or drink too much (Titus 2:3). It is their duty, after all, to teach younger women how to be submissive, self-controlled, chaste, good household managers, and kind (Titus 2:5). Women are expected to do all these things, but the prevailing view of the larger culture is that they cannot, by nature, remain self-controlled all the time. Women are considered weak, ruled by emotions, and irrational. Because they are deemed incapable of controlling their desires, particularly their sexual desires, women have to be protected, or more precisely, households have to be protected from the potential shame that women can bring upon them.[22] The anxiety of caring for a daughter is expressed in Sir 42:9-14:

> A daughter is a secret anxiety to her father, and worry over her robs him of sleep; when she is young, for fear she may not marry, or if married, for fear she may be disliked; while a virgin, for fear she may be seduced and become pregnant in her father's house; or having a husband, for fear she may go astray, or, though married, for fear she may be barren. Keep strict watch over a headstrong daughter, or she may make you a laughingstock to your enemies, a byword in the city and the assembly of the people, and put you to shame in public gatherings. See that there is no lattice in her room, no spot that overlooks the approaches to the house. Do not let her parade her beauty before any man, or spend her time among married women; for from garments comes the moth, and from a woman comes woman's wickedness. Better is the wickedness of a man than a woman who does good; it is woman who brings shame and disgrace.

Thus, protecting a female from her own wickedness and potential to bring shame required the control of the paterfamilias. Seen in this light, the instructions in the Pastoral Epistles (as well as the household codes)

---

22. Carolyn Osiek and David L. Balch, *Families in the New Testament World: Households and House Churches* (Louisville: Westminster John Knox, 1997), 39.

assume the need for the paterfamilias's control and for the wife's submission for the sake of the household's reputation. It also helps make sense of why male leaders would be partially judged by their ability to control or lead their own household: "for if a man does not know how to manage his own household, how can he care for God's church?" (1 Tim 3:5; cf. 3:4, 12). The model female in the Christian household could help win the respect of outsiders.

There is more, however, to the instructions in 1 Timothy than a negative caricature of women. In fact, 1 Tim 2:8 gives instructions regarding prayer and begins with men who should lift holy hands and pray without anger or quarreling (2:8). Then, in 1 Tim 2:9, the instructions to women begin with "likewise," suggesting that the author is continuing the topic of public prayer.[23] The problem that is occurring when these women pray regards their apparel. They are still donning high status markers—gold, pearls, and expensive clothes—*when they pray in the assembly*. (This advice sounds remarkably like 1 Cor 11:2-16.) Thus, the women are not silent or told to be silent in the whole service. Rather, the context for silence and submission is the time when they should be learning: "Let a woman learn in silence with full submission. I permit no woman to teach or to have authority over a man; she is to keep silent." It appears that some women are interrupting the teaching.

The surrounding verses reveal some important information about the women in the Ephesian church who need to sit down and be ready to learn. These women are not your average housewives. In fact, they enjoy some social privileges. First and foremost, they have the ability to marry legally, a privilege not granted to slaves or noncitizens.[24] They are not of the working class and, thus, have the free time to roam from house to house and to create scandal with their gossip (1 Tim 5:13). The author has to tell them to dress modestly and decently, not with elaborate hairstyles, gold, pearls, or expensive clothes (1 Tim 2:9). Considering that the vast majority of the population of the first-century world contained people living near the subsistence level, it is amazing that some women in the Ephesian church have the ability to wear elaborate outfits with expensive jewelry. These are not

---

23. See also Craig Keener, *Paul, Women & Wives: Marriage and Women's Ministry in the Letters of Paul* (Peabody, MA: Hendrickson, 1992), 102-3.

24. Though the word for woman and wife is the same in Greek, it appears that the women in question are indeed wives who are expected to bear children (1 Tim 2:14-15).

the housewives of peasants. When taken with the evidence of 1 Tim 5, these are women whose households have some status in their society. They are living comfortably and do not have to work for a living. They have multiple outfits and jewelry to match. They have slaves to do their hair, and most interestingly, they have too much time on their hands. If they were part of the twenty-first century, we might cast them in a reality TV show, *The Real Housewives of Ephesus*.

And these women are trying to call the shots in the church. They are clearly in a world where they are used to certain privileges and status. They are used to managing their households, and, based on the need for instructions regarding their dress, they are clearly captured by a need to maintain their social appearances, even in the church. In *Struggles for Power in Early Christianity*, Elsa Tamez argues that the description of the women in this passage implies a social position above that of some of the male leadership. Though *anēr* can mean "husbands" in 2:12, the term can also simply refer to men in general. Tamez argues that "men" here would be those whose teaching is being interrupted. The dilemma behind this passage involves a struggle for power between some wealthy women and the male leadership or, more specifically, males in a teaching role.[25] The prohibition in 2:12 is against teaching and "domineering" (*authentein*) or having authority over men. Women in lower social status are not accustomed to wielding authority in their daily lives, but wealthy women whose households have honor and social standing are used to getting their way because of the patronage system.

The patronage system ensured that it was nearly impossible for someone of lower social status to engage in any behavior that could be interpreted as disrespectful to a patron. According to Seneca, benefaction was "the practice that constitutes the chief bond of human society" (Seneca, *On Benefits* 1.4.2). The benefactor was encouraged to select clients who would show the giver honor and respect with appropriate gratitude (Isocrates, *To Demonicus* 29). Failure to show appropriate gratitude would incur the patron's wrath (Aristotle, *Rhetoric* 2.2.8). Only intense and complete personal loyalty would do (Seneca, *On Benefits* 2.22.1; 2.24.2). What happens, though, when wealthy members of the church use their resources to support the congregation?

It certainly appears that there are wealthy families in the Ephesian

---

25. Elsa Tamez, *Struggles for Power in Early Christianity*, trans. Gloria Kinsler (Maryknoll, NY: Orbis, 2007), 8–9.

church who are accustomed to being treated as benefactors. In 1 Tim 6:3-10, they are connected with some of the dissensions in the community. Otherwise, there would be no need to charge the rich in the church to be generous and to perform good deeds (1 Tim 6:17-19). Given that the church must meet in houses—and not all in the first century have the luxury of a house large enough to host a gathering—the church needs the generosity of wealthy families in order to assemble. The problem is that cultural etiquette would dictate that those who are supporting the church would be in the role of benefactors. In other words, they have power. The women who are interrupting the male teachers are clearly wealthy women, intent on maintaining their social status by appearance and by actions. They are the ones whom "Paul" tells to be quiet (1 Tim 2:11-12). I suspect that, if I were part of that church, I would be tired of the people of privilege always getting their way, and if I were a slave or a freedwoman of the working class, I might even secretly cheer when this letter was read publicly, right in front of these rich housewives with their tailored dresses, golden jewelry, and perfectly tamed locks. The author, thankfully, is more gracious than I am.

The author does not just tell them to be quiet, he offers a remedy: let them *learn* (1 Tim 2:11). In my twenty-first-century context of privilege, it might be easy to overlook how scandalous this advice truly is. The author is commanding the education of *women*. As Craig Keener argues in *Paul, Women & Wives*, learning in silence and full submission is expected of every serious student. Furthermore, Keener points out that Paul's word for "silence" is the same word used to exhort the whole church to a kind of quiet life just a few verses earlier in 1 Tim 2:2, where the believers are instructed to be quiet and godly and respectful in every way.[26] The author is actually proposing something quite remarkable. The women are not considered *irrational*, but *teachable*.

Indeed, there seems to be a dire need to train them. False teachers have come into the community and have targeted women (2 Tim 3:6-7). Likely, these women, the ones who are managing households, are the only women in the church with time on their hands to speak to the teachers. They seem to be spreading the false teaching from household to household, particularly to their female counterparts in the church (1 Tim 5:13). This false teaching, though, is wreaking havoc on the community. It is allowing false doctrine to infiltrate the church and giving credence to teachers whom the author does not deem to be people of integrity. There appears

---

26. Keener, *Paul, Women & Wives*, 107-8.

to be a real need for the wisdom of older women in the church who could help guide and perhaps even curtail the divisive behavior of the younger, wealthy wives until they are able to learn. These wealthy women are commanded to don the appropriate posture of a student, and they will be entrusted with sound teaching and sacred doctrine. They have already put themselves in the role of teaching other women. The author wants to give them material that is worthy to be spread.

Ripped out of context, 1 Tim 2:11–12 has been used to silence all women—across generations and socioeconomic classes. Taken in its first-century context, though, the instructions here offer sound advice to women who are using their status to interrupt and possibly try to "correct" sound teaching. After all, the false teachers have invested time in training these women. From the author's perspective, though, these women are not worthless to the mission of the gospel. Rather, they are integral to the mission of the church. Not only are they helping to support the church, but they are also naturally in positions of teaching others. First, though, they must be trained.

Submission to the Hubs? The Role of Women in the Family

Though the role of women in the church has consumed much of our discussion, the discussion of women in leadership in the early churches cannot be divorced from women's positions in their homes. The early believers met, after all, in house churches, and the house, as Carolyn Osiek and Margaret MacDonald remind us, was the woman's place.[27] Wives have authority to manage their households. Would that authority translate to the church? What does it mean to have a female head of the household as the one who welcomes the church movement? Nympha seems critical to the early church in Colossae (Col 4:15) and Lydia to Philippi (Acts 16:14–15). Of course, as heads of their households, these women are in a different position than most. They appear to be of high enough social status that they do not need to remarry,[28] and they can support an early church gathering in their homes. But what about the women who are not heads of their house-

---

27. Osiek and MacDonald, *A Woman's Place*, 144–63.

28. Since women were expected to marry, there is little evidence for Roman women who chose to remain single. Choosing not to remarry, however, was far more common. "A woman of one husband" was offered respect (Ann Hanson, "The Roman

hold? Where do they stand in this early church movement? While much of the discussion on Paul's views of family centers on the household codes in Ephesians and Colossians, those texts should also be read in light of 1 Cor 7, the only chapter in Paul's undisputed letters where the apostle is forced by the church to offer some housekeeping advice.

1 Corinthians 7: Bad Housekeeping

Paul's words concerning marriage and singleness are anything but a message to focus on the family. It is not that the apostle is anti-family. Rather, he is pro-mission. The urgency of the gospel is too great for him to be bothered by household matters. And yet, the household is where believers live. They have placed trust in this gospel, but they have so many uncertainties concerning how to live out this faith when no one is sure when Jesus will come back.

It is easy to see why First Church Corinth would include household matters in their letter to Paul. The household provided the locus of identity in the first-century world. The goal of those within a household was to secure the household for the next generation. In essence, the household was the top priority. Honor and shame were attached to the honor of the family. The building blocks of the household—husband and wife, parents and children, master and slave—were the building blocks of society. The household—and one's place in it—marked status, power, rank, and place in the world. The household connected a family to generations past and provided the only security one had for the future. The concerns behind Paul's advice in 1 Cor 7 reflect the church's struggle with dual allegiances to their own household and to the household of God, when the master of that house could return at any moment.

The bulk of the chapter concerns instructions on marriage and singleness in light of the parousia. The chapter is not only odd for its content, but also odd for its presentation. Paul's instructions here are not dogmatic. Rather, the apostle moves forward cautiously, giving what he believes to be Spirit-filled advice, but also concessions (see 7:6). Though he echoes Jesus's teaching on divorce (7:10), he recognizes that in other matters, he is moving into territory where he does not have a command from the Lord

---

Family," in *Life, Death, and Entertainment in the Roman Empire*, ed. D. S. Potter and D. J. Mattingly [Ann Arbor: University of Michigan Press, 1999], 34).

(7:12). So he gives his opinion "as one who by the Lord's mercy is trustworthy" (7:25) and who has the Spirit of God (7:40). Paul's advice in this chapter is geared toward the church's devotion to the Lord (7:35) and the holiness of the community (e.g., 7:34, 36), in view of the reality that "this world is passing away" (7:31). He recommends singleness, not because it is somehow a higher calling, though he does call it a gift (7:7), but because the one who is single has time to be devoted to the Lord and committed to the mission of the gospel, whereas those who are married must be concerned with running a household (7:25-40).

Paul's instructions here regarding women within marriage and women remaining single deserve more attention. The advice runs counter to culture. Nowhere in 1 Cor 7 does Paul tell women to submit to their husbands, virgins to obey parents, or slaves to serve masters. In each of these relationships, Paul gives advice that runs against the norm.

Regarding the husband-wife relationship, the language of authority in marriage is applied to both parties (7:2-4). The husband has authority over the wife's body, and likewise the wife has authority over the husband's body (7:4). Paul also speaks of sex as an "obligation" or "duty" (*opheilē*, 7:3) incumbent on each spouse. The mutuality of the gender relationship is striking. By law and by custom, the paterfamilias wielded supreme power over his entire family. Yet here Paul offers no sign that a husband has more authority than the wife. Paul's concern, rather, is to guard against sexual immorality (*porneia*, 7:2). If the couple agrees not to engage in sexual intercourse for a while, Paul advises that this agreement is mutual, temporary, and for the purpose of prayer (7:5). No concern is expressed here that the marriage produce heirs. The repeated concern is a lack of self-control that leads to temptation to go beyond the marital bed to fulfill desires. This advice comes after Paul has already warned against visiting prostitutes (6:15-16). What the Corinthians do with their bodies matters, because their bodies are the temple of God (6:19). Yet he gives no advice here for one party to submit to the other without reciprocation. Both husband and wife have responsibility in this marital relationship. Both must guard against *porneia*.

Paul's encouragement to remain single could cause friction in the parent-child relationship. In the first-century world, marriage was a family matter. Parents arranged unions to safeguard their children's future.[29]

---

29. Suzanne Dixon, *The Roman Family*, Ancient Society and History (Baltimore: Johns Hopkins University Press, 1992), 63.

Women and the Pauline Mission

Girls—especially from political families—could be in the early to mid-teens when they wed. According to Dio Cassius, a girl could be ten years old at her betrothal and considered marriageable at the age of twelve (*Roman History* 54.16). It is questionable how much say virgins—male or female—would have in plans to marry. According to Susan Dixon, brides and grooms were at least consulted in theory, but a bride's refusal to marry could be discounted.[30] The purpose of the marriage was to secure alliances, especially for political families or those of the upper classes, and to produce heirs to secure the legacy of a family from one generation to the next. Love was not part of the equation in the selection of a spouse, though it was expected that respect and conjugal love would develop in the course of the union.[31] Yet Paul's advice in 1 Cor 7 disregards the concern for the household to last to another generation. "This world is passing away," he warns the Corinthians in 7:31. There simply is not time to worry about marrying off daughters or producing heirs. The implications of his advice regarding staying single, though, would be staggering.

Not only were virgins expected to marry, under some periods of Roman rule, they were legally required to do so. Augustus even offered prizes for marriage and the begetting of children (Dio Cassius, *Roman History* 54.16):

> The basic premise of this legislation was that marriage was a duty incumbent on all Roman men between 25 and 60 years of age, and on all Roman women between 20 and 50. Widowed and divorced persons within these age limits were expected to remarry. Exemptions were granted to free-born persons who had procreated at least three children, and to freed persons who had procreated four; in general these numbers represented the "quota" expected of each citizen.[32]

Of course, for Augustus, Roman citizens producing more Roman children served the best interest of the Roman Empire. Paul also demonstrates imperial concerns, but not for Roman rule. Paul is concerned about the

---

30. Dixon, *Roman Family*, 63-64; see also Osiek and Balch, *Families in the New Testament World*, 61-62.

31. See discussion in Dixon, *Roman Family*, 61-64.

32. Richard I. Frank, "Augustus' Legislation on Marriage and Children," *California Studies in Classical Antiquity* 8 (1975): 45; quoted in Andrew D. Clarke, *Secular and Christian Leadership in Corinth: A Socio-Historical and Exegetical Study of 1 Corinthians 1-6* (Eugene, OR: Wipf & Stock, 2006), 82.

holiness of the community in light of the coming reign of Christ and about the freedom of the church to live as witnesses of the gospel. Everything else—customs, household obligations, and even Roman law—pales in comparison. However, for the unmarried—the widowed, the virgins, and the divorced—to remain unmarried meant that the church had to function as a household to offer protection—particularly to unmarried women—as they all await the revelation of Christ (1 Cor 1:7-8).

Though slaves are not the focus of this chapter, the mention of slaves in 1 Cor 7:21-23 seems to be an extension of the household matters. Slaves are encouraged to gain freedom (7:21), and the believers are told not to enter into servanthood (7:23). The rationale complements Paul's instructions on marriage; freedpersons would have more liberty to do the work of the gospel. Everyone is a slave of Christ. Unlike the household codes in Ephesians and Colossians, there is no concern here to uphold the power of human masters. Furthermore, if married people take Paul's advice to "have" one another only as an outlet for sexual desire, the slave in a Christian household would not be considered sexually available. Paul's concern here, though, as in the chapter as a whole, is not that the household run smoothly according to societal standards, but that every member of the household—even slaves—can be free to carry out the work of the gospel.

Ephesians 5: Submission and Sacrificial Love

In a world where "family" is being redefined with each generation, my seminary students find the household codes particularly troubling. The codes of Ephesians, which go into more detail about the husband-wife relationship than any other passage, have been used to support women staying in abusive relationships.[33] Telling women to submit to their husbands at all costs, though, does not take into account the command for husbands to love their wives as Christ has loved the church. Furthermore, before we ever hear anything about husbands and wives in Eph 5, both parties must first submit to Christ. Though the headline in the twenty-first century is the command to women, in the first century the truly countercultural command would have been for husbands to love their wives—

---

33. See, e.g., Debi Pearl, *Created to Be His Help Meet: Discover How God Can Make Your Marriage Glorious*, 10th Anniversary ed. (Lobelville, TN: No Greater Joy Ministries, 2014), 54, 132-33, 263.

particularly with the cruciform love of Christ. In fact, Christ's love for the church dominates the instructions to husbands (vv. 25-27), a point to which we will return below.

In many ways, the rules for the Christian household reflect conventional thought on household management that can be found in Greco-Roman and Hellenistic Jewish literature. Since the household was considered the building block of the empire, the pieces of the household—the relationships between husbands and wives, slaves and masters, children and parents—had to run seamlessly for the success of the whole familial unit. It is not hard to find similar instructions and assumptions about the household in other literature from the period. Since the household—and one's place within a household—comprised people's primary identity and their future security, it is understandable that the management of a household would be of particular import. A well-run household would preserve the family name and legacy from generation to generation.

The household was also critical to the development of the early church. Since Christians did not have the legal right of public assembly, the early church relied on households for its continued existence. It is no surprise, then, that the New Testament preserves codes that would enable the household to survive in its environment (see also Col 3:18-4:1; 1 Pet 2:18-3:7; cf. 1 Tim 2:1-15; 5:1-16; 6:1-2, 17-19; Titus 2:1-3:8). We do not have codes like this in the undisputed letters of Paul. In fact, in these early letters, as noted above, the instructions for the household do not seem a primary concern. In 1 Cor 7, for instance, Paul addresses household matters only because it has become important to the members of the church who have raised questions (1 Cor 7:1). If Paul penned Ephesians and Colossians, it could indicate that, with the delay of the parousia, instructions for the household had become necessary to the continued success of the mission. Most scholars, however, question whether Paul wrote these letters. Aside from authorship, one scholarly consensus remains: The household codes should be read in light of the sociohistorical and political situation of these letters.

In his commentary on Ephesians, Stephen Fowl challenges the idea that the household codes were written to keep Christians from being perceived as a threat to the Roman Empire. He argues that, although many moral philosophers make the connection between the household and the larger political climate, this connection is absent from the writings of others who give advice on household management (specifically, Plutarch, Dio

Chrysostom, and Musonius Rufus).[34] Thus, unless a writer explicitly links the household as the basic unit of the city or political order, there is no reason to assume that the writer is concerned about how the household helps contribute to the running of the Roman Empire. He raises a fair point. Fowl argues: "To the extent to which Christians found themselves in conventionally structured patriarchal households, Ephesians gives them guidance about how best to live in those households as followers of Christ."[35]

Whether Paul is here concerned with how the believers appear before the government is difficult to say. There are certainly indications that the writer sees God's power as greater than every other rule or authority (Eph 1:19–23). The letter also reveals an understanding of the cosmos where God is at battle and declaring victory over evil (Eph 2:2; 4:27; 6:10–20; cf. 5:11–20). The writer is trying to convince believers that they already participate in that victory (2:6). In Rom 13:1–7, Paul's advice to pay taxes seems to help the church stay under the radar and at the very least avoid another possible expulsion from the city (cf. Acts 18:2). If the writer of Ephesians is the same author as that of the Pastoral Epistles, then the good manager of a household is also supposed to be respectable in his environment, be subject to the ruling authorities, and lead a quiet and peaceable life (Titus 3:1; 1 Tim 2:1–2; cf. 1 Tim 3:2, 4–5, 7; Titus 2:5, 8). Being respectable implies that the leader is considered worthy in light of larger social conventions, and not just what the followers of Jesus would consider laudable.

Fowl's observation, however, sheds light on a critical reality: The early believers must find a way—within their current ways of existence—to bear witness to a household whose paterfamilias no longer takes as his cue what the world deems as wise and noble and good, but must now pattern his behavior after one who has given himself sacrificially for the other. As Carolyn Osiek and Margaret MacDonald argue, "the household code provides a type of balance between flight from society and confrontation with society." It is important not to forget that these idealized households are the very ones who are commanded to battle evil in 6:10–20.[36] Osiek and MacDonald view the teaching in Ephesians as "an important sociopolitical statement": "The symbolic use of marriage to explain the relationship between Christ and the church meant that in the church, as in

---

34. Stephen Fowl, *Ephesians: A Commentary*, NTL (Louisville: Westminster John Knox, 2012), 180.

35. Fowl, *Ephesians*, 181.

36. Osiek and MacDonald, *A Woman's Place*, 123.

the larger society, the married couple was idealized as a microcosm of the society as a whole." The wives are expected to submit and to respect their husbands. This would not be newsworthy in the ancient world. There is a tension, however, between conventional marriage and the larger theme of Ephesians that emphasizes the rupture of traditional forms of identity and upholds the need for separation from the gentile world.[37] If there is a connection between the Christian household and the household as a building block of the political sphere, then the primary political sphere in which the church is called to operate is not the Roman Empire, but "the kingdom of Christ and of God" (Eph 5:5). The Christian married couple, modeling Christ's sacrificial love, would be a microcosm of God's kingdom rather than a microcosm of an empire built on strong power differentials designed to keep some in authority and others in servitude.

In the kingdom of God, the one with the most power in the marital relationship (and within society at large) is not called to lord his power over the other but to *love* as Christ has loved the church. Unquestionably, in the Roman world, the male head of the household, the paterfamilias, had power over all within the household. Though not every male is a paterfamilias, the paterfamilias serves as the model husband. In his *Advice to Bride and Groom*, Plutarch compares this power to the rule of a monarch, since every house is under one "head" (*Moralia* 142e). While there are exceptions to having a male in charge of the household (such as Chloe or Lydia), this is the typical model for most households in the first century. A clear hierarchy exists with the husband having the most power. The wife, thus, is to submit to the husband (5:22). The paterfamilias serves as husband, parent, and master. The question that remains for the community, however, is what those relationships look like when all submit first to Christ (5:21).

Christ's cruciform love is the lens through which the author presents the codes. The husband and wife are to relate to one another in submission to Christ, and the husband is to model his love for his wife after Christ's love for the church. The charge to model Christ has already been made for the whole church. In Eph 5:1-2, the believers are called to be "imitators of God" and to "walk in love, as Christ loved us and gave himself up for us, a fragrant offering and sacrifice to God." By repeating the charge of 5:2, it is as if the author is saying that no one—not even the head of the family—is exempt from displaying the kind of self-sacrificial love that Christ embodies. In fact, due to the high regard that society places upon the husband, it

---

37. Osiek and MacDonald, *A Woman's Place*, 120–22, quoting 120.

is that much more critical that the one in position of authority recognize his responsibility to love.

The teaching about Christ's love is elaborated. No other piece of these codes receives as much instruction as does the husband in regard to the kind of love he is to show his wife (5:25-33). The wife is to be subject to her husband as the church is to Christ (5:24). This analogy, however, has prompted the author to clarify what that submission looks like. Christ does not lord his authority over others but has loved the world and given himself up for the church (5:25). As the Philippian hymn makes clear (Phil 2:5-11), Christ is the one who has power, status, and privilege to relinquish for the sake of another. Christ's sacrifice is presented for the benefit of the church, for the church's sanctification (5:26-27). Failure of the husband to love the wife sacrificially is likened to failure to love his own body (5:29). The author even cites Gen 2:24 for support (Eph 5:31). The husband is to love the wife for her sake as well as his own. A few writers in the ancient world would command husbands to love their wives, but the instructions here still stand out.[38]

The author uses *agapē*, a love that is given with no expectation of anything in return. This is the same word for love used in 1 Cor 13 to speak of the love of the believers for one another. One might expect the use of *erōs* or *philia*. Sarah Ruden explains well the oddness of *agapē*: "in Greek there was *erōs* for sexual desire and being 'in love'; *philia* for the affection of family and friends; and *agapē*, a marginal word adapted to carry the central message of Christianity. *Agapē* is selfless love that people can feel even for enemies or strangers. It is utterly impractical and makes no sense, but it is real."[39]

In many ways, *agapē* itself is countercultural. It is a kind of love that does not make sense because it is like an act of charity where the graciousness of the gift cannot be returned in kind. It is the kind of love that does not seek its own benefit or expect any gain. It will not buttress the power of the giver, but only make him look weaker and perhaps even appear foolish. It is not the kind of love expected of a paterfamilias. In fact, it is hard to imagine whether the early church would have known how to put this advice into practice. The author offers the only example at his disposal, Christ, who is the real Master of the household (6:9).

For my students who shy away from these verses due to how they have

---

38. Fowl, *Ephesians*, 188-89.
39. Ruden, *Paul among the People*, 171.

Women and the Pauline Mission

been used to support women staying in abusive relationships, there is hope. In Eph 6:9, the author warns the "master" that all actions will be judged by the one who has real authority and power and who shows no partiality. The author does not shy away from claiming the wrath of God to come upon those who disobey (5:6). When read in their context, the household codes of Ephesians cannot support abusive and oppressive behavior in any way. Instead, these verses offer a glimpse of a community of believers trying to bear witness to the kingdom of God in the midst of the circumstances in which they find themselves. After wrestling with this text and pleading with her audience not to cut it out of their Bibles, Frances Taylor Gench writes, "After all, as we come before this text, it *is* the new community that we see envisioned here, however imperfectly, engaged in acts of discernment that we continue in our time and place, also imperfectly. We see faith being enacted in love and love seeking to effect its transforming power in the midst of this age."[40] The household codes of Ephesians challenge all would-be followers today to ask, what would it look like for households (however they might be defined) to take Christ's self-sacrificial love as the paradigm for "familial" relationships?[41] What kind of love are our Christian homes modeling, however imperfectly, in our world?

Women and the Eschatological Community

I confess that Paul has a much higher view of the church than the one with which I normally operate. The vision of the church at the ending of Romans is one of my favorite texts in the whole biblical witness. Paul uses the voices of Scripture to describe all nations praising God with one voice (Rom 15:7-13). Somehow, for Paul, the diversity of humanity is not an obstacle to God, but rather part of the glory of how God creates and blesses creation. I think that Paul, if he knew what we have done to oppress and suppress others in our interpretation of his letters, would cringe at how the structures and hierarchies of the "present evil age" (Gal 1:4) have limited

---

40. Gench, *Encountering God in Tyrannical Texts*, 34.

41. In her classic article on the household codes, Clarice J. Martin challenges the church, particularly "African American believing communities," not to absolutize, universalize, or eternalize these codes but to promote "equitable, just, and liberative faith communities" ("The *Haustafeln* (Household Codes)," in *Stony the Road We Trod: African American Biblical Interpretation* (Minneapolis: Fortress Press, 1991), 228.

our thinking, caused us to want uniformity rather than unity, and hindered us from seeing the Spirit of God move among the least expected. After all, as a first-century Jew, Paul, like Peter or others of the Jesus movement, was surprised to meet the God of Israel's Spirit working among the unclean and idolatrous gentiles. Somehow, Paul's revelation of the risen Lord expanded his vision of God's work and God's grace.

What we see in the undisputed letters of Paul, or what others might consider as Paul's earlier letters, are churches where the Spirit has indeed fallen upon all believers. What was perhaps most remarkable in the first century was not that First Church Corinth contained women or that Paul tells the Galatians that there is neither male nor female in Christ, but that the Spirit of the God of Israel honors no boundaries. God's Spirit falls upon *all*. It extends beyond the house of Israel to those of foreign tongue and practices, to those who follow after other gods. What we see in these earliest congregations is indeed a fulfillment of Joel 3:1–5, a scriptural passage that gets cited by the author of Acts in Peter's Pentecost speech: "In the last days it will be, God declares, that I will pour out my Spirit upon all flesh, and your sons and your daughters shall prophesy, and your young men shall see visions, and your old men shall dream dreams. Even upon my slaves, both men and women, in those days I will pour out my Spirit; and they shall prophesy" (Acts 2:17–18). The apostle Paul believes that he and those early churches are living in the last days. The Spirit is at work, and Paul has no desire to quench the work of that Spirit (1 Thess 5:19)—even among women.

While from our twenty-first-century perspective, we might want the biblical texts to give us more information about the roles of women in the Pauline mission, the fact that women are mentioned at all is remarkable. Furthermore, women are serving in leadership capacities—as patrons, deacons, apostles, and coworkers of Paul (Rom 16). What we see in these letters are the struggles of real believers who are trying to navigate life in the tension of their conventional roles and in the freedom of their service to Christ. These are not easy tensions to traverse—for the first century or the twenty-first century.

Perhaps the baptismal formula of Gal 3:28 should offer us a challenge. This passage is often lifted up as the model of gender equality. Though an equalizing factor is at play in this text in the sense that all are equal before God, the text should not be limited to male and female being equal in Christ. The concept of being equal has led to the expectation of an androgynous eschatological body.⁴² The argument, however, is much more challenging. The male-female dichotomy—which was created by God—will not be erased, but *redeemed*. Gender is not removed; the relationship between the genders is rectified. God is not a creator of uniformity, but diversity. As Kendall Soulen argues in *The God of Israel and Christian Theology*, "What the church rejects is not the difference of Jew and gentile, male and female, but rather the idea that these differences essentially entail curse, opposition, and antithesis. Understood in this way, the church is the social embodiment of the doctrine of justification, for justification in its social dimension means the reconciliation of different kinds of people. Reconciliation does not mean the imposition of sameness, but the unity of reciprocal blessing."⁴³

The focus of Soulen's argument is the way in which the church provides a provisional form of relationship between Jew and gentile that reflects the promises of God. It is a relationship of mutual blessing where God is magnified. The vision Soulen describes is not unlike the vision with which Paul ends Romans in 15:7–13. Yet this Jew and gentile relationship can also teach us something about the male and female dichotomy. If the distinction between the nations is not erased but redeemed to become relationships of mutual blessing, then the gender relationship too can be redeemed in God's reign. While the church, which still struggles with the power of sin, may not be the perfect embodiment of God's reign where ethnic and gender distinctions are sources of blessing, the church is still called to bear witness to that mutual blessing, to life in new creation. That new creation does not look like a God whose power is limited, but a God who can work through and among the most unexpected people—including the least among us.

FURTHER READING

Gench, Frances Taylor. *Encountering God in Tyrannical Texts: Reflections on Paul, Women, and the Authority of Scripture*. Louisville: Westminster John Knox, 2015. Gench's study considers the interpretation of key texts in the Pauline and deutero-Pauline epistles that have impacted the roles of women

---

42. See discussion in Wayne A. Meeks, "The Image of the Androgyne: Some Uses of a Symbol in Earliest Christianity," *History of Religions* 13 (1974): 165–208.

43. R. Kendall Soulen, *The God of Israel and Christian Theology* (Minneapolis: Fortress, 1996), 170.

in the life of the church: 1 Tim 2:8–15 and 5:3–16; Eph 5:21–33; 1 Cor 11:2–16 and 14:33b–36; and Rom 16:1–16.

Martin, Clarice J. "The *Haustafeln* (Household Codes)," in *Stony the Road We Trod: African American Biblical Interpretation*. Minneapolis: Fortress Press, 1991. This classic womanist reading of the household codes challenges the hierarchical structures of the codes and urges "African American believing communities" to seek an antihierarchical and liberative approach.

Osiek, Carolyn, and Margaret Y. MacDonald, with Janet H. Tulloch. *A Woman's Place: House Churches in Earliest Christianity*. Minneapolis: Fortress, 2006. This book examines the roles of women in the early church and in the houses that give shape to the early church movement.

Ruden, Sarah. *Paul among the People: The Apostle Reinterpreted and Reimagined in His Own Time*. New York: Pantheon, 2010. This book tackles controversial topics in the interpretation of Paul's letters—for example, homosexuality, women, slavery, and the state. Chapter 4, "An Apostolic Oinker: Paul and Women," examines 1 Cor 7; 11:2–16; and 14:33–36 in light of their cultural context.

Tamez, Elsa. *Struggles for Power in Early Christianity*. Translated by Gloria Kinsler. Maryknoll, NY: Orbis, 2007. Tamez reconstructs the probable situation behind the circumstances of 1 Timothy through the lenses of patronage and power that were prevalent in the first-century world. Her reading is both faithful to the biblical text and challenging to all who claim to seek God's justice today.

CHAPTER FOUR

The Galatian Heirs

When considering Paul's ministry with the "least of these," it might be easier to limit that study to Paul and poverty, but such limitations would overlook the various ways in which people might be considered "least" in the first-century world.[1] Roman perspectives varied widely about the people groups subjugated under Rome's power. History, of course, preserves the perspectives of the powerful. What the Roman elite have to say about the so-called Galatians, however, is appalling. Paul's letter offers an example of the apostle's relationship with a group of people who have been negatively stereotyped by Greco-Roman writers as barbaric, uncivilized, and war-mad. The gospel's effect on a subjugated people is worthy of our attention in Paul's mission to the least.

In spite of the negative caricatures of the Galatians, Paul refers to them as nothing less than "children of the promise, like Isaac" (Gal 4:28). Though it is arguable whether Rome might have seen this identity shift as a promotion of status, Paul presents it as such to the believers. According to Paul, being "in Christ" has granted the Galatians the status of inheriting promises from a forefather whom they would have never claimed by birth. As this chapter will argue, for a landless people, the implications of this inheritance are staggering. Rome may possess their lands, but the gospel has offered the Galatians something more—abundant life in a redeemed world.

To appreciate what the good news might sound like to the Galatians, we will first investigate how these people have been perceived by their larger culture. Then we will examine Paul's claim that the Galatians are indeed

---

1. Parts of this chapter have been presented at the Fourteenth Oxford Institute for Methodist Theological Studies and published in a collection of those presentations by *Holiness: The Journal of Wesley House Cambridge* 4.2 (2014): 7–24.

"children of the promise, like Isaac." This label has multiple ramifications, not only for the Galatians' identity, but also for their promised inheritance.

Galatians, Gauls, and Celts: Oh My!

There are many debates regarding the location of the recipients of Paul's letter. Placing the churches either in the north or the south of the Roman region of Galatia has a bearing on reconstructing Paul's mission and dating the letter. We need not take a side in that debate, however, since *Galatai*, Paul's label in Gal 3:1, could be used to describe people inhabiting the province of Galatia within Asia Minor and as an ethnic term to refer to people within that province and in lands far beyond. While the references to the churches of Galatia in 1:2 seem to indicate the province of Galatia, the term *Galatai* in 3:1 addresses the people as an ethnic designation.[2] As will be shown below, this title might obscure more than it describes.

In her groundbreaking study on Galatians, *Galatians Re-Imagined*, Brigitte Kahl demonstrated that the term "Galatian" was not limited to the people group who lived within the Roman province of Galatia. The Galatians were often confused with the Gauls and the Celts by the ancient writers. For example, Livy calls the people who had attacked Delphi in 279 BCE and who had later been defeated by Manlius Vulso in 189 BCE "the Gauls who inhabit Asia" (39.6.3), while Polybius refers to these same people as *Galatai* (1.6.5).[3] In her survey of the ancient writers, there seems to be no consistency in the use of the labels to describe the people groups or the region(s) to which they are related. Kahl is not the first to make this observation. After trying to differentiate between Celtic and Galatian territories in Europe, Diodorus Siculus concludes, "The Romans, however, include all these nations together under a single name, calling them one and all Galatians (*Galatas hapanes*)" (*Library of History* 5.32.1).[4] Perhaps some of the

---

2. While J. Louis Martyn argues, based on the ethnic and regional label, that *Galatai* would refer to Celtic cities in the northern part of the province (*Galatians*, AYB 33A [New York: Doubleday, 1997], 15–17), the common use of the label to describe multiple people groups in various regions complicates naming the location of these churches.

3. See larger discussion in Brigitte Kahl, *Galatians Re-Imagined: Reading with the Eyes of the Vanquished* (Minneapolis: Fortress, 2010), 49.

4. See also Appian, *Roman History* 6.1.

historiographers can be forgiven since they do not hail from the area that would become the province of Galatia in the first century. Yet it is telling that Strabo, a native of Asia Minor, refers to the same people, the people group in his homeland, as both "Gallic" and "Galatian" (*Geography* 4.4.2). His ignorance regarding the distinctions between these groups might be considered innocent lack of knowledge had he not also indicated that he found these groups unworthy of his attention.

What is most important for our study is that all these people groups—the Galatians, Gauls, and Celts—that are lumped together under the title "Galatian" bore negative stereotypes from Greco-Roman authors. Perhaps because the Galatians were a formidable foe, the Roman writers took delight in portraying them as a savage people. The Galatians are acknowledged as "bold fighters" (Lucian, *Zeuxis or Antiochus* 8-12) who "seemed invincible" (Julian, *Oration* 1 [*Panegyric in Honor of Constantius*]), but their ability to fight is linked to being a "race insatiable of wealth" (Plutarch, *Pyrrhus* 26.6). Plutarch claims that they strike terror wherever they go with their "furious violence" (*Camillus* 28.3). Dio Cassius writes, "For the Gauls, who are unreasonably insatiate in all their passions, know no moderation in either courage or fear, but plunge from the one into hopeless cowardice and from the other into headstrong audacity" (*Roman History* 39.45.7). They are deemed "men of ungoverned passion and uncontrollable impulse" (Dio Cassius, *Roman History* 12.2). Strabo calls them "war-mad," "high-spirited," and "quick for battle" (*Geography* 4.4.2). Pausanius portrays the Galatian warriors as the worst of all criminals, who slaughter the vulnerable elderly and women, who drink the blood of suckling newborns, and who sate their lust on the bodies of the dead (*Description of Greece* 10.22.3-4). Not only do they disrespect the dead among their enemies, according to Pausanius, they fail to collect their own fallen warriors after battle (Pausanius, *Description of Greece* 10.21.6).

As a whole, the Galatians are portrayed as barbarians whose violence can be tamed only by a more civilized and advanced (i.e., Roman) society. Strabo makes this judgment, "At present time they are all at peace, since they have been enslaved and are living in accordance with the commands of the Romans who captured them" (4.4.2). Polybius describes them as a people who enjoy a period of peace only when Rome has subjugated them, but who suffer again when the younger generations grow up to revolt (Polybius 2.21.1-3). Similarly, Dio Cassius writes about a certain group of Gauls who seemed more "peaceable" than the rest because they adopted Roman garb rather than their native dress and long hair (*Roman History* 46.55.5).

The Galatians had become a favorite topic—a portrait of barbarism—not only in Roman literature, but also in visual art. Kahl traces the negative stereotypes of the Galatians through images on sarcophagi, architecture, coins, and sculptures. Perhaps the most famous graphic examples of Galatian defeat include the Dying Gaul, the Suicidal Galatian, and the Great Altar of Pergamum. What is clear from the evidence is that Rome celebrates its victory over the Galatians by publicly portraying this people's gruesome defeat.

> Worldwide *Galatia* was the prototypical battlefield of the Roman ideology of domination that derived its law and legitimacy from the triumph over the barbarian Other, the quintessential topos signifying hostile and inferior barbarian Otherness that needs to be conquered. When entering the ancient world as readers of a letter to Galatia—north or south, east or west, wherever Paul's Galatians were situated geographically—we have to keep in mind that on the *mental* map of the first century C.E., *Galatia* was a well-defined territory: it was *Roman* territory and it was enemy territory, burnt earth and fertile ground where civilization—and the worldwide Roman Empire—could thrive on the ashes of barbarism.[5]

Through this lens of domination, Kahl rereads Paul's letter as a coded discourse to an enslaved people for whom the apostle's good news offers more than spiritual renewal in a distant future, but also redemption and restoration from Roman rule.[6] Kahl's study depicts the Galatians among the "least" in the oppressive Roman regime.

Paul's address in 3:1, *Galatai*, is accompanied by descriptors that, at first glance, may seem to reflect wider culture. He refers to the believers as "foolish" (*anoētoi*) and "bewitched" (3:1). Paul, however, is describing the Galatians' *current* status, as people who have been led astray to "another gospel" (1:6-9). In other words, Paul is not marshaling preconversion stereotypes. Rather, their present situation—as believers who are behaving as though they have been bewitched—reflects the impact of the opposing teachers' message, a message that, from Paul's perspective, is a perversion of the gospel (1:6-9). Equating "foolishness" with a perversion of truth coincides with how Paul speaks of foolishness in his other letters. Being

---

5. Kahl, *Galatians Re-Imagined*, 31-75, quoting 75.
6. Kahl, *Galatians Re-Imagined*, 256.

The Galatian Heirs

foolish is the opposite of acting in wisdom (Rom 1:14). For Paul, to act with wisdom is to be guided by the scandal of the cross (1 Cor 1:18–2:16).[7] Thus, Paul does not consider foolishness a distinctively Galatian characteristic. As Martinus de Boer has argued, the use of the term "foolish" in Gal 3:1 refers to people who are not in their right minds, who lack insight, or who have a failure of spiritual discernment: "The rhetorical questions that follow in vv. 2 and 5, to which the Galatians already know the answers, are intended to shake them out of their mental stupor so that they can see that the bewitching message of the new preacher in Galatia is false and in fact irrelevant to their own experience."[8] In short, the address "O foolish Galatians" in Gal 3:1 is intentionally jarring.

We do not have any idea how the Galatians would have heard the address in 3:1 or whether this rhetorical technique was effective. After all, they have made significant sacrifices—for example, circumcision (as adults!) and a new diet—to follow the message of faithfulness presented by teachers who have come to the region since Paul's departure. It should not go unnoted that, as a result of the teachers' message, a people who have been portrayed as the epitome of lawless barbarians have willingly adopted laws that not only make them look more Jewish, but also more disciplined and, from the Roman perspective, more civilized. Perhaps, as Kahl has argued, appearing more Jewish had its privileges: "Only if they could pass as proper Jews would they be entitled, at least theoretically, to participate in the arrangement available only to Jews with regard to imperial and civic religion. Otherwise, they—and the Jewish communities along with them—would risk possible persecution and repression."[9] If the success of the opponents' mission is any indication, the Galatians may have also thought it better to appear Jewish—either for social reasons or for spiritual ones. Now, Paul is telling them that their sacrificial zealousness, whatever the rationale, is wrongheaded.

Regardless of whether the teachers' message had the result of helping the Galatians appear more civilized to their Roman oppressors, Paul's portrait of the Galatians within this letter defies the profiles of their culture. They have not acted with savagery toward Paul, but with hospitality and love. These so-called barbarians nursed Paul back to health. These people,

---

7. While Romans uses the same root for "foolishness," in 1 Cor 1:18–2:16 the terms that Paul uses for "foolishness" derive from *mōria*.

8. Martinus C. de Boer, *Galatians*, NTL (Louisville: Westminster John Knox, 2011), 170.

9. Kahl, *Galatians Re-Imagined*, 226.

who have been characterized as heartless, insatiably greedy, and fiercely violent, have loved Paul with such tenderness that the apostle proclaims, "though my condition put you to the test, you did not scorn or despise me, but welcomed me as an angel of God, as Christ Jesus" (Gal 4:14). He claims that they would have plucked out their very eyes and given them to him (Gal 4:15). These acts of kindness run counter to the stereotypes perpetuated by their conquerors. To the least in this Roman province, Paul—an ill missionary from another subjugated people, a foreigner in their midst—shares good news.

Paul's gospel has welcomed the Galatians as they are and has promised the divine Spirit to the Galatians *as* Galatians. His gospel does not involve their transformation into being more Roman or more Jewish. Rather, the gospel is open to all—whoever they are, male or female, slave or free, Jew or Gentile. All are one in Christ (Gal 3:28). All can be "children of the promise, like Isaac," even the *least* of the subjugated peoples in the Roman Empire.

Three's a Crowd: Paul, the Galatians, and the Teachers

As stated above, the letter to the Galatians assumes the message of an opposing group of teachers. James Dunn refers to the letter as "theology in the raw."[10] The letter is raw indeed. It is the only Pauline letter that is missing a thanksgiving in the beginning salutation. In other words, it is the only epistle where the apostle does not even pause at the beginning to thank God for the recipients. Paul moves immediately to the problem: The Galatians have defected from the one true gospel (1:1–9). Paul even characterizes their behavior as a betrayal of his own relationship with them. In Gal 4:16, Paul wonders, "Have I then become your enemy by telling you the truth?" How could these people, who would have done anything for the apostle, now consider Paul an enemy? Paul declares what other readers of this letter may be wondering, "*What has happened?*" (Gal 4:15). What has happened is that a group of rhetorically savvy teachers have come to town preaching a different gospel (1:6–9), and Paul wishes that they would go castrate themselves (Gal 5:12)!

Who are the teachers? They appear to be Christian Jews who claim some connection or authority from the Jerusalem church in support of their

---

10. James D. G. Dunn, *The Theology of Paul's Letter to the Galatians*, New Testament Theology (Cambridge: Cambridge University Press, 1993), 2.

gentile mission.[11] Early in the body of the letter (2:1-10), Paul reminds the Galatians of the Jerusalem church's support of his own gentile mission, though he is adamant that no one in that church taught him the gospel that he received (1:18-24). What he has taught the Galatians has been a revelation from God (1:11-17). Of course, we do not have the teachers' message, but there are glimpses of what Paul assumes their message to be (Gal 1:1-9; 3:1-5; 4:17; 5:7-12; 6:12-14). For instance, the Sarah and Hagar allegory (Gal 4:21-5:1)—an allegory that finds no parallel in Paul's other letters—would support the notion that the teachers have made much of the Galatians becoming descendants of Abraham, a point to which we will return. At every turn, this letter is an impassioned rebuttal of the teachers' message that, from Paul's perspective, places emphasis on human deeds rather than the power of God to act through the cross.

Though we do not get to hear the Galatians' rationale for following the advice of the teachers, it is not far-fetched that the Galatians would be attracted to their message. Paul has proclaimed the gospel, and after he leaves town, these teachers arrive who are also talking about Jesus. Perhaps in a US context where multiple churches are scattered throughout even the smallest of towns, we might lose sight of how few people had even heard about Jesus in the lands that the Galatians inhabited. With Paul nowhere in sight, the believers must have rejoiced to meet other travelers who were talking about a crucified and resurrected Jew from Nazareth, especially when those travelers seem well versed in the same sacred texts that Paul had cited. It is likely that the Galatians wanted to do everything that they could to demonstrate their faithfulness to the God of Israel. No doubt the teachers used the sincerity of the Galatians' faith to encourage what might have been proclaimed as the next faithful step—circumcision. Paul has encouraged them to walk in the Spirit, but this advice, while worthy, is not always so clear. The teachers are offering practical guidelines, clear-cut rules (pun intended) for living.

---

11. Martyn prefers "teachers" to "opponents" (see *Galatians*, 117). The neutral language is used here to leave open the possibility that the teachers did not view themselves as opponents of Paul's mission, but rather as building upon the foundation that Paul had already laid. Of course, Paul does not portray their message in a neutral light, since he equates their "gospel" as a defection from the truth (1:6-9)! Regardless of whether Paul saw them as opponents, the teachers have effectively managed to sway Paul's congregations toward the gospel that they are preaching. This would likely not be possible if they had come to town and introduced themselves as critics of Paul's mission.

When considering Rome's provisions for Jewish practices, it might have been more advantageous for the Galatians to appear Jewish rather than to be a Galatian "barbarian." As noted in the previous section, Brigitte Kahl has argued that there would be social and civic incentives for appearing to convert to Judaism. Jews, for instance, had the legal right of assembly. Perhaps some of the Galatians were concerned about proclaiming the sovereignty of a Jew from Nazareth who had been crucified on a Roman cross. Maybe appearing to follow an ancient God with ancient laws had some appeal.

Although enjoying a few civic rights may have been an incentive, Paul is more focused on other rewards for inheriting the promises to Abraham. For instance, the apostle highlights the receipt of the divine Spirit (Gal 3:2–5, 14). Furthermore, in Gal 3:8, the gentiles are not just claiming Abraham as father, they are also sharing in the *blessings* of Abraham. To be descendants of Abraham is to partake in the inheritance of these promised blessings, and the promise is not contingent upon deeds of the law: "for if the inheritance comes from the law, it no longer comes from the promise; but God granted it to Abraham through the promise" (3:18). Fear of losing this inheritance may have offered just the incentive that the Galatians needed to do whatever it took to be considered "children of Abraham." After all, the Galatians have been convinced by the other teachers to change their diets and to undergo circumcision. These are not insignificant sacrifices.

Descendants of Abraham, Children of God

Central to the teachers' message was the need for the Galatians to join the children of Abraham. Becoming Abraham's descendants was the means by which these foreign people could inherit the promises of Abraham. From the teachers' perspective, it is through Christ that the law has been made available to the gentiles. Thus, now even the Galatians can follow the law and call Abraham their ancestor.[12] Since the Galatians believe that God has worked through Christ, the next step, according to the teachers, is for them to follow the law so that they too might participate in the abundant blessings that God has promised to all Abraham's children.

---

12. For an excellent summary of the teachers' message based on Paul's counterargument in Galatians, see Martyn, *Galatians*, 302–6.

Paul combats the notion that the law is the means to inherit Abraham's blessings (3:6–29) and insists that through Christ the Galatians have received the promise. The law was never intended as the guarantee of abundant life; it was given as a guide (3:19–29). Paul finishes the letter with the exclamation that circumcision or uncircumcision is nothing (6:15) and accuses his opponents of desiring the Galatians' circumcision for their own glory (6:13).

Paul, however, agrees with the teachers that the believers are heirs of the promise to Abraham. The highest concentration of promise language in all of Paul's letters occurs in Romans and Galatians where he develops his argument in reference to Abraham (Rom 4:1–25; Gal 3:6–4:7; 4:21–5:2). In both letters, Paul emphasizes the faith of Abraham and the faithfulness of God. In Rom 4, Abraham takes center stage in Paul's argument. This ancestor is reckoned as righteous based on faith rather than performing any deeds. The blessing of God was given *before he was circumcised* (Rom 4:9–12). The timing is crucial to Paul's argument. Since the divine blessing predated circumcision, which Paul equates to the "sign or seal" of his righteousness (4:11), the blessing was not contingent upon circumcision or any human deed. So too in Galatians, Abraham "believed God, and it was reckoned to him as righteousness" (3:6; cf. Rom 4:3). The promise of God to Abraham predated the law—by 430 years (!) according to Gal 3:17. Plus, the law is incapable of nullifying the promise (3:18) and is not opposed to the promises of God (3:21). Importantly, in both Romans and Galatians, all who share in Abraham's faith are considered children of Abraham and heirs to the promises. Both letters cite Scripture to demonstrate that Abraham is the father of both the circumcised and the uncircumcised (Rom 4:11–12, 16–17), indeed, the father of many nations (Rom 4:17; Gal 3:8).

Abraham may be lifted up as an example of human faithfulness, but it is God who is the main actor in this cosmic drama. God gives life to the dead and calls into existence things that do not exist, such as granting heirs to a barren couple (Rom 4:17). The blessing to Abraham is a promise of God that reveals God's glory and power to bring life in the midst of death and barrenness (4:13–25). God is the one who reckons Abraham as righteous. God is the one who makes an old man who is "as good as dead" a father of many nations (4:19). God is the one who brought life to Sarah's infertile womb (4:19) and who raised Jesus from the dead (4:24). God is capable of producing heirs and reckoning heirs of the promise (4:25). The promise rests entirely on grace and is guaranteed to all Abraham's descendants—including all who share in the faith of Abraham, "for he is the father of us all" (4:16). This guarantee stems from *God's* faithfulness, not from human effort.

Though the teachers seem fixated on descent from Abraham, Paul's argument shifts the emphasis from being children of Abraham to being children of God. Paul does not see the church's primary identity as descendants of Abraham, but as those who have been clothed in Christ, who is the singular seed of Abraham (3:16). Through Christ, the Galatians are connected to the God who reckoned Abraham righteous and blessed him and his seed (Gal 3:16, 21). God has justified the gentiles (3:8), ratified a covenant, and created a promise that is irrevocable (3:17). Indeed, God is *one* (3:20). In Christ, the Galatians become more than children of Abraham; they become children of God (3:26). It is "through God" that they have become "sons" like Isaac and heirs (4:7). It is because of God's actions—rather than any human deed—that they inherit the promises spoken by God to Abraham.

The Power of the Promises

Though Paul cites only a few verses from the Genesis narratives (particularly, Gen 15:6 and 12:3; cf. Gen 18:18), the theme of promise courses throughout his argument in Gal 3 and 4. What was promised to Abraham, Paul claims, was promised to his "seed" in the singular, and that seed is Christ (Gal 3:16). Through Christ, the Galatian gentiles are inheritors. What are they inheriting? To put it another way: What is the reward of being children of Abraham? Why would the Galatians want to circumcise themselves simply to demonstrate that the God of Israel—the God of a foreign people in a foreign land—is a promise-keeping kind of God? What is the incentive for the Galatians to mutilate their own flesh just to prove that they are Abraham's offspring?

What exactly is the promise to Abraham? There is more to the Abrahamic promise than progeny. The promises to Abraham (e.g., Gen 12:1–3; 15:1–6, 17) and to his descendants (e.g., Gen 22:18; cf. 12:7; 13:15; 17:7) include progeny *and* land. *Land is the inheritance* of Abraham's descendants.

Herein lies the problem: Paul makes no explicit reference to the land in Galatians. If both land and progeny are integral to God's promises to Abraham, how is Paul appropriating the promise of land for the gentile Galatians? Furthermore, how can the Galatians possibly be, as Paul claims, "children of the promise, like Isaac" (Gal 4:28), if land is *not* part of the inheritance? In short, what on earth has happened to the promise of land in Paul's theology? And second, how does this promise relate to a non-Jewish people who have been vanquished by Rome and thus who find themselves landless?

The land promises to Abraham, though reinterpreted by Paul, have by no means disappeared from Galatians or from Pauline theology. Rather, the promise of land finds its fulfillment in the hope of *new creation*—a creation that is not simply spiritualized, but is nothing short of the consummation of God's created order. This new creation is not only marked by resurrection, but also includes land and all the blessings of life in God's redeemed cosmos. It is new creation that Paul emphasizes as the real incentive for the Galatians to stay the course in the faith that he first taught them.

The Absence of "Land" in Paul's Language

First, it must be acknowledged that Paul avoids talking about the "land" explicitly. If land is part of God's promise to Abraham, why does Paul not mention land as part of the inheritance? In his meticulous study of land in the New Testament, W. D. Davies highlights the lack of land language in Paul's letters.[13] In Romans, Davies argues, Paul would have good reason to avoid the mention of land as part of the Abrahamic promises. The apostle's cautionary words in Rom 13:1-7 demonstrate sensitivity to the political environment. Perhaps Paul did not desire to stir up trouble in a letter written to believers in the heart of the Roman Empire. But, as Davies notes, the letter to the region of Galatia would not necessarily share the same political cautiousness. Davies writes: "In Galatians we can be fairly certain that Paul did not merely ignore the territorial aspect of the promise for political reasons: his silence points not merely to the absence of a conscious concern with it, but to *his deliberate rejection of it*. His interpretation of the promise is a-territorial" (*italics* mine).[14] The promise, in essence, becomes a blessing to all nations and, therefore, unboundaried. Furthermore, Davies argues, Christ is the key to Paul's argument: "For Paul, Christ had gathered up the promise into the singularity of his own person. In this way, 'the territory' promised was transformed into and fulfilled by the life 'in Christ.' All this

---

13. W. D. Davies, *The Gospel and the Land: Early Christianity and Jewish Territorial Doctrine* (Berkeley: University of California Press, 1974), 167.

14. Davies, *Gospel and the Land*, 178-79.

is not made explicit, because Paul did not directly apply himself to the question of the land, but it is implied." Thus, Davies concludes, "the land, like the Law, particular and provisional, had become *irrelevant*."[15]

There is much to commend in Davies's observations. First, Davies acknowledges that land is a concept that gets redefined apart from a particular nation or territory not only in Paul's letters but also in the Hebrew Bible. Calling the non-Jewish audience "heirs" of the promise, therefore, emphasizes the multinational blessings that the promises to Abraham were meant to facilitate. In Gal 3:8, Paul cites Gen 12:3: "In you shall all the nations be blessed."[16] This citation highlights the Abrahamic promise as inclusive of all nations and not limited to one nationality or, as Davies has pointed out, one territory or land.

Second, Davies argues that Paul avoids explicit language of land due to his own thought transformation about the land via Christ. For Davies, being "in Christ" personalizes and universalizes the promise, thereby dislocating the promise from one people and one place and relocating it "in Christ."[17] Without a doubt, Paul's argument in Gal 3 and 4 hinges on the Galatians being "in Christ" and therefore part of Abraham's seed. Being in Christ by faith is absolutely essential to Paul's counterargument to the teachers who want the Galatians to join the children of Abraham through law observance.

There are problems, nonetheless, with claiming that the promise of land is now irrelevant—a dated promise that falls away now that Christ is on the scene. Land, after all, is a promise of God. According to Gal 3:17–18, not even the law—which is holy and good (Rom 7:12, 16)—can annul a covenant ratified by God or void a promise. And Paul, according to Rom 11:29, sees the promises of God as *irrevocable*. Rather than interpreting Paul's lack of land language as a dismissal of the land promise, what happens if we *assume* the land promise in Paul's argument? In Gal 3:16, it is interesting that Paul does not refer to a single promise made to Abraham, such as progeny, but refers to the promise*s* (plural) that were made to Abraham and to his offspring. What if the promise of land is inherent in being "children of the promise"? Would a landless and subjugated people not be more tempted to become children of Abraham in any way possible, including circumcising themselves, if they believed that doing so would make them Abraham's heirs?

---

15. Davies, *Gospel and the Land*, 179.
16. Also Gen 18:18.
17. Davies, *Gospel and the Land*, 179.

Revisiting Land

When God made the promise to Abraham, the promise included all the land that he could see. The territory is not neatly demarcated with borders. In fact, even as the story progresses, the physical territory is not consistently defined. At least two "maps" are in the Hebrew Bible:[18] (1) the land of Canaan[19] and (2) an extension of that land, during the united monarchy, to include both sides of the Jordan (minus Moab and Ammon) as well as north to the Euphrates River (Deut 11:24).[20] It is telling that the text does not consistently speak of the same boundaries. Rather, the *idea* of land takes on a significance that is bigger than either of these maps.

The biblical text speaks of the land both *literally* and *symbolically*—both the fertile soil that sustains life *and* the symbolic notion of prosperity, security, and abundance.[21] The literal and symbolic concepts are not easily disentangled since land as territoried space finds its meaning and purpose in land as symbol. Brueggemann defines land as a place with the Lord, "a place well filled with memories of life with him and promise from him and vows to him. It is land that provides the central assurance to Israel of its historicality, that it will be and always must be concerned with actual rootage in a place which is a repository for commitment and therefore identity." As for promise, Brueggemann claims, God's promise to God's people is always God's land.[22] Plus, that physical territory, the longing for it or the loss of it, consumes much of the plotline from the Abrahamic promises onward. It is little wonder that Brueggemann would see in the land a central, if not *the* central, theme of the text.

Life on the land depended completely on the Lord. The Lord provided rain. The Lord provided security. The Lord sustained life. The land was always so deeply connected to the Lord that in a profound way the land always belongs to God. Israel never "owns" the promised land. Even the year of Jubilee was meant to ensure that the land returned to the users

---

18. Gary M. Burge, "Land," in *The New Interpreter's Dictionary of the Bible* (Nashville: Abingdon, 2008), 571. See also Davies, *Gospel and the Land*, 17, n. 3.

19. The land from the Jordan River to the Mediterranean Sea and from the Wadi of Egypt to Hamath (Num 34:1-12).

20. Burge, "Land," 571.

21. Walter Brueggemann, *The Land: Place as Gift, Promise, and Challenge in Biblical Faith* (Philadelphia: Fortress, 1977), 2.

22. Brueggemann, *Land*, 6.

God had elected as its tenders from the beginning.²³ In short, the Lord is sovereign over the land. That sovereignty is not confined to borders. The bordered space was always intended to be a witness, and thus a blessing, to the nations.

What might it look like to fulfill the land promise? Fulfillment requires more than just the granting of land. The land as territory is always meant to be the land as a space where people can prosper. The land is even characterized as a place flowing with milk and honey—an area that produces more than enough to support life (Exod 3:8, 17; 13:5; Lev 20:24; Num 13:27). Fulfillment of the land promise must look like people living and thriving on a land of plenty—a land that can support a growing population. For the land to serve this function, its inhabitants must be good stewards of the land and its resources—hence the land's connection to the covenant (Gen 17:8–9).²⁴

The intertwining of covenant and promise reflects God's good intentions for the created order. In his book *The God of Israel and Christian Theology*, R. Kendall Soulen highlights the importance of God's blessings for God's creation. Rather than seeing the great plotline of the biblical story as the redemption of humanity, Soulen argues persuasively that God longs for the consummation of creation. Through land, God blesses Israel with life and the fullness of life.²⁵ The gift of land embodies the kind of blessed life that God wants not just for Israel, but for all nations.²⁶ Soulen writes: "By electing Israel and blessing it 'in the land,' God elects Israel together with the whole human family in all its time-, place-, and season-bound earthiness as the object of God's consummating work."²⁷ Thus, the land is both a means and a symbol for God's blessing. As such, life on the land serves as a microcosm of God's desire for all creation.

How does land then factor into the good news for the Galatians? If Paul is ministering during a time of Roman occupation both of the promised land and of the Galatians' homeland, could the land promise not seem like a distant wish, a pie-in-the-sky hope, with no grounding in reality? Would it not be easier on God if the land promise could just be spiritualized so

---

23. Burge, "Land," 571–72.

24. The firstfruits and first crops were sacrificed to the Lord (Lev 27:30–33; Deut 14:22; 26:9–15), and the Sabbath was even observed *by* the land (Lev 25:2).

25. R. Kendall Soulen, *The God of Israel and Christian Theology* (Minneapolis: Fortress, 1996), 123.

26. Soulen, *God of Israel*, 124.

27. Soulen, *God of Israel*, 123.

that God does not have to be invested in the actual created order? Based on most interpretations of the land in Christian theology, it seems that interpreters have wanted to protect God's reputation. The land, like the law, has fallen to the wayside. What happens, though, if we take seriously the land as a tangible vehicle of God's blessing for creation? Paul's promise of new creation is not a promise divorced from the created order. Rather, new creation for Paul is just as tangible as slicing foreskin.

Back to the Future

To return to the Abrahamic promises in Galatians, why would Paul assume that God would honor one promise—the promise of progeny—and dismiss the promise of land?

Paul's failure to mention land explicitly does not mean that Paul was unconcerned about the land or that he found the land promise irrelevant post-Christ. Davies, I believe, is correct that Paul reveals no concern to promote a nationalistic pride in a particular territory. Furthermore, he has no interest in transforming the gentiles into Jews. Though Paul is committed to the Jerusalem saints and to connecting the gentile believers to the Jewish Christians via the God of Israel, this commitment stems from his understanding of what God is doing through Christ for all nations. There is no sign that Paul's "new creation" has as its goal a nation-state with boundaries. Nonetheless, we should not so quickly dismiss the concept of land from Paul's understanding of inheritance. Paul's references to the promise in Galatians indicate that Paul is reinterpreting the promise via Christ. The promise itself—the incentive for grown men to have themselves circumcised and radically change their diets (!)—is not divorced from God's rectification of the whole created order. If the land promise is implied in Paul's references to the Abrahamic promise, as I believe it is, we need to consider Paul's language for what is being inherited. *What is the promised inheritance that is being passed on to the Galatians as heirs?*

In Galatians, the promise is directly related to at least three interrelated realities: life in the Spirit, the kingdom of God, and new creation. It is significant that all three of these synonymous realities employ land imagery. First, Paul connects the promise to the presence of the Spirit. In Gal 3:14, after claiming that the nations will be blessed through Abraham (3:8; citing Gen 12:3 and 18:18), he says that in Christ, the blessing of Abraham comes to the gentiles, who receive the "promise of the Spirit" through faith.

What is the promise of the Spirit? It is nothing short of life. Paul consistently contrasts the Spirit, which brings life, with the power of sin, which brings death (Rom 8:2; 5:12-21). According to Gal 3:21, the problem with the law is that it can only point out sin; it cannot overcome sin to produce life. Rather, by being "in Christ," the promise comes to those who believe (Gal 3:22), since Christ is the singular seed of Abraham. If the Galatians are in Christ, Paul claims, then they too are Abraham's seed and "heirs of the promise" (3:29). Thus, being "in Christ" is the locus of life, as Davies has argued.

Even the promised life of the Spirit, however, is illustrated with land imagery. In Gal 6:8, the apostle uses imagery of sowing seed—in other words, imagery of life on the land, to illustrate the work of the Spirit: "For the one who sows to the Spirit will reap from the Spirit eternal life" (cf. Rom 7:6). This verse is surrounded by extensions of the sowing and reaping metaphor. In the first half of the verse, the agricultural metaphor is applied to life in the flesh: "The one who sows to the flesh will reap from the flesh corruption" (6:8a). Paul ends the metaphor with the exhortation in 6:9 not to grow weary in doing good, for in the *kairos* time, which the NRSV aptly translates as "harvest time," "we will reap, if we do not give up." Before this metaphor in chapter 6, Paul has already described the work of the Spirit as *karpos*, "fruit," in Gal 5:22. Though the metaphor is intelligible without reference to the land promise, one wonders whether the land promise itself has inspired Paul here.

Second, the promise is also wed to the kingdom of God through the language of inheritance. In Gal 5:21, Paul warns: "Those who walk according to the flesh rather than live by the Spirit will not inherit the kingdom of God." Here the kingdom is associated with life in the Spirit. It is often assumed that Paul's reference to eternal life or even his rare mentions of the kingdom of God refer to a nonspatial, spiritual kingdom. Yet the kingdom language in Jesus's teaching assumes a kingdom on earth. The Lord's Prayer, for instance, teaches followers to pray for the kingdom to come, for God's will to be done *on earth* as it is in heaven.

Paul's view of the promise is not divorced from the created order. In Rom 4:13—within the discussion of God's promises to Abraham—Paul refers to the Abrahamic promise as the promise to inherit the *cosmos*: Paul writes, "The promise to Abraham and his descendants, that they should inherit the *world*, did not come through the law but through the righteousness of faith." Paul avoids saying "land," as though "land" is simply not big enough to encompass the extent of God's power and grace. Instead, the inheritance of Abraham is the whole world!

Paul's expansion of the promise to incorporate the world is not unique. In Genesis, the promise is for the land that Abraham can see. By the time of Paul, though, the boundaries of that land have broadened to incorporate the whole world (cf. Sir 44:21; Jub. 19:21; Philo, *On the Life of Moses* 1.155; cf. 1 En. 5:7b).[28] For example, Sir 44:21 reflects this extension of the land promise:

> Therefore the Lord assured him [Abraham] with an oath that the nations would be blessed through his offspring; that he would make him as numerous as the dust of the earth, and exalt his offspring like the stars, and give them *an inheritance from sea to sea and from the Euphrates to the ends of the earth*. (NRSV; italics added for emphasis)

Similarly, Jub. 22:14 expresses Abraham's blessing for Jacob in terms of inheritance of "all the earth." This promise is reiterated in Jub. 32:19: "And I shall give to your seed all of the land under heaven and they will rule in all nations as they have desired. And after this all of the earth will be gathered together and they will inherit it forever." In 1 En. 5:7, the chosen will receive this great inheritance: "But to the elect there shall be light, joy, and peace, and they shall inherit the earth." These elect will "not return again to sin," but live long peaceable lives according to wisdom (1 En. 5:7-10). Wisdom will create peace and happiness on the earth (1 En. 5:7-10).

The hope of inheriting this peace is related to the eschatological blessing of the earth's renewal. In 2 Bar. 14:7, the anticipated inheritance is the world to come: "Therefore, they [the righteous] leave this world without fear and are confident of the world which you have promised to them with an expectation full of joy." Baruch laments that the wicked seem to prosper while the righteous suffer (2 Bar. 14:1-19; cf. 4 Ezra 6:55-59), yet it is for the righteous that God created the world (2 Bar. 14:19; cf. 4 Ezra 6:55). In his pleading with the Lord, Baruch bemoans, "For if only this life exists which everyone possesses here, nothing could be more bitter than this" (2 Bar. 22:13). The text is written during a time of foreign occupation of the land,[29]

---

28. For an excellent survey of the expansion of the metaphor, see Brendan Byrne, *Romans*, SP (Collegeville, MN: Liturgical, 2007), 157. Even during the Second Temple period, the language of inheritance is tied to the land (cf. 2 Macc 2:17-18; Wis 12:21; 18:6; Pss. Sol. 12:6; 4QapGen 21:8-14).

29. It seems that the author lives after the destruction of the Second Temple in 70 CE, if 2 Bar. 32:2-4 is interpreted to presuppose two destructions. This work also

and there is fear that "the Mighty One does not anymore remember the earth" (2 Bar. 25:4; cf. 32:9). Baruch's hope is placed in an Anointed One who will resurrect all who sleep in hope of him (2 Bar. 30:1). Ultimately, "the Mighty One will renew his creation" (2 Bar. 32:7), and the righteous will inherit this renewed earth (2 Bar. 44:12-14; 51:3; cf. 4 Ezra 7:9). In 2 Bar. 57:1-3, the renewal of the earth is equated with the promise of life for the righteous.

Likewise, in Sib. Or. 3, the world to come is a renewal of the created order. The Sybil pronounces the transformation of the earth with a land of plenty (3:619-23), a renewed temple (3:701-30), and a just kingdom on earth (3:767-95). The transformation is equated with God's promise "to open the earth and the world and the gates of the blessed and all joys and immortal intellect and eternal cheer" (3:669-771). This coming kingdom is marked by peace (3:780), "just wealth" (3:784), and the judgment and dominion of God (3:784). In language reminiscent of Isaiah, the oracle imagines a time when wolves and lambs will feed together, bears will sleep with calves, lions will feast on husks, like an ox, and "mere infant children will lead them with ropes. For he will make the beasts on earth harmless. Serpents and asps will sleep with babies and will not harm them, for the hand of God will be upon them" (3:787-95; cf. Isa 11:6-8; 65:17-25). This coming kingdom will exhibit God's justice on earth and abundant life in a world of peace.

In sum, Paul's language of inheriting the world, though bigger than land as territoried space, is congruent with other Hellenistic Jewish literature. Far from spiritualizing the promise of the land, this literature expands the physical space of inheritance to incorporate the whole earth. Far from abandoning the created order, there is an expectation that God will renew it. This expectation lives on in the early church. Severian, bishop of Gabala in Syria in the late fourth and early fifth centuries, describes the world to come as a world that has been renewed: "Paul says that the righteous will inherit the world because the ungodly will be thrown out and handed over to punishment on the day of judgment, but the righteous will possess the universe which remains, and will have been renewed, and the good things of heaven and earth will be theirs."[30]

---

has many parallels with 4 Ezra. If a common source or literary dependence is possible, then 2 Baruch may date to the beginning of the second century. For a discussion, see A. F. J. Klijn, "2 (Syriac Apocalypse of) Baruch: A New Translation and Introduction," in *The Old Testament Pseudepigrapha: Apocalyptic Literature & Testaments*, ed. James H. Charlesworth (Garden City: Doubleday, 1983), 1:616-17.

30. Severian, "Pauline Commentary from the Greek Church," in *The Ancient*

Finally, in Gal 6:15, Paul links the promise to "new creation." Paul concludes the body of his argument by reiterating that the fruit of the Spirit rather than the marks of circumcision are the outward signs of God's work in the Galatians. God is renewing and rectifying the whole cosmos, not just the physical descendants of Abraham. In 6:15, Paul exclaims: "For neither circumcision counts for anything, nor uncircumcision, but a new creation." This "new creation" stands in contrast to the "present evil age" of Gal 1:4, which has been subjugated under sin's power (Rom 5:12-21). New creation is the reign of God's grace that is marked by abundant life in a redeemed world. This redemption has already begun. According to 2 Cor 5:17, those who are "in Christ" are already a new creation. Yet God's rectification does not stop with humanity. In Rom 8, Paul writes that all creation is suffering under the power of sin. As Beverly Roberts Gaventa has argued, the longing of creation must include more than the plight of human creatures.[31] Rather, the longing of creation must indeed be *all* God's creation—both human and nonhuman. All have suffered under the reign of sin.

To recall Soulen's argument, God has not abandoned any of God's creation, but works toward its consummation. The God of Israel invests and reveals Godself in creation by electing a human family (the family of Abraham), by granting that family children, and by giving those children land. These specific gifts were intended to be a blessing to all nations. For Paul, the land promise has been magnified. The borders are bigger than one territory. The whole cosmos is in view, because the whole cosmos stands in need of rectification. In short, to claim that the land promise is now irrelevant misses the reality that the gift of land is a divine investment in the created order. The problem with hope in a nonspatial, spiritual kingdom is that God never consummates creation. Only humanity finds redemption, while the rest of creation suffers.

This anthropocentric reading runs counter to the vision of new creation in Isa 65. There, the new world imagined by the prophet includes peaceful and abundant existence on the land—where people live long lives, build houses, plant vineyards, and reap the benefits of their own harvest, where even the predators live at peace with their former prey (Isa 65:17-25). The new heavens and new earth are characterized by God's abundant blessings (65:23).

Christian Commentary on Scripture: Romans, ed. Gerald Bray (Downers Grove, IL: InterVarsity, 1998), 118.

31. Beverly Roberts Gaventa, *Our Mother Saint Paul* (Louisville: Westminster John Knox, 2007), 53-55.

Conclusion

What on earth has happened to the land in Paul's theology? It is nothing short of abundant life in a redeemed world. The gift of land embodies blessing—God's commitment to the blessing of abundant life that God desires for God's creation. Paul's appeals to the promises of Abraham do not dismiss God's promise of land. Rather, Paul *assumes* the blessing of land as testimony of God's faithfulness and as witness to God's intention to rectify creation. Through faith, the Galatians are indeed heirs and children of the promise, and what they are inheriting is life—the kind of abundant life that rectifies and reclaims human and nonhuman creation alike.

This must have been a remarkable piece of good news for a people group who had found themselves landless. According to Euphorion, the name "Galatian" stems from *Gaizētai*, from "those who are searching (*zētountes*) for land (*gēn*)."[32] Perhaps these Galatians are more like Abraham than they realize. Abraham has the promise and trusts in it in a way parallel to the Galatians, who, though foreigners and landless themselves, have placed their faith in this same God. Abraham and his family did not have land but were constantly moving toward it and living in anticipation of it. They were, as Brueggemann says, "empowered by anticipation."[33] The Galatians, too, live with the firstfruits of new creation, the Spirit, while they anticipate God's kingdom come. If the teachers' message has threatened their status as inheritors of the cosmos, it is little wonder why these vanquished people would do anything that the teachers asked to preserve their status as descendants of Abraham. Paul's gospel, however, assures the least of these in the empire that they are more than descendants of Abraham, they are "children of the promise" and, even more important than that, "children of God."

FURTHER READING

Gaventa, Beverly Roberts. "The Singularity of the Gospel." Pages 101–12 in *Our Mother Saint Paul*. Louisville: Westminster John Knox, 2007. Gaventa gives an overview of Paul's gospel and the importance of God's act of rectifying the "present evil age" and bringing about "new creation."

---

32. Euphorion, *Poetic Fragments* 42.
33. Brueggemann, *Land*, 15.

Kahl, Brigitte. *Galatians Re-Imagined: Reading with the Eyes of the Vanquished*. Minneapolis: Fortress, 2010. Kahl's work seeks to place the Galatians within their social, historical, and imperial context and rereads the letter in light of a vanquished people under Roman rule.

Martyn, J. Louis. *Galatians*. AYB 33A. New York: Doubleday, 1997. Martyn constructs a plausible reconstruction of the teachers' message based on the assumptions in Paul's argument in Galatians. The comment sections in this commentary are just as valuable as the verse-by-verse exposition.

CHAPTER FIVE

The Church as the Least of These?

Paul calls the Corinthians "babes," or "infants," in 1 Cor 3:1: "And so, brothers and sisters, I could not speak to you as spiritual people, but rather as people of the flesh, as infants in Christ" (NRSV). With this metaphor, Paul likens the church to the least in the developmental chain, infants who depend on others for feeding and nurturing. Though the image would be readily accessible, how to interpret this metaphor—or even how the Corinthians might have heard it—is more complex than the dominant readings might make it seem. This metaphor of weakness invites the Corinthian church to see themselves in a position of humility and vulnerability.

It has become commonplace to see the label "infants" as a caricature of the Corinthians' childish behavior.[1] David Garland articulates this point well: "Their behavior reveals that they are not wise and mature, but childish and foolish."[2] Indeed, the focus on childish behavior captures a critical facet of the infancy metaphor: The foolish behavior of the Corinthians is a symptom of their spiritual immaturity or, as Paul says, of being "fleshly" (1 Cor 3:1, 3). Reading the infancy metaphor in a pejorative fashion fits well with the preceding argument. In 1 Cor 1:18–2:16, Paul draws dichotomies between wise and foolish, *pneumatikos* (spiritual) and *psychikos* (unspir-

---

1. Though some will highlight the Corinthians' failure to comprehend their position in Christ (J. Francis, "As Babes in Christ—Some Proposals Regarding 1 Corinthians 3:1-3," *JSNT* 7 [1980]: 41-60; David Garland, *1 Corinthians*, BECNT (Grand Rapids: Baker Academic, 2003], 107) as opposed to their failure to progress in the faith (Reidar Aasgaard, "Like a Child: Paul's Rhetorical Uses of Childhood," in *The Child in the Bible*, ed. Marcia J. Bunge [Grand Rapids: Eerdmans, 2008], 267), the effect is still a focus on the behavioral aspect of the metaphor.

2. Garland, *1 Corinthians*, 107.

itual), as well as mature and immature. To follow the world's wisdom is to be like the *psychikos* (unspiritual) person, who neither receives the gifts of God's Spirit nor understands them (2:14); whereas, to be guided by the "mind of Christ" is indicative of the *pneumatikos* (spiritual), who is considered mature (2:6). In contrast to the spiritual ones, the Corinthians' quarreling serves as proof of their immaturity (3:3). Surely, the apostle's plea for them to exhibit the mind of Christ (2:16) still lingers in the opening lines of 1 Cor 3, when Paul refers to the Corinthians as "infants." In effect, reading "infants in Christ" with the preceding argument reinforces the interpretation of the Corinthians' behavior as childish and foolish. The sentiment created by this common interpretation might be paraphrased as Paul telling the Corinthians, "Stop acting like babies!"

By acknowledging only the behavioral aspects of the metaphor, however, have we too quickly placed the Corinthians in "time out"? If "infants in Christ" connotes only foolish behavior, then why does Paul expand the metaphor to include concrete details of childcare—for instance, the role of a wet nurse, the care of *paidagōgoi* (guardians), or the discipline of a father? While the role of a guardian or father evokes the need to discipline a bunch of whiny children, the task of giving milk or solid food does not suggest behavioral immaturity, but rather their vulnerability and dependency at this early stage of development. Far from being sages, the Corinthians are likened to the "least" on the developmental scale, mere babies.

Within the same breath that Paul calls the Corinthians infants, he refers to them as *sarkinoi*, "fleshly" people. Though calling them fleshly would fit well with the idea of spiritual immaturity, there is more in this text than the chiding of children. Flesh connotes weakness. The Corinthians are *sarkinoi* as the "Day" is coming (3:13), a day of revelation and judgment. Being of the "flesh" is a dangerous position, a position that is antithetical to being of the Spirit (*pneumatikoi*) and a situation that stands in direct opposition to God's will (Rom 8:5-8). After all, in 1 Cor 5:5, it is the "flesh" that faces destruction on the Day of the Lord.[3] Given the expansion of the

---

3. The translation of 1 Cor 5:5 raises a number of issues regarding the salvation of the *pneuma* (spirit) and the destruction of the *sarx* (flesh). Rather than take *sarx* as a reference to the man's body (contra Hans Conzelmann, *First Corinthians*, Hermeneia [Philadelphia: Fortress, 1975], 97; C. K. Barrett, *The First Epistle to the Corinthians*, Black's New Testament Commentary [Peabody, MA: Hendrickson, 1996], 126-27; F. F. Bruce, *1 and 2 Corinthians* [Grand Rapids: Eerdmans, 1971], 54-55; Ivan Havener, "A Curse for Salvation—1 Corinthians 5:1-5," in *Sin, Salvation, and the Spirit*,

metaphor to include concrete references to childcare and the urgency of the coming Day, could the metaphor "infants in Christ" be more complex than telling the Corinthians to stop acting like babies?

This chapter argues that the metaphor of infancy is, in fact, multifaceted. Calling the church "infants" connotes childishness, but being childlike involves more than immaturity or foolishness. The metaphor cannot be limited to foolishness any more than the actual experience of being a child can be limited to child's folly. According to Norman Friedman, metaphor is a "device which speaks of one thing (tenor) in terms which are appropriate to another (vehicle), with the vehicle serving as the source of traits to be transferred to the tenor."[4] Put differently, Lakoff and Johnson claim, "The essence of metaphor is understanding and experiencing one kind of thing in terms of another."[5] This means that the metaphor works only when the audience has familiarity with the concepts that are being used.[6] That familiarity cannot be limited to other metaphorical uses of the same term or concept, but must also consider how the complexities of real life inspire the comparison. If metaphors rearrange the furniture in our minds, as Kittay suggests,[7] then this infancy metaphor invites us to see the audience in a whole new perspective—the perspective of the vulnerable, a position of the "least of these." To understand how Paul is using the infancy metaphor in 1 Cor 3 we will consider not only how other writers refer to infants—either concretely or metaphorically—but also how evidence from everyday life might illuminate the comparison between the Corinthians and "babes."[8]

---

ed. D. Durken [Collegeville, MN: Liturgical, 1979], 340-41), *sarx* should be read in concert with its use in Gal 5:13, 19, 24; Rom 7:5-6, 18, 25; 8:1-17 (see Adela Yarbro Collins, "The Function of 'Excommunication' in Paul," *HTR* 73 [1980]: 259; Richard B. Hays, *First Corinthians*, IBC [Louisville: Westminster John Knox, 1997], 86).

4. Norman Friedman, *Form and Meaning in Fiction* (Athens: University of Georgia Press, 1975), 289; cited in Beverly Roberts Gaventa, *Our Mother Saint Paul* (Louisville: Westminster John Knox, 2007), 25.

5. George Lakoff and Mark Johnson, *Metaphors We Live By* (Chicago: University of Chicago Press, 1980), 5. See also George Lakoff and Mark Johnson, *Philosophy in the Flesh* (New York: Basic, 1999); Gilles Fauconnier and Mark Turner, *The Way We Think: Conceptual Blending and the Mind's Hidden Complexities* (New York: Basic, 2002).

6. Aristotle, *Rhetoric* 3.10.4; see also *Poetics* 1457b.

7. Eva Fedder Kittay, *Metaphor: Its Cognitive and Linguistic Structure* (Oxford: Oxford University Press, 1979), 124-35; cited in Gaventa, *Our Mother Saint Paul*, 11.

8. As Reidar Aasgaard has noted, Paul's attitudes toward children and childhood are reflected both in the concrete references as well as the metaphorical uses ("Paul

The Church as the Least of These?

All this evidence comprises the social context from which Paul's audience would interpret "infants in Christ." If metaphors have the ability to teach and inform by setting things "before the eyes," as Aristotle suggests,[9] then this infancy metaphor invites the recipients to see themselves in a whole new perspective—the perspective of the vulnerable.

The Imagery of Infancy in the Writings of Paul's Contemporaries

Ancient writers used infancy metaphors to convey two interrelated facets of childhood: (1) the lack of understanding and (2) the vulnerability of the infant.[10] The term *nēpioi* in Greek or *infantes* in Latin referred to "non-speakers."[11] This inability to communicate was linked to the absence of *logos*.[12] Babies and, indeed, all who were deemed irrational were considered particularly vulnerable, dependent on others for their protection, provision, and care.

The lack of *logos* could be viewed neutrally, positively, or negatively. The inability to reason placed the infant in an impressionable position, capable of being swayed in any direction. Philo, for instance, claims that the infant child shares neither in virtue nor vice because the soul of the infant is stripped of all evil or goodness (*Allegorical Interpretation* 2.53; also 2.64).[13] This bareness can have positive connotations to suggest innocence.

---

as a Child: Children and Childhood in the Letters of the Apostle," *JBL* 126 [2007]: 129–59 [esp. 132]).

9. Aristotle, *Rhetoric* 3.10.2, 6.

10. Ancient writers are not consistent with their references to children. The term *nēpioi* gets used to refer to newborns as well as slightly older children. For instance, Philo refers to *nēpioi* as having the capacity to do and say many things that reasonable people also do and say, but *nēpioi* lack the capacity to reason (*Allegorical Interpretation* 3. 210). The term is used to refer to children with the ability to speak as an adult might speak. Similarly, Paul uses *paidia* interchangeably with *nēpioi* in 1 Cor 14:20 and refers to infants (*nēpioi*) speaking, thinking, and reasoning in 1 Cor 13:11. Regarding Paul's use of *teknon*, see Larry O. Yarbrough, "Parents and Children in the Letters of Paul," in *The Social World of the First Christians: Essays in Honor of Wayne Meeks*, ed. L. Michael White and O. Larry Yarbrough (Minneapolis: Fortress, 1995), 127.

11. Thomas Wiedemann, *Adults and Children in the Roman Empire* (New Haven: Yale University Press, 1989), 21.

12. Wiedemann, *Adults and Children in the Roman Empire*, 21.

13. Herm. Mand. 2.1.1, "He said to me, 'Be simple and guileless, and you will be

In 1 Cor 14:20, Paul appeals to the notion of innocence when he tells the church to be like infants in evil, but in thinking to be mature.[14] Often, however, the absence of *logos* was associated with negative traits. Thus, metaphorical references to an infant (*nēpioi*) frequently connote unwise behavior. In this context, "childish" serves as a synonym for "foolishness" (e.g., Philo, *On the Cherubim* 63). If the dominant reading of 1 Cor 3:1 is correct, then calling the Corinthians "infants" would certainly have negative connotations.

Since infants can be considered blank slates for evil or goodness, they are also portrayed as those who are in need of instruction. This training is deemed necessary to develop into a mature person. Philo argues that the perfect or mature person (*teleios*) is not in need of instruction, because this person reflects the image of God, while the *nēpios* stands in need of rules and guidance (see Philo, *Allegorical Interpretation* 1.94).[15] Similarly, in 1 Cor 13:11 Paul contrasts reasoning like a child with thinking as a more mature adult. Both Paul and Philo are inspired by the need for childhood instruction even though the infancy metaphor is being applied to adults. The image serves to encourage adults to be like the mature person rather than like *nēpioi*, who are incapable of reason.

Due to the lack of *logos*, infants are commonly considered in the same category as old men and women—in other words, as those considered weak or irrational.[16] Josephus preserves this stereotype when conveying a conversation between Ptolemy and Joseph regarding the actions of the young Onias: "Forgive him, on account of his age; for you cannot certainly be unacquainted with this, that old men and infants have their minds exactly alike; but you shall have from us, who are young men, everything you desire, and shall have no cause to complain" (*Jewish Antiquities* 12:172).[17] The deteriorating mental acuity of the elderly was considered parallel to the growing mental acuity of infants

---

as the children (*nēpioi*) who know not the wickedness that ruins the life of people.'"

14. Even Paul in 1 Cor 13:11 uses *nēpios* in contrast to *anēr*, who does not reason like a *nēpios* or think like a *nēpios* or speak like a *nēpios*. According to the Shepherd of Hermas, infants are likened to those in whose "hearts no evil originates" and who do not know what wickedness is (Herm. Sim. 9.29.1).

15. See also Philo, *Who is the Heir?* 73.

16. See discussion in Wiedemann regarding the protection of the divine for those deemed weak (*Adults and Children in the Roman Empire*, 176).

17. Cf. Sib. Or. 13:8.

The Church as the Least of These?

because the mental capacities of both required provision and care, whereas young men were supposed to be the very epitome of health and wellness.

People who took advantage of the vulnerable were considered particularly brutal. The deaths of women, children, and the elderly frequently served to highlight the atrocities of war (Philo, *Against Flaccus* 62). Philo refers to enemies who do not even spare "the innocent helplessness of babes" (*Against Flaccus* 62).[18] An example of such a foe can be found in 3 Macc 3:12, where King Ptolemy Philopater's letter "to the commanders and soldiers in Egypt and in all places" (3 Macc 3:12) issues the command to torture anyone who would shield any Jew, whether an old man or a suckling (3 Macc 3:27). No one—no matter how vulnerable or helpless—was to be spared.

A similar topos exists in literature that imagines divine judgment—whether the destruction is caused by an enemy's army or attributed to the hand of God. In the Testament of Judah 23:3, the Lord's judgment is portrayed in the rising of one's enemies, the robbery of possessions, the ruin of health, the burning of the temple, the desolation of the land, the death of infants, and the capture of spouses.[19] In the Sibylline Oracles, divine judgment is looming as the immortal God hosts a great tribunal to judge all humankind (2:214-20).[20] In light of this day of reckoning, when the earth will be destroyed by fire (2:196-214), the Sibyllist laments: "Alas, for as many as are found bearing in the womb on that day, for as many as suckle infant children, for as many as dwell upon the wave; alas, for as many as will see that day. For a dark mist will cover the boundless world east and west and south and north" (2:190-95).[21] The hope for the future that infants might ordinarily bring will not exist on that day.

---

18. *Against Flaccus* 68; cf. *Jewish Antiquities* 1:352; 2:307, 465, 496; 3:201; 6:138, 262; 9:231; 13:345; 14:480.

19. In the Sib. Or. 3:268, one of the signs of coming evil and destruction of the impending exile is to watch innocent children and wives being led away in slavery to hostile men.

20. Although Sib. Or. 2 shows signs of later Christian redaction, the imagery of vulnerability found here still demonstrates a topos that considers the lives of the most vulnerable when looking forward to coming judgment. For a discussion of the hand of Christian redaction, see John J. Collins, "The Sibylline Oracles, Books 1 and 2," in *The Old Testament Pseudepigrapha: Apocalyptic Literature and Testaments*, ed. James H. Charlesworth (New York: Doubleday, 1983), 1:330-34.

21. The fate of the wicked in the judgment also notes the vulnerability of children: "Then they will wail here and there at a distance in most piteous fate, fathers and infant children, mothers and weeping children at the breast" (Sib. Or. 2:297-99). The

When faced with judgment that brings desolation, the good news of pregnancy is no longer good news, and the despair of barrenness is replaced with a sense of relief. Who can protect children in the midst of such overwhelming defeat? In view of Jerusalem's destruction, Baruch writes,

> Blessed is he who was not born, or he who was born and died....
> And you, wives, do not pray to bear children, for the barren will rejoice more. And those who have no children will be glad, and those who have children will be sad. For why do they bear in pains only to bury in grief? Or why should men have children again? Or why should the generation of their kind be named again, where this mother is lonely, and her children have been carried away in captivity? (2 Bar. 10:10, 13-16)[22]

The same kind of sentiment is found in the Gospels on the lips of Jesus: "Woe to those who are pregnant and to those who are nursing infants in those days! For there will be great distress on the earth and wrath against this people" (Luke 21:23; cf. Matt 24:19; Mark 3:17). Instead of hope, children's existence in a time of "great distress" and "wrath" only maximizes the despair. According to 1 En. 99, great horrors will occur on the day of the destruction of the unrighteous: "In that very time, women who give birth will cast out and give away and abandon their infants, and those with child will abort, and those nursing will cast down their children and will not return to their infants or the nursing babies" (1 En. 99:5).[23] Those who cannot take care of themselves will be abandoned by the very ones charged with their care. For a world that relies on heirs to secure the future of a household or an empire, these images of coming judgment are grave portraits indeed.

Fortunately, however, the hopelessness described in portrayals of the coming judgment is not the last word. The helplessness of the most vulnerable also illustrates the power of what only God can make possible. God will bring about a kingdom where the most defenseless of creatures

---

imagery suggests that none of the wicked will be spared—not even those to whom the most vulnerable cling.

22. See also 2 Bar. 33:9, where, after hearing about the end of times, the people lament and cry out to Baruch when he is leaving them, "Do you leave us as a father who leaves his children as orphans and goes away from them?"

23. See also Sib. Or. 2:298; 3:482.

will be accompanied by their predators unharmed: "Wolves and lambs will eat grass together in the mountains. Leopards will feed together with kids. Roving bears will spend the night with calves. The flesh-eating lion will eat husks at the manger like an ox, and mere infant children will lead them with ropes. For [God] will make the beasts on earth harmless. Serpents and asps will sleep with babies and will not harm them, for the hand of God will be upon them" (Sib. Or. 3:788-95).

This imagery echoes that of Isa 65, where the wolf and lamb eat together and the lion grazes on straw (Isa 65:25).[24] Third Isaiah's vision of the new heaven and new earth also looks forward to a time when infants will live longer than a few days and will not be doomed to misfortunes (65:20, 23). Likewise, an old man will live out his years (65:20). In other words, even the most vulnerable of creation will thrive under God's provision and care, and no harm will befall them.

In this sketch of how other writers employ infancy language, it can be concluded that the references to infants—whether metaphorical or concrete—stem from the perception that infants lack *logos*. The immaturity of babes—physically, mentally, and emotionally—places them in a vulnerable position. They are dependent upon others for their instruction, care, and provision. These realities inspire metaphors of childhood that highlight innocence, foolishness, irrationality, or other childlike qualities. Yet it is also evident that writers who wish to portray the severity and impartiality of impending doom readily appeal to the helplessness of children, the weakness of women, and the feebleness of old men. According to 2 Bar. 28:1, those who understand that destruction, desolation, and violence mark the end of times are those who will be deemed "wise," the very opposite of what it means to be childlike. The Corinthians, though, by their foolishness and lack of understanding, demonstrate that they are not indeed wise, but immature and vulnerable, as the Day approaches.

Evidence from Daily Life

The children of the house churches would have provided abundant inspiration for Paul's teaching. There was no nursery room with a one-way mirrored window for young mothers to rock their babies in privacy and still watch the worship service. Babies would be cooing and crying. Small

24. Cf. Isa 11:6-8.

children would be toddling around the house. Nurses would be feeding infants. The noises of children and their caretakers must surely have been part of the cacophony of sounds competing for the attention of the Corinthian assembly. Unfortunately, though, little is known about children in everyday life, especially children in lower-income families, as most of the Corinthians would appear to be.[25] It seems that children—particularly infants (*nēpioi*)—are in a vulnerable position, regardless of their families' social standing.

Roman writers considered vulnerability or feebleness—*infirmitas*—a basic characteristic of childhood.[26] Concerning the powerlessness of a human baby at birth, Pliny says,

> But man alone on the day of his birth she [Nature] casts away naked on the naked ground, to burst at once into wailing and weeping and none other among all the animals is more prone to tears, and that immediately at the very beginning of life. . . . This initiation in the light is followed by a period of bondage such as befalls not even the animals bred in our midst, fettering all his limbs; and thus when successfully born he lies with hands and feet in shackles, weeping—the animal that is to lord it over all the rest, and he initiates his life with punishment because of one fault only, the offence of being born.

---

25. According to Rom 16:23, Gaius's house was large enough to host the whole Corinthian church, yet not all had homes (1 Cor 11:17-22). Gerd Theissen highlighted the divisions between the haves and the have-nots (*The Social Setting of Pauline Christianity: Essays on Corinth*, ed. and trans. John H. Schütz [Philadelphia: Fortress, 1982]). Though there is not a consensus in determining the economic status of Paul's congregations, many would at least consider the majority of the congregants to be living at the subsistence level or below. For discussions of the economic status of Paul's churches, see Steven Friesen, "Poverty in Pauline Studies: Beyond the So-Called New Consensus," *JSNT* 26 (2004): 323-61; John Barclay, "Poverty in Pauline Studies: A Response to Steven Friesen," *JSNT* 26 (2004): 363-66; Peter Oakes, "Constructing Poverty Scales for Graeco-Roman Society: A Response to Steven Friesen's 'Poverty in Pauline Studies,'" *JSNT* 26 (2004): 367-71; J. J. Meggitt, *Paul, Poverty and Survival* (Edinburgh: T&T Clark, 1998); Bruce W. Longenecker, *Remember the Poor: Paul, Poverty, and the Greco-Roman World* (Grand Rapids: Eerdmans, 2010).

26. Cicero, *On Old Age* 10.33; Wiedemann, *Adults and Children in the Roman Empire*, 11.

Alas the madness of those who think that from these beginnings they were bred to proud estate!²⁷

Likewise, Artemidorus of Daldis, in his interpretation of dreams (*Oneirocritica*), claims that the appearance of a child in a dream was an indicator that the dreamer would soon become helpless like a child or that the dreamer would soon die.²⁸ After all, the infant mortality rate was staggeringly high. By some estimates, as many as 5 percent of all live-born babies died in their first month.²⁹ For those who survived beyond the first month, close to 30 percent died in the first year.³⁰ Death was such a normal part of childhood that no formal mourning was prescribed for infants who died in the first year.³¹ Furthermore, Romans did not think it appropriate to observe full mourning for children between the ages of three and ten.³²

With only 50 percent of children living to the age of ten,³³ free fami-

---

27. Pliny, *Natural History* 7.1 (Rackham, LCL); for a discussion of other ancient writers, see also Wiedemann, *Adults and Children in the Roman Empire*, 18-19.

28. Wiedemann, *Adults and Children in the Roman Empire*, 19.

29. Beryl Rawson, *Children and Childhood in Roman Italy* (Oxford: Oxford University Press, 2005), 103-4. If stillbirths or in-childbirth deaths were added to that figure, then it would be 8 percent.

30. Rawson, *Children and Childhood in Roman Italy*, 104. It is not possible to know whether these figures account for those infants who were abandoned. Infant exposure or abandonment did not necessarily lead to death. See Rawson for places where infants were commonly left (*Children and Childhood in Roman Italy*, 118). When found, abandoned children could be raised as slave or free (W. A. Strange, *Children in the Early Church: Children in the Ancient World, the New Testament and the Early Church* [Eugene: Wipf & Stock, 1996], 21-22).

31. Suzanne Dixon, *The Roman Family*, Ancient Society and History (Baltimore: Johns Hopkins University Press, 1992), 14. Even Augustus's law took into consideration the high rate of infant mortality (see Rawson, *Children and Childhood in Roman Italy*, 96-97; cf. also Dixon, *Roman Family*, 120).

32. In some circles, it was not until age ten that a child's identity was fully recognized. Although mourning infants was frowned upon as a social practice, still 1.3 percent of the epitaphs in Rome and Italy are for infants. Social pressures or, more likely, the lack of financial resources would be important variables in preventing public mourning. Rawson, *Children and Childhood in Roman Italy*, 104. See also Dixon, *Roman Family*, 99.

33. Wiedemann calculates a similar figure when considering mortality rates of other preindustrial societies, rather than relying strictly on literary, epigraphical, and

lies needed to produce more children in an attempt to secure an heir. According to Ann Hanson, the average Roman woman had to give birth to five or six children to ensure that she and her husband would have an heir and someone to care for them in their old age.[34] This means that most women were giving birth throughout their adulthood for as long as they were fertile.[35]

Energy and attention were devoted to helping the strongest survive.[36] The paterfamilias took responsibility for the decision to rear a child.[37] Unless the child was unhealthy or adultery was a factor, the father was expected to welcome the child into the family, and the parents made appropriate provisions for the baby's care.[38] In the second book of *Gynecology*, Soranus gives explicit instructions to midwives for the immediate care of the newborn and detailed instruction for how to determine whether a child is healthy enough to raise.[39] He goes on to describe the qualities one should look for in the most desirable wet nurse—one who is most likely to give the healthiest milk and who has already gained wisdom by bearing at least two or three children of her own.[40] The point of the advice is that families should choose someone with experience—not too young herself,

---

archaeological evidence for the Roman Empire (*Adults and Children in the Roman Empire*, 11-17).

34. Ann E. Hanson, "The Roman Family," in *Life, Death, and Entertainment in the Roman Empire*, ed. D. S. Potter and D. J. Mattingly (Ann Arbor: University of Michigan Press, 1999), 33.

35. Rawson, *Children and Childhood in Roman Italy*, 97.

36. Though Christians were forbidden from exposing or abandoning an infant, there is no evidence to discern what happened in actual practice. See Carolyn Osiek and Margaret MacDonald, *A Woman's Place: House Churches in Earliest Christianity* (Minneapolis: Fortress, 2006), 51-53; Carolyn Osiek and David Balch, *Families in the New Testament World: Households and House Churches* (Louisville: Westminster John Knox, 1997), 163.

37. Rawson, *Children and Childhood in Roman Italy*, 105; Amy Wordelman, "Everyday Life: Women in the Period of the New Testament," in *The Women's Bible Commentary*, exp. ed., ed. Carol A. Newsom and Sharon H. Ringe (Louisville: Westminster John Knox, 1998), 487; Strange, *Children in the Early Church*, 20.

38. Osiek and MacDonald, *A Woman's Place*, 53.

39. *Gynecology* 2.6. *Soranus' Gynecology*, trans. Owsei Temkin (Baltimore: Johns Hopkins University Press, 1956).

40. *Gynecology* 2.12.

The Church as the Least of These?

but not too old either. The healthier the wet nurse, the better chance the child has for survival.

The rituals for welcoming a new child also recognize the vulnerability of life in its beginning stages. Naming happened after a child had been alive for eight days for girls and nine days for boys. Other rituals to ensure an infant's well-being involved propitiating divine powers, driving off evil spirits, and cleansing the child or home of any pollution.[41]

Beyond the earliest days of infancy, attention turned to education and training. The young child would be passed from the charge of the wet nurse to the charge of early teachers and supervisors (*paidagōgoi*) who were usually male dependents of the household or slaves.[42] As the child matured, particular attention was given to instruction and discipline. Ultimately, it was the paterfamilias who was responsible to make provisions not only for raising the infant, but also for the infant's continued care, discipline, and education.[43]

Paul's designation of himself as the paterfamilias implied that it was on his authority—given through Christ—that the weak and struggling Corinthian "infants" were offered nourishment. They were certainly not the strongest—not even capable of progressing to solid food at the appropriate time (1 Cor 3:2). Though in most households resources might be reserved for the healthier children, these infants—even with their stunted growth—have been chosen despite their obvious handicaps. Their weakness only further illustrates the scandal of the cross: God has chosen the weak to display God's power (1 Cor 1:27).

Revisiting "Babes in Christ" in 1 Corinthians 3

In light of the above evidence, it can be argued that there are many connections between Paul's infancy metaphor in 1 Cor 3 and the social context from which this metaphor is taken. It has already been noted that the immaturity of infants can have negative connotations for behavior that is

---

41. Rawson, *Children and Childhood in Roman Italy*, 109–10.
42. Hanson, "Roman Family," 40.
43. Noting the ultimate authority of the paterfamilias should not, in any way, discount the roles that the mother and various women played in assisting in births, nursing and caring for infants, and overseeing the rearing and education of children (Osiek and MacDonald, *A Woman's Place*, 68–94).

deemed "childish" or "foolish." This interpretation reflects the dominant reading of "infants in Christ" in 1 Cor 3. It is not my concern to dispute this interpretation, but rather to expand the understanding of the metaphor to include another facet of infancy: vulnerability.[44] Vulnerability is evoked both by the illustrations from everyday life and by the reference to a coming day of judgment.

The infancy metaphor in 1 Cor 3 is surrounded by abundant references to the everyday life of children: the offering of milk and the feeding of solid food in verse 2, the acknowledgment of many *paidagōgoi* but only one father (4:15), the reference to the church as "my beloved children" in 4:14, the acknowledgment of the father as disciplinarian (4:14, 21), and the concern over the children's inheritance in 6:9 (cf. 4:20). Interestingly, Paul has taken upon himself the role of nursing the Corinthians.[45] Instead of a separate wet nurse, he is the one determining whether it is time for solid food. Though Paul's metaphor raises questions about whether milk and solid food could correlate to aspects of Paul's teaching, Morna Hooker has well argued that the food from Paul is nothing short of the gospel of Christ crucified.[46] The Corinthians' developmental failure reflects their own weakness and continued dependency on the world's wisdom—wisdom that cannot provide sustenance or growth—rather than the life-giving message of God's scandalous grace. Although they have believed the gospel, they are not letting the "foolishness of the cross" serve as a guide for how they treat one another or how they interact with the world. As a result, they are developmentally challenged, not yet ready for solid food.

Paul's metaphor insists that the Corinthians, who think that they are mature, are still at a vulnerable stage in their development. The references from everyday life highlight the vulnerability of being babes who need nourishment, protection, education, and discipline. Though they have a myriad of *paidagōgoi*, who are responsible for tutoring and guiding

---

44. Aasgaard notes that the instances where Paul places himself in the role of the infant may be more than rhetorical cleverness; they may also show Paul's way of demonstrating his own vulnerability as he is "left to the mercy of his addressees" ("Like a Child: Paul's Rhetorical Uses of Childhood," 276).

45. For a discussion of this motherly imagery and male wet nurses, see Gaventa, *Our Mother Saint Paul*, 41–50; Keith Bradley, *Discovering the Roman Family: Studies in Roman Social History* (New York: Oxford University Press, 1991), 37–75.

46. Morna Hooker, "Hard Sayings: 1 Cor 3:2," *Theology* 69 (1966): 21; cf. Francis, "As Babes in Christ," 41–60.

them,[47] they only have one father who loves them and disciplines them (4:14, 21). Paul not only serves as a wet nurse; he also steps into the role of a paterfamilias who has chosen to raise them in spite of their obvious weaknesses. This father will admonish them, instruct them, and guide them toward their inheritance, which is nothing short of the kingdom of God (4:14, 20–21; 6:9).

The references to childcare are not the only indicators of the Corinthians' vulnerable position. Interestingly, Paul calls the Corinthians babes in the face of coming judgment. In 1 Cor 3:10–15, he uses a construction metaphor to talk about his ministry, which builds on the foundation of Christ (3:11). After extending the metaphor to include other workers, he warns in 3:13 that the "Day" will disclose the work of each builder with fire. Even if the work is shoddy, the builder might be saved, "but only as through fire" (3:15). If anyone is guilty of destroying God's temple, however, God will destroy that person (3:17). This Day is going to be a day of God's wrath against all wickedness and ungodliness (1 Thess 1:10; cf. Rom 1:18).

The warning of coming judgment is not limited to 1 Cor 3.[48] Paul's eschatological expectations weave throughout the letter from the beginning (1:7–8) to the end (16:22). In 1 Cor 4:4–5, Paul looks forward to judgment when the Lord will come and bring to light the things now hidden in darkness and disclose the purposes of the heart. The apostle believes that the form of this world is passing away (7:31; 7:29), and the church lives at the end of the age (10:11). Because the Day is coming, Paul urges the church to live faithfully and reminds them to act in a manner that is commensurate with their status as those who have been washed, sanctified, and justified "in the name of the Lord Jesus and in the Spirit of our God" (6:11). He does not want them to stumble from the faith or to make the same mistakes as their faith ancestors, who were struck down in the wilderness for their unfaithfulness (10:5).

The reminder of a coming day is all the more sobering when considering another qualifier the apostle gives to the Corinthians: "people of the flesh" or "fleshly." Rather than being *pneumatikoi*, "spiritual," the Corinthians are *sarkinoi*, "fleshly." In 3:3, Paul points to their quarreling and jealousy as evidence that they are still of the flesh (*sarkinoi*). While "fleshly" could certainly indicate "spiritual immaturity," "spiritual immaturity" alone cannot bear the gravitas that *sarkinoi* connotes. For Paul, "flesh" is

---

47. See Bradley, *Discovering the Roman Family*, 37–43, 49–55.
48. Consider 1 Cor 4:4–5; 5:5.

fundamentally at odds with the Spirit. This dichotomy between the Spirit and the flesh takes center stage in Rom 8 and in the contrast between the fruit of the Spirit and the deeds of the flesh in Gal 5. Those who are in the flesh cannot please God (Rom 8:8). To live according to the flesh leads to death (Rom 8:13). Similarly, in 1 Cor 5:5 it is the sinful man's flesh that must die in order that his spirit may be saved on the Day of the Lord Jesus.[49] Thus, the fleshly activities of bickering and quarreling must come to an end. There is no time for such activities. Those who are "in Christ" must crucify the flesh with its passions and desires (Gal 5:24). Rather than live according to the flesh, the church is called to live by the Spirit (Gal 5:16). In contrast to those who behave according to the flesh, those who are *pneumatikoi* bear the "mind of Christ" (2:16; cf. Phil 2:1-11). On this point, J. Francis has noted that the problem of the Corinthians is a failure to comprehend.[50] They are not bearing the mind of Christ, but Paul seems to believe that through the Spirit they are capable of doing so.[51] After all, Paul is convinced that they were all baptized into the same Spirit (12:12-13). It is their bickering that indicates not spiritual behavior, but the behavior of the world. Rather than continue to feast on the goodness of the gospel, they have chosen to sustain themselves with the world's wisdom.[52]

The Corinthians have no reason to boast in their own knowledge or wisdom. They are far from being mature or wise. In fact, they owe their very existence to the Lord (1:30). Their behavior has proven them to be not only childish, but also "fleshly."[53] According to the literature that anticipates judgment, to be children in days of judgment is dangerous. Paul is adamant that to be "fleshly" is antithetical to God's will and incompatible with inheriting God's kingdom (6:9-11; Gal 5:16-21). Instead, the Corinthians are called to recognize that they belong to Christ (3:23) and to be unified in the same mind and purpose (1:10). Paul urges them to act according to the Spirit and bear the mind of Christ (2:6-16).

---

49. On whether *pneuma* refers to his spirit or the Spirit in the community, compare Barth Campbell, "Flesh and Spirit in 1 Cor 5:5: An Exercise in Rhetorical Criticism of the New Testament," *JETS* 36 (1993): 331-42; Hays, *First Corinthians*, 85-86; and Collins, "Function of 'Excommunication' in Paul," 259.

50. Francis, "As Babes in Christ," 43.

51. Cf. Phil 2:1-11.

52. Hooker, "Hard Sayings: 1 Cor 3:2," 21.

53. Francis also reads "childish" as the opposite of spiritual ("As Babes in Christ," 43).

A Multifaceted Metaphor

It is perhaps time to pause and question whether this multifaceted interpretation of 1 Cor 3:1 is too complex—a metaphor that simultaneously connotes immaturity and vulnerability. After all, many of the ancient writers employ childhood imagery to emphasize one aspect of the metaphor—innocence *or* foolishness, immaturity *or* vulnerability. Yet this reading incorporates both the immaturity of the Corinthians, which connects nicely with Paul's preceding argument, *and* the vulnerability of infancy—as indicated in the expansion of the metaphor around issues of childcare and the acknowledgment of coming judgment. Is this interpretation too complex?

Paul's metaphor sounds remarkably like Deut 32:1-43. The song of Moses places the children of Israel in a position similar to Paul's description of the Corinthians. Moses calls Israel's unfaithful behavior foolish and unwise (32:6) even as he emphasizes Israel's status as children of the Lord (32:5, 18). As in 1 Cor 3, the childhood metaphor is developed with imagery of infancy—imagery that highlights the Israelites' vulnerability and dependency. In fact, the song of Moses is rife with parental and childhood imagery. God is the Father of the Israelites (32:6). The Lord not only fathered them, but also gave birth to them (32:18). Like an eagle hovering over her young (32:11), God cared for them, shielded them, and guarded them (32:10). God fed them fruit from the fields (v. 13) and nourished them with honey, oil, and milk (vv. 13-14) until they grew fat and were kicking (32:15).

Here childhood imagery does more than connote the people's lack of maturity; it calls the people to be faithful to the God who birthed them, reared them, and sustained them. Why is the call to remembrance necessary? A day of judgment is at hand (Deut 32:35-36). Angered by his sons and daughters, the Lord will hide from his unfaithful children (32:19-20). The coming judgment is portrayed in fierce imagery: wasting famine, consuming pestilence, deadly plagues, consumption by wild beasts, the venom of vipers, and the death of infants, old men, and youth (32:23-26). God's anger against Israel's unfaithfulness is dire, but God vows not to blot out their memory (32:26-27). This Father will judge his children but also have compassion on them (32:36). God will take vengeance on his enemies and make atonement for his land and people (32:43). Though Moses calls Israel a nation who lacks wisdom and understanding (32:28-29), there is still hope for the Lord's salvation. The Israelites must rely on the Lord who has given them life (32:39).

As the Israelites are children of the Lord, so the Corinthians are babes "in Christ." Because the Corinthians belong to Christ, they also belong to God (1 Cor 3:23). God's judgment is coming (3:13), and their work and motives will be revealed (3:13-15). Like Israel, even they may be saved as though through fire (3:15). As a coming judgment approaches, both the Israelites and the church must look to the Lord as their very source of life.

Although there is no evidence that Paul used Deut 32 in the writing of 1 Cor 3, he is clearly influenced by this text elsewhere. He cites Deut 32 at least three times in Romans (10:19; 12:19; 15:10). Plus, the imagery of God's jealousy in 1 Cor 10:22 echoes Deut 32:21.[54] Whether Deut 32 is the source behind the imagery of 1 Cor 3 cannot be conclusively determined. Paul does not cite the passage here. Nonetheless, the song of Moses in Deut 32 provides an important piece of evidence—evidence of which Paul was aware—that the metaphor of childhood is a multifaceted way both to demonstrate a people's immaturity *and* to highlight the vulnerability of remaining childlike—or foolish—when a day of judgment is coming. Like 1 Cor 3, Deut 32 portrays the people as both vulnerable and foolish.

The Church as the Least of These?

If the metaphor implies vulnerability, then whom is Paul putting in the position of the "least"? Who are the "infants in Christ"? In 1 Cor 3, Paul's rhetoric is directed at those who are quarreling and who consider themselves wise and mature. Those who are behaving like ordinary folks rather than the Spirit-filled community are the targets of the metaphor. Though people from all social strata may be involved in the quarreling, those who are in inferior positions—clients of patrons, slaves of masters, persons freed from households—might find it difficult to be in open conflict with those who are socially superior to them. They are, after all, duty bound to honor their benefactors or masters. Openly quarreling with a person who is seen to be in a benefactor's position could have grave economic and social repercussions. Indeed, the fact that Paul refuses from this congregation financial support for his own ministry (1 Cor 9:1-27) suggests that those with resources are part of the problem. It is also far more likely for those who are socially superior to be in positions of leadership and influence. As Gerd Theissen has well argued, the divisions in First Church Corinth are due in large part to divisions between the haves and the have-nots.[55]

---

54. E. Earle Ellis, *Paul's Use of the Old Testament* (Grand Rapids: Baker, 1981), 153.
55. Theissen, *Social Setting of Pauline Christianity*.

The Church as the Least of These?

In 1 Cor 8:1-13 and 11:17-34, Paul's instruction is aimed at those who have resources, who think that they are knowledgeable, and who are boasting in their knowledge. This profile fits well those who think they are mature and wise in 1 Cor 3. Certainly, not all well-to-do people are causing problems. Gaius helpfully provides his home (Rom 16:23). Nor do all who are in an inferior position remain silent. For instance, some are giving voice to the position of the "weak" in the argument over the consumption of idol food (1 Cor 8:1-13). Nevertheless, some who have homes to eat in and plenty of food and drink have demonstrated a lack of ability to consider the needs of those who have nothing (11:17-34). More than likely, those leading the divisions around certain leaders are not folks who take up some form of servanthood, since Paul likens the leaders, himself included, to mere servants (1 Cor 3:5; cf. 4:1). Those guilty of carrying on these divisions or, worse, those who might be guilty of creating factions around certain teachers are the very ones whom Paul calls "babies."

Those who have placed themselves in positions of leadership and who have declared a certain amount of knowledge or wisdom would be stung by this metaphor. Infants cannot be leaders. Infants cannot be knowledgeable. Infants cannot boast in wisdom. Infants are completely dependent on others. The inability to eat solid food indicates that they are not even thriving infants. Ignatius uses the infancy metaphor to highlight the danger of stunted growth: "Am I not able to write to you of heavenly things? But I fear to do so, lest I should inflict injury on you who are but babes in Christ. Pardon me in this respect, lest, as not being able to receive such doctrines, you should be strangled by them" (Ignatius, *To the Trallians* 5:1). Ignatius highlights the fragility of infancy. Far from being sages, these Corinthians are incapable of reason. Far from being in positions of caring for others, the Corinthians are in the position of those who need care. Paul's rhetoric in 1 Cor 3:1 reframes the thinking of any who have fostered division and disunity at Corinth.

Furthermore, the need for maturity is urgent. The jeopardy of being people of the flesh or suckling babes on the Day of the Lord is not a danger of appearing foolish, but a real peril likened to the peril of the idolatrous wilderness wanderers in 1 Cor 10:1-22 or the man who has been sleeping with his stepmom in chapter 5. The normal time frame for "babes" to grow up is a luxury that the Corinthians do not possess. The "Day" is coming (3:13-15). Yet the Corinthians are still living as those in the "flesh" rather than those in whom the Spirit abides.

In sum, while it is undeniable that the Corinthians need to be more mature, the metaphor of "babes in Christ" also places the Corinthians in the position of the "least." The dominant reading of 1 Cor 3 engages well one facet of the infancy metaphor, immaturity, but neglects to consider how the infants' lack of *logos* also involves vulnerability. This neglect is all the more surprising since Paul extends the infancy metaphor to include imagery of childcare. Paul mentions the role of giving milk and solid food (3:2), the instruction of *paidagōgoi* (4:15), and the discipline of the father (4:14-15, 21). These images suggest that the metaphor is inspired by real-life circumstances. In the first-century world, as today, infants were vulnerable. Particular attention was given to ensure their survival. Plus, the Corinthians are "babes" and "fleshly" people as the Day is coming. In light of the social context of the imagery, the infancy metaphor is serving multiple purposes: to illustrate that the Corinthians are not walking according to the Spirit, to demonstrate the vulnerability of their position, and to call them to exhibit the mind of Christ. To read Paul's metaphor only as a statement of the Corinthians' foolishness is to miss the vulnerability of their position as ones who are called to faithfulness even until the end of the age. If the Corinthians who are boasting in their knowledge and taking pride in their wisdom are failing to humble themselves and consider the needs of their brothers and sisters, Paul's metaphor instantly places them in a posture of humility as the "least of these."

FURTHER READING

Gaventa, Beverly Roberts. *Our Mother Saint Paul*. Louisville: Westminster John Knox, 2007. Gaventa surveys the maternal imagery in Paul's letters.

Osiek, Carolyn, and David L. Balch. *Families in the New Testament World: Households and House Churches*. Louisville: Westminster John Knox, 1997. This book gives an overview of the material and social environment of the Greco-Roman household and considers how early Christian families might have functioned within their world.

Rawson, Beryl. *Children and Childhood in Roman Italy*. Oxford: Oxford University Press, 2003. Rawson considers the life stages of a child in the Roman world.

Strange, W. A. *Children in the Early Church: Children in the Ancient World, the New Testament and the Early Church.* Eugene, OR: Wipf & Stock, 1996. This brief volume considers the evidence of the life of children in the New Testament world and provides a survey of the attitudes about children in the New Testament.

CHAPTER SIX

Paul as the Least of These?

Like the people of Lystra (Acts 14) or Malta (Acts 28), we often view Paul as though he were a god. Though our reverence may not be attached to his ability to shake off a snakebite or perform Jesus-like miracles, we are a culture easily impressed by the written word. Paul is a best-selling author. Thirteen epistles attributed to him make it into our New Testament canon, a canon that boasts of only twenty-seven books. Plus, the interpretation of one of Paul's letters, his Epistle to the Romans, has indelibly shaped church history. Surely, this is good reason to place Paul on a pedestal. But from this pedestal, we get a skewed portrait of Paul's ministry. Paul had no idea that we would be reading and wrestling with his letters two thousand years later. As successful as we might see Paul's mission, his evangelistic achievement is not measured in three-piece tailored suits or stadium seating for church services. His nonglamorous life included multiple imprisonments, frequent beatings, and homelessness.

When we survey the Pauline epistles, we encounter someone who works with his own hands to fund his ministry, who faces danger from all fronts to carry out his mission (2 Cor 11:25–27), and who will suffer any hardship for the sake of the gospel. To use modern terms, Paul was a bivocational minister who worked from sunup to sundown to support his ministry. Though he stayed in a few places—like Corinth or Ephesus—for extended periods of time, he was homeless—a recipient of another's hospitality. When he was not enjoying the hospitality of friends and supporters, he was either traversing land and sea at the mercy of robbers and the stormy waves or wasting away in prison, wondering when he would have his next meal, when he would get a trial, or when he might see his beloved churches again.

Whatever importance Paul might have claimed for himself was rooted in the experience of his calling. Evidence from his letters and

Paul as the Least of These?

from Acts indicates that the revelation on the Damascus road turned his life upside down. The religious zealousness that drove him to persecute followers of the Way was redirected by a voice from heaven and a blinding light that brought him to his knees. According to 1 Cor 15, he never felt worthy of this experience—this epiphany. And he would never be the same. Due to this revelation (Gal 1:12, 16), he willingly faced hardships, went hungry, suffered stonings and beatings—all because of this encounter with the risen Christ. Paul takes to heart the humiliation of the cross as his leadership paradigm (Phil 2:5-11). Christ took the form of a servant, and Paul seeks to imitate Christ's service. This is evident in how he depicts his apostleship.

Paul is well aware that he has authority as both an apostle (Rom 1:1; 11:13; 1 Cor 1:1; 4:9; 9:1-2; 15:9; 2 Cor 1:1; 12:12; Gal 1:1; 1 Thess 2:6; cf. Eph 1:1; Col 1:1; 1 Tim 1:1; 2:7; 2 Tim 1:1; 1:11) and as the symbolic paterfamilias of these various house churches (1 Cor 4:14-15; cf. 1 Thess 2:11). Yet this first-century evangelist gravitates toward models of servitude and humility to depict his ministry. Metaphors inspired by those who might be considered "least" course throughout his letters: a slave (Rom 1:1; 7:25; 1 Cor 3:5; 4:1-2; 9:19; 2 Cor 3:6; 4:5; 6:4; 11:23; Gal 1:10; Phil 1:1; cf. Eph 3:7; Col 1:23, 25; Titus 1:1), a nursing mother or wet nurse (1 Thess 2:7; 1 Cor 3:1-2), a premature infant (1 Cor 15:8), an orphan (1 Thess 2:17), a farmer (1 Cor 3:6), a coworker (Phlm 1) or laborer (1 Cor 4:12; 1 Thess 2:9), a prisoner (Phlm 1; 2 Cor 11:23), a debtor (Rom 1:14), a fellow soldier (Phlm 1; Phil 2:25), the scum of the earth and the refuse of the world (1 Cor 4:13). In light of these images, it is perhaps not surprising that Paul also characterizes himself as "nothing" (2 Cor 12:11), "last of all," as a man "sentenced to death" (1 Cor 4:9), "weak" (2 Cor 11:29-30; 12:10), and a "fool" for Christ (1 Cor 4:10; 2 Cor 11:19). His own accounts of ministry include hunger, nakedness, homelessness, sickness, shipwrecks, imprisonments, beatings, and lashings (1 Cor 4:11; 2 Cor 11:23-30). He was stoned at least once and suffered countless beatings, often near death (2 Cor 11:23).

Though this book has highlighted Paul's concern for the "least," the apostle's concern for the "least" must also be considered alongside his willingness to become the least. It is not enough that Paul stood in solidarity with those who were on the fringes of society or that Paul's communities included those who had no voice elsewhere. Paul's rhetoric and life demonstrate that he not only considered himself in the category of the least, but that Paul was simultaneously the leader and the least. In fact, Paul referred to himself as the "least of the apostles, unfit to be called an apostle because I persecuted the church of God" (1 Cor 15:9). This chapter will examine Paul's perspective of his preconversion life, his role as an apostle, and his willingness to suffer hardship for the sake of the gospel. Though he shares few details of his past, it is telling that he always mentions his life as a persecutor. Perhaps, as he shares in 1 Cor 15:9, his background makes him feel unworthy of God's calling. As an apostle, he willingly takes on the paradigm of a servant. In fact, other than "apostle," Paul most often refers to himself as a slave of Christ. For this reason, examining the metaphor of servanthood will consume most of this chapter. Finally, it is worth considering Paul's willingness to become the least by examining his time as a prisoner. According to church tradition, Paul's lengthy final imprisonment ended in capital punishment. Regardless of whether church tradition is correct, Paul's ministry lands him in jail on multiple occasions. The one who imprisoned the earliest followers of Jesus became a prisoner himself for the sake of the gospel. Though his prison experiences will vary significantly, prisoners live at the mercy of others. His imprisonment makes him vulnerable, a characteristic that we might not always associate with this bold missionary whose mission helped change the world.

Paul the Persecutor

The Bible provides few details about Paul's life before he arrives on the scene as a persecutor of the Jesus movement. In Acts, the character of Paul claims to be a Jew from Tarsus of Cilicia (Acts 21:39), a Roman citizen by birth (Acts 16:37; 22:25–29), who has been educated strictly according to the law (Acts 22:3). In Phil 3:4–6, as he is facing a trial that seems likely to end in death, he reflects back on features of his identity that he esteemed highly before his encounter with Christ: "If anyone else has reason to be confident in the flesh, I have more: circumcised on the eighth day, a member of the people of Israel, of the tribe of Benjamin, a Hebrew born of Hebrews; as to the law, a Pharisee; as to zeal, a persecutor of the church; as to righteousness under the law, blameless" (Phil 3:4–6). This passage offers a summary of identity features that recur elsewhere. For instance, Paul never shies away from his Jewish heritage (Gal 2:15; 2 Cor 11:22), and his knowledge of the law is evident throughout the letters. Yet neither Acts nor the letters of Paul provide many details of Paul's upbringing. What can be gleaned from Paul's preconversion life stems from the period immediately prior to his encounter with the risen Christ.[1] In 1 Cor 15:9, Paul says that he is unfit to be called an apostle, the least of the apostles, because he persecuted the church of God. Interestingly, though Acts and Paul's letters sometimes have discrepancies in reconstructing a life of Paul, Paul's work as a persecutor is well documented in both. Paul's attempt to destroy the church is a critical part of his testimony.

Paul never allows himself to forget how he treated the followers of Jesus (1 Cor 15:9; Gal 1:13, 23; Phil 3:6; cf. 1 Tim 1:13). He talks about his "conversion" experience only a few times (Gal 1:11–17; Phil 3:4–17; and 1 Cor 15:8–11; cf. 1 Tim 1:12–17), and he mentions his persecution of the church every time (1 Cor 15:9; Gal 1:13, 23; Phil 3:6; cf. 1 Tim 1:13). It is a fundamental feature of his testimony, a reminder of just how far God's grace extends (1 Cor 15:10). He claims even that he was trying to destroy the church of God (Gal 1:13). Likewise, in the three accounts of Paul's conversion experience in Acts, Saul's persecution of the church is central to the story. Though the details of the Damascus road experience vary, the core speech of Jesus remains essentially the same, "Saul, Saul, why do you persecute me?" This question is followed by Saul's response, "Who are you, Lord?" Then the voice says, "I am Jesus, whom you are persecuting" (Acts 9:4–5; 22:7–8; 26:14–15). Thus, in each of the three accounts, the speech of Jesus twice accuses Paul of persecution. Even Jesus's identity is tied to Saul's acts of persecution. The threats against the church are interpreted as actions against Jesus himself. Acts portrays Saul as attempting to eradicate the Jesus movement. He seeks out authority from the Jerusalem leaders to hunt down the believers, to arrest them, and to kill them (9:1–12; 22:4–5; 26:10–12). He even takes a leading role in the stoning death of Stephen (Acts 7:58–8:3). He is ruthless in his zealousness. It is little wonder that the disciples were afraid of him (Acts 9:26; Gal 1:23).

In his preconversion life, the religious authorities respected him as an educated leader who had been granted authority over matters of life and death. He enjoyed some status as a highly trained Pharisee. The rhetoric of his letters also suggests that he has had some rhetorical training, as would be expected from a citizen family from a significant town.[2] Regardless of whether greater society would have counted being of "the tribe of

---

1. I will use the term "conversion" to refer to his Damascus road experience. There is open debate about whether this experience is a conversion or call.

2. For more on Paul's likely rhetorical training, see Dale B. Martin, *The Corinthian Body* (New Haven: Yale University Press, 1995), 47–55.

Benjamin" and a Pharisee as high-status indicators, Paul mentioned the status markers in Philippians as badges of honor that he counted as nothing after meeting Jesus (Phil 3:7–11). Those status markers did not prevent him from persecuting the followers of Jesus. They only gave him more credibility as a critic of the church. Paul's encounter with the risen Christ changed his entire perspective. In the revelation of Christ (Gal 1:12, 16), he then saw God more clearly. He felt compelled to share this revelation with everyone.

In 1 Cor 15:8, Paul says that the risen Christ appeared to him after he had appeared to Cephas, then to the twelve, then to more than five hundred others, then to James and to all the apostles. Finally, after visiting all these other folks, "he appeared also to me." In this verse, we encounter one of the most graphic images that Paul uses to describe his preconversion life. He likens himself to a premature infant (*ektrōma*). The power of the image of a premature or miscarried infant is often lost in translation. Typically, English versions translate this term as an untimely birth, thus: "as to one untimely born, he appeared also to me" (1 Cor 15:8 RSV). This translation could suggest a chronological dilemma. Paul met Christ after the crucifixion and resurrection. If he had been born a little earlier (and perhaps raised in Galilee?), then maybe he could have walked among the earliest disciples. He was born too late, at the wrong time, but he became a faithful disciple nonetheless. To be sure, Paul does hint at a chronological timetable in the previous verses. In the litany of post-resurrection appearances in 1 Cor 15:5–7, he places himself last among the apostles who have seen the resurrected Lord. Perhaps, had he been born earlier, he would not have been last. The connotation of this translation is that Paul was overdue, but alive and well.

What happens, however, when we read this image in light of the more common understanding of *ektrōma*? While it is true that *ektrōma* has the connotation of an untimely birth, it is not an overdue birth. The Revised English Bible (REB) comes closer: "Last of all he appeared to me too; it was like a sudden, abnormal birth." Even this translation does not allow us to hear the precariousness of life inherent in the metaphor. The term *ektrōma* usually means a baby who is born prematurely and without life—a stillbirth or a miscarriage. Paul does not use this term elsewhere, nor is it found anywhere else in the New Testament. The term, however, appears three times in the Septuagint (Num 12:12; Eccl 6:3; and Job 3:16), and in each case, the untimely birth results in death. Without the advances of modern medicine, it is unlikely that a baby who survived a premature birth would live. Since nearly half of all children died before the age of ten,[3] households faced incredibly difficult odds with all the babies born under their care—from heirs to slaves alike. From finding the right wet nurse to learning how to tell signs of weakness, families in the ancient world invested their resources in helping the strongest infants survive. With the household's future on the line, heirs had to be protected and nurtured. The paterfamilias had the right to decide which child would receive the utmost care. The term *ektrōma* refers to a premature birth with little chance of survival. *In other words, Paul should be the last person whom one would expect the paterfamilias to raise.* But God chose him anyway. He likens himself to a baby who would not even be nursed, much less ever live to eat solid food. When compared to the infant imagery of 1 Cor 3:1-2, where the metaphor highlights the church's stunted growth, the imagery that Paul applies to himself as a miscarried fetus only heightens the apostle's weakness. This image of weakness fits well with his insistence on being "least" among the apostles, not worthy to be called an apostle (1 Cor 15:9).

When we turn to Paul's other letters, we see that the apostle, perhaps inspired by the scandal of the gospel, willingly describes himself with images that evoke vulnerability and weakness. Elsewhere, Paul likens himself to an infant (1 Thess 2:7),[4] a wet nurse (1 Thess 2:7), and even an orphan (1 Thess 2:17). In 1 Cor 15:9b, Paul states the rationale for his unworthiness: "because I persecuted the church of God." The one who was hunting down and imprisoning others was as good as dead. What hope could there be for one who was not only hostile to the church, but who was also actively trying to eradicate it?

In the context of 1 Cor 15, a lengthy section of the letter devoted to the power of resurrection, the reader should hear in the *ektrōma* metaphor the certainty of mortality. In effect, this God who chose to reveal Godself through the foolishness of the cross has also revealed Christ to the very epitome of weakness, a premature infant who is barely clinging to life. God who chose the scandal of the cross has also chosen a miscarried fe-

---

3. Thomas Wiedemann, *Adults and Children in the Roman Empire* (New Haven: Yale University Press, 1989), 11-17; see also Beryl Rawson, *Children and Childhood in Roman Italy* (Oxford: Oxford University Press, 2005), 103-4; Suzanne Dixon, *The Roman Family*, Ancient Society and History (Baltimore: Johns Hopkins University Press, 1992), 14.

4. Though a manuscript variation reads "gentle," the better attested reading is "infant."

tus to call as an "apostle." If God can bring life to this infant—if God can resurrect Paul the persecutor, whose past might justly reckon him as unworthy of life—then there are no limits to the powerful grace of this God. This God is a God who brings life to the dead. The imagery of weakness highlights the power of God rather than the humility of Paul.[5] Paul is not trying to be humble here. He is being honest. Christ's story is not the only resurrection narrative in this passage. Paul's story serves to demonstrate the power of this God. God can change the life of Paul, and this same God brings life to *all*.

Paul's Apostolic Role: A Slave to All?

In the undisputed letters, Paul introduces himself as an apostle or a slave, but these titles are linked to how he sees his ministry. Paul often refers to his apostleship, particularly in the salutation (Rom 1:1; 11:13; 1 Cor 1:1; 4:9; 9:1-2; 15:9; 2 Cor 1:1; 12:12; Gal 1:1; 1 Thess 2:6; cf. Eph 1:1; Col 1:1; 1 Tim 1:1; 2:7; 2 Tim 1:1, 11). He also frequently uses the language of service to depict his ministry (Rom 1:1; 7:25; 1 Cor 3:5; 4:1-2; 9:19; 2 Cor 3:6; 4:5; 6:4; 11:23; Gal 1:10; Phil 1:1; cf. Eph 3:7; Col 1:23, 25; Titus 1:1). In fact, in the salutation of Philippians, Paul and his cosender Timothy are merely introduced as slaves (*douloi*) of Christ Jesus, with no other titles listed. Paul has likely been influenced by the abundant servant images of Israel's Scriptures that depict the faithful as servants of the Lord (e.g., Exod 32:13; Num 11:11; 12:7; 14:24; Deut 3:24; 9:27; 32:36; Josh 1:1; 5:14; 1 Sam 1:11; 3:9; 1 Kgs 8:22-40; 11:13).[6] Being a slave to the divine also means being a servant of one another (Gal 5:13; 2 Cor 4:5). This is perhaps most visible in his claim to be a "slave to all" in 1 Cor 9:19-23.

Slave to All? 1 Corinthians 9:19-23

The fact that Paul calls himself a slave of Christ or a steward of God's mysteries is not surprising, but in 1 Cor 9:19-23 he expands the metaphor to being a slave to *all*. The reference comes in a section where the apostle claims

---

5. See also Anthony C. Thiselton, *The First Epistle to the Corinthians*, NIGTC (Grand Rapids: Eerdmans, 2000), 1208-9.

6. Consider also Israel as God's slaves in Lev 25:42, 55.

to become "all things to all people" so that "by all means" some might be saved. Paul alleges that he becomes like a Jew to win Jews, like one under the law to win those under the law, and like one outside the law to win those outside the law. He even tells the Corinthians that he becomes "weak" in order to win the weak. Paul's lesson in versatility is directed at the church's engagement with one another. The apostle wants the Corinthian elite, the so-called knowledgeable, to renounce their social privileges when the exercising of those privileges, in this case eating idol food in the local temple, is destroying their brothers and sisters in Christ by encouraging them to return to their former gods (1 Cor 8:1-13). Paul's chameleon-like behavior is not a sycophantic strategy to please people and, thereby, make the gospel somehow less offensive. In fact, the rhetoric assumes that becoming "weak" or becoming a "slave to all" would be offensive. Paul's claim to become weak comes in a section where he is highlighting his voluntary self-lowering of status. This apostle of the crucified Lord has renounced his apostolic rights in order to preach the gospel free of charge. Not only has he renounced his rights, but he has also humbled himself. Paul, the free man, *enslaves* himself to *all*—knowledgeable or ignorant, lawful or lawless (9:19).

How can one be a slave to all? This metaphor raises questions of status and expectations for a slave at the time—questions that are fraught with difficulty since the institution of slavery in the Roman world was extraordinarily complex. Being a slave does not necessarily place a person at the lowest end of the social spectrum. However, being a slave to *all* implies being a slave to slaves and to those whom Roman society considered outcast or expendable. For a free person willingly to adopt the status of a slave is worthy of note.

It is hard to imagine what a "slave to all" might look like in reality. Slaves in the Roman Empire served a variety of functions and attained varying levels of social standing. Scholars such as Wayne Meeks and Dale Martin have drawn attention to the possibilities of upward social mobility of a free person who sold himself (or herself) to a respectable family and, thereby, became affiliated with a particular household.[7] It is even possible, though admittedly rare, that slaves in respectable households received an education and later, as freedpersons, enjoyed social standing in their communities. In 1 Cor 7:17-24, Paul may very likely be addressing the phenom-

---

7. Wayne Meeks, *The First Urban Christians* (New Haven: Yale University Press, 1983), 19-23; Dale B. Martin, *Slavery as Salvation: The Metaphor of Slavery in Pauline Christianity* (New Haven: Yale University Press, 1990), 35-42, 50-85.

enon of selling oneself into slavery to gain social standing, when he urges the Corinthians to remain where they were when they were called (with the exception of allowing freedom, 1 Cor 7:21-23).[8] Thus, while there seems to be some evidence of using slavery to gain status in Roman society, Paul is making the opposite claim. Becoming a slave to all would surely be going the opposite direction in the social hierarchy.

Slaves, whatever their status, had an identity intertwined with the slaveholder. Slaves represented a household and particularly the master. In some instances, slaves could even serve the punishment that should have been inflicted on the slaveholder for failing to pay dues or for other infractions.[9] In this way, slaves served as a type of surrogate body for their owners. In the late second century, Artemidorus asserted that, in dreams, the appearance of one's slaves often represented the body of the master.[10] Though it would be dangerous to assume that the identity of all slaves was so closely intertwined with the slaveholder's identity, this evidence does indicate the vulnerability of the slave's circumstances and the close connection between the servant and the one served.

When Paul claims to be a slave of Christ or a "steward of God's mysteries" (1 Cor 4:1), the slave metaphor demonstrates the apostle's close connection with the one whom he claims to serve. He is affiliating himself with a master of the greatest possible status and seeing himself as doing the master's bidding. Martin argues that the title "slave of Christ" is not a title of self-abasement, but a title used to demonstrate the superiority of the household that Paul serves.[11] It is paradoxically a title of high status among slaves because, from Paul's perspective, there is no higher household.

In 1 Cor 9:19-23, Paul, however, does not highlight his servitude to Christ, but his servitude to *all*: "Though being free from all, I made myself a slave to all, in order that I might gain the more" (author's translation). Paul's status as a free person is critical to his argument. While some may elect to sell themselves into slavery in the hope of upward social mobility, Paul's rhetoric assumes that he has renounced his higher status of a free person in order to become a slave, not for his own benefit, but for the benefit of others.

---

8. Bruce Winter, *Seek the Welfare of the City: Christians as Benefactors and Citizens* (Grand Rapids: Eerdmans, 1994), 145-64.

9. Jennifer A. Glancy, *Slavery in Early Christianity* (Oxford: Oxford University Press, 2002), 15-16.

10. Glancy, *Slavery in Early Christianity*, 9.

11. Martin, *Slavery as Salvation*, 50-85, 117.

The concept of being a "slave to all" was prevalent in the writings of Greco-Roman moral philosophers regarding leaders. In his study *Slavery as Salvation*, Martin has emphasized the role that this metaphor of servitude played among politicians of Paul's time and has argued persuasively that Paul is deliberately using rhetoric of leadership that would be jarring to the elite at Corinth. Martin surveys two common types of leaders in the Greek world: the benevolent patriarch and the demagogue. Most leaders presented themselves as "benevolent patriarchs," that is, as fatherly but kingly figures, who led compassionately and thoughtfully from a position of authority, while never betraying their superior social status or compromising their power.[12] This respected leader was noble born, a steward of the city's welfare, who exhibited a lifestyle of means, maintained social hierarchies, avoided manual labor or the appearance of servitude, and enjoyed the best education.[13] This is, by far, the most dominant model of ideal leadership in Paul's world. In contrast to the benevolent patriarch is a demagogue or populist leader, who portrays himself in a lower-status position to his subjects, as their servant.[14]

Both types of leadership had to choose their words and actions carefully in order to persuade others and to maintain their power. Persuasive orators skillfully adapted behavior, speech patterns, appearance, customs, or even beliefs in order to win over their audience.[15] Philo relates the adaptability of a politician to a physician who varies treatment according to what is best for the patient (*On the Life of Joseph* 34). It was incredibly difficult, however, for orators to judge when the opportune time had come to make such adaptations.[16] Orators could easily succumb to the accusation of flattery if the timing was off or the performance was not well received by the audience.[17] The efficacy of the speech depended on the character of the

12. Martin, *Slavery as Salvation*, 88-91, 125.
13. Consider Philo, *On the Life of Joseph* 67; Martin, *Slavery as Salvation*, 114-15.
14. Martin, *Slavery as Salvation*, 92-116, 125.
15. Clarence E. Glad, *Paul and Philodemus: Adaptability in Epicurean and Early Christian Psychagogy* (Leiden: Brill, 1995), 45-46. See also David Armstrong, "All Things to All Men: Philodemus' Model of Therapy and the Audience of *De Morte*," in *Philodemus and the New Testament World*, ed. John T. Fitzgerald, Dirk Obbink, and Glenn S. Holland (Leiden: Brill, 2004), 15-54.
16. George Kennedy, *The Art of Persuasion in Greece* (Princeton: Princeton University Press, 1963), 63-67; Glad, *Paul and Philodemus*, 46.
17. For more examples of the charge of flattery related to the adaptability of the speaker, see Martin, *Slavery as Salvation*, 94-95.

orator and the rapport he had with his audience.[18] To win the audience's favor, rhetoricians were taught to avoid any gestures or show any emotions that made them appear like slaves or women when speaking.[19] Persuasive speakers were in complete command of their emotions as well as skilled at eliciting the feelings they hoped to evoke (Quintilian, *Institutes of Oratory* 11.1.3). They epitomized the honorable, virtuous male in their speech (*Institutes of Oratory* 11.1.14). Neither slaves nor women were thought to embody the virtues valued by the dominant culture—virtues that were indistinguishable from being a free, adult male.

Unlike the benevolent patriarch, who took advantage of his high status, the demagogue is repeatedly portrayed as a flatterer who is simply a slave of the people. Cicero negatively refers to this leader as a "smooth-tongued, shallow citizen" (*On Friendship* 95). According to Philo, the demagogue always keeps the whims of the people in mind and ultimately becomes a slave with ten thousand masters (*On the Life of Joseph* 35). This facade of service is nothing more than vanity (*On the Life of Joseph* 34-36). The populist leader is often accused of being obsequious to the masses to secure power for himself.[20] Aristotle equates a demagogue with a flatterer who is truly sovereign only over the opinion of the masses (*Politics* 4.1292a). The demagogue claims to help the people but fails to act (Dinarchus, *Demosthenes* 1.31), because he is concerned to say only whatever pleases the masses (Diodorus Siculus, *Library of History* 9.4). Because the demagogue stands in opposition to the aristocracy, he gains the favor of the people (Demosthenes, *4 Philippic* 10.44). Yet Polybius accuses this leader of simply being a "mob-orator" with no real military training or ability to act for the people's security (Polybius, *History* 3.80). Instead, the demagogue displays unreasonable confidence in his own abilities and rises to a position of despotic power (Polybius, *History* 15.21). Plutarch asserts that the true character of a king is neither a demagogue nor a despot (*Comparison of Romulus with Theseus* 2).

All characteristics of the demagogue topos are not negative. Although the demagogue walks a fine line between being versatile to persuade the crowd and being accused of flattery, the populist leader seeks to protect the

---

18. Glad, *Paul and Philodemus*, 47.

19. Joy Connolly, "Mastering Corruption: Constructions of Identity in Roman Oratory," in *Women and Slaves in Greco-Roman Culture: Differential Equations*, ed. Sandra R. Joshel and Sheila Murnaghan (London: Routledge, 1998), 135.

20. Martin, *Slavery as Salvation*, 94-95, 99.

people and to serve their interests. From the perspective of the common people, this leader is worthy of praise. In his vast survey of literature, Martin is able to produce only two texts that speak approvingly of the enslaved leader topos: Nicolaus of Damascus's account of Cyrus and Antisthenes's "Odyssean" speech.[21] In both cases, the leaders are praised for versatility and adaptability.

In light of the overwhelming weight of negative comments about the demagogue, the paucity of positive references is striking. This is no doubt due to the reality that the surviving literature preserves the perspective of the elite, who would feel the most threatened by the demagogue's power.[22] Perhaps more beneficial than praise for this topos are the writers who include some positive aspects of populist leadership even while they ultimately support the rule of a benevolent patriarch. As mentioned above, Philo noted that, as captains of a ship negotiate winds and physicians consider best treatments, all leaders have to make adjustments in their style for the common advantage (*On the Life of Joseph* 33–34). Thus, populist leaders might be praised for considering the needs or desires of the people and for reacting nimbly. What creates a distinction between a good leader and a demagogue ultimately seems to be one of motive. All leaders must occasionally vary their style, but Philo accuses demagogues of voluntarily lowering themselves for their own good rather than the good of the poor masses. In other words, these leaders fail to consider the good of the rich or the good of the whole.[23] Since they must keep the masses content to maintain their power, populist leaders are usually characterized as slaves to the ever-changing will of the people (*On the Life of Joseph* 67). To put it another way, they are slaves to all.

Paul's adaptability might be a virtue of any politician, but his voluntary enslavement to all would not be considered virtuous by those of high social standing. In fact, this voluntary act of self-lowering echoes some of the criticisms leveled at the demagogues, leaders who were slaves to the populace. Paul's claim to save some (1 Cor 9:22) recalls the demagogue's pretext to seek the good of the people. Likewise, becoming all things to all people could sound like empty flattery to some of the Corinthians. Paul, however, differentiates himself from some of the scathing criticisms of the demagogue by demonstrating the sincerity of his words and by seeking the

---

21. Martin, *Slavery as Salvation*, 98, 103–7; see also Glad, *Paul and Philodemus*, 272.
22. Martin, *Slavery as Salvation*, 100.
23. Martin, *Slavery as Salvation*, 114.

benefit of others rather than his own benefit. Paul's metaphor evokes the enslaved leader topos, but Paul is careful in his use of this image. He adopts the language of being a slave to all, language that would likely make the Corinthian elite uncomfortable, but he has to avoid the charges of flattery and vanity. Ironically, he avoids these charges by emphasizing his servitude.

Paul has emphasized his freedom only to renounce it (1 Cor 9:1, 19). In 1 Cor 9:1-27, Paul notes that his apostleship does not look like the apostleship of others. He refuses the financial support of the Corinthians (9:15-18), likely because he does not want to be beholden to anyone in the congregation. To accept the money of wealthy benefactors would make Paul indebted to them in a patron-client relationship.[24] It would be difficult for Paul to correct the social elite, as he is doing in 1 Cor 9, if he were in this honor-bound relationship.

Instead of receiving the wage that he is entitled, Paul chooses to work with his hands. In light of the leadership models above, Martin argues persuasively that Paul adopts the rhetoric of being a "slave to all" from the demagogue model, but rather than merely appearing to lower himself for the good of the people, he actually humbles himself socially.[25] Because of Paul's trade as a tentmaker,[26] it might be assumed that Paul was a commoner. His Roman citizenship and his education would normally be indicative of the upper classes.[27] Working as a tentmaker would be considered demeaning work by the upper classes and would make him appear slavish.[28]

There is debate, however, about whether Paul himself would have looked down upon his labor. According to Hock, Paul's use of the slave metaphor (1 Cor 9:19) and the language of humbling himself for work (2 Cor

---

24. For discussions of the patron-client relationship, see Anthony Clarke, *Secular and Christian Leadership in Corinth: A Socio-Historical and Exegetical Study of 1 Corinthians 1-6* (Leiden: Brill, 1993), 73-88; see also J. Chow, "Patronage in Roman Corinth," in *Paul and Empire: Religion and Power in Roman Imperial Society*, ed. R. A. Horsley (Harrisburg: Trinity, 1997), 104-25.

25. Martin, *Slavery as Salvation*, 117-35.

26. Paul acknowledges working with his own hands in 1 Cor 4:12 and in 1 Thess 2:9. Though Paul never refers to making tents, there is little reason to question the reliability of Acts 18:3 on this point.

27. Adolf Deissmann, *Paul: A Study in Social and Religious History* (New York: Hodder and Stoughton, 1926), 4. For a survey of church fathers, see Ronald Hock, "Paul's Tentmaking and the Problem of His Social Class," *JBL* 97 (1978): 556-57.

28. Hock, "Paul's Tentmaking and the Problem of His Social Class," 555-64.

11:7) portray upper-class stereotypes of manual labor. Hock argues that these stereotypes suggest that Paul is not from a background accustomed to labor. Thus, Paul's status as an educated, Roman citizen would indicate that the apostle has enjoyed some social standing in the past and that he has truly demeaned himself to offer the gospel free of charge (1 Cor 9:18). In other words, in light of the rhetoric of an enslaved leader who speaks about lowering himself, taking up manual labor actually knocks Paul down the social ladder. The issue is not whether Paul lowers himself socially, but whether Paul sees his labor as degrading and uses upper-class stereotypes regarding work that would have put him on the side of the Corinthian elite.

While Paul's rhetoric assumes that the elite would have found his labor demeaning, nothing indicates that Paul resents working with his own hands. In 1 Cor 9, he demonstrates that he is well aware that there is another way for him to carry on his mission without supporting himself as a bivocational minister. He could accept money from the church—even Jesus's teaching would support this (9:14). He is not fundamentally opposed to financial support. After all, he accepts support from the Philippians and asks the Romans to partner with him in his mission to Spain. Working with his own hands, though perhaps appearing slavish to the upper classes, actually grants him more freedom to present the gospel "free of charge." He is free to correct his would-be patrons. As Todd Still notes, if he did find work demeaning and used language that denigrated part of the congregation, he would not be very effective in creating unity in this congregation: "By confirming and even affirming the wise, powerful, and noble in the aristocratic arrogance and upper-class snobbery, Paul would have been shaking the very hands he was seeking to slap in Corinth! Far from puncturing their pride and placing their feet back on spiritual terra firma, by sharing the Corinthian elite's jaundiced view of work(ers) he would have only widened the chasm he was seeking to bridge."[29]

Paul seems to view work as a means to support his ministry, but, though the elite might find it denigrating, Paul labors to fund his letter writing, travel, and daily needs. Paul cannot be accused of merely flattering his audience by claiming to be a "slave to all"; his daily work demonstrates that he is seeking the good of others without the desire for personal gain. The churches can trust that he is not seeking the interest of any rich patron, but rather represents the household of God. Perhaps, as Still concludes, Paul

---

29. Todd D. Still, "Did Paul Loathe Manual Labor? Revisiting the Work of Ronald F. Hock on the Apostle's Tentmaking and Social Class," *JBL* 125 (2006): 787.

is "ambivalent" about the work itself.³⁰ Labor is a means to an end and one that allows the fewest conflicts of interest for his mission in Corinth.

Working with his own hands has more benefits than freeing Paul from the patronage system. It provides Paul opportunities that he might not otherwise have. Through this trade, he has clearly met people, like Prisca and Aquila, who have partnered with him in ministry. Plus, he is actually making money that he is using to fund the mission, and he hopes that others will be inspired to do the same. Not only does he ask the Corinthian elite to seek the good of the so-called weak, but in the Thessalonian correspondence, Paul advises those who live off the benefaction of a patron to break the benefaction cycle by working with their own hands and tending to their own business (1 Thess 4:10-12; 2 Thess 3:6-13). As Bruce Winter notes, working rather than relying on the benefaction of the wealthy would free the congregation from being indebted to a patron and would allow them to help others in their midst. In the church, then, those who are able to work could themselves become benefactors to others, but benefactors who seek the good of others rather than patrons who expect reciprocity or repayment in return.³¹

Labor is only part of a larger portrait of Paul's apostleship—a portrait that demonstrates his dedication to his mission but seems to run counter to the elites' vision of an apostle. The glimpses of his hardships show that he will go to great lengths to preach the gospel even when those hardships make him appear foolish (see, e.g., 1 Cor 4:8-12; 2 Cor 11:22-33; 1 Thess 2:2). In 1 Cor 4:8-12, Paul creates a stark dichotomy between the knowledgeable Corinthians, who are puffed up in judgment over one another (4:5-7), and the "weak" apostles. He characterizes the Corinthians as "kings," while the apostles are "last" of all, "like those sentenced to death," a "spectacle to the world and to angels and to humanity" (4:9), "fools for Christ," disreputable (4:10), like "the rubbish of the world," and "the dregs of all things" (4:13). To add to the humility, Paul says that he labors, working with his own hands (4:12), and is still hungry and thirsty, ill-clad and homeless (4:11; cf. 2 Cor 11:27). He does not stand up for himself when he is reviled. Instead, he blesses those who revile him and endures when persecuted (4:12). He does not retaliate when he has been slandered; instead, he seeks reconciliation (4:13). He willingly endures beatings, stonings, imprisonments (2 Cor 11: 23-25), having experienced shipwrecks and danger on multiple fronts:

30. Still, "Did Paul Loathe Manual Labor?," 795.
31. Winter, *Seek the Welfare of the City*, 41-60.

Paul as the Least of These?

"danger from rivers, danger from bandits, danger from my own people, danger from Gentiles, danger in the city, danger in the wilderness, danger at sea, danger from false brothers and sisters" (11:26). To return to Martin's two portraits of leaders, it is fair to say that this portrait of Paul's apostleship looks nothing like the model of the benevolent patriarch. Moreover, his opponents in Corinth later accuse him of being weak in bodily presence and having "contemptible speech" (2 Cor 10:10). Harrill argues that this insult is aimed at discrediting his authority by attacking his moral character as a servile flatterer, who says one thing but does another.[32] Accusing Paul of looking weak was akin to stripping him of his status as a free, adult male and instead treating him like a slave.[33] Paul is undaunted by this charge. He is fully aware of his weakness and even boasts in it (1 Cor 2:3; 2 Cor 11:16-30; 12:7-10).

In light of Paul's use of the metaphor of slavery to all in 1 Cor 9:19-23, Paul's charge in 1 Cor 4:8 that the Corinthians are kings calls to mind the good leaders, the benevolent patriarchs who rule from their elevated status.[34] It would be beneath these leaders to become weak, to be in need of basic life necessities, or to perform manual labor (see above). Hays argues that the true sage is depicted by Cynic and Stoic philosophers as being a king and a master: "But some think that the Stoics are jesting when they hear that in their sect the wise man is termed not only prudent and just and brave, but also an orator, a poet, a general, a rich man, and a king; and then they count themselves worthy of all these titles, and if they fail to get them, are vexed" (Plutarch, *On the Tranquility of the Mind*).[35] Paul

---

32. J. Albert Harrill, *Slaves in the New Testament: Literary, Social, and Moral Dimensions* (Minneapolis: Fortress, 2006), 36-57.

33. Harrill, *Slaves in the New Testament*, 45-53.

34. The charge of being like kings and already ruling has been interpreted through the lens of over-realized eschatology. For an overview, see Thiselton, *First Epistle to the Corinthians*, 357-59. In other words, the Corinthians, according to this reading, are claiming that the eschaton has already come. The Corinthians certainly are proud (4:6) and are probably claiming wisdom (4:10; 8:1-6), but the sarcasm of verse 8 does not require that the believers have actually portrayed themselves as kings who had "already" arrived at the glorious kingdom of God. In fact, there are many warnings in this letter that the eschaton is coming (e.g., 1:7; 2:6; 3:13-15; 4:5; 7:29, 31; 10:11; 11:26; 16:22). Perhaps the Corinthians are lacking in eschatological fervor, and Paul must remind them of the coming judgment to urge them on to faithfulness. Richard B. Hays, *First Corinthians*, IBC (Louisville: Westminster John Knox, 1997), 70.

35. Hays, *First Corinthians*, 70-71. Plutarch, *Moralia* 472a (Helmbold, LCL).

may here be playing on the topos of the wise leader who lives like a king.[36] What is clear is the stark contrast between the wise Corinthians who live like kings and Paul's characterization of himself and his colleagues as the scum of the earth (4:13).

If the topos of the leader as "slave to all" was such an overwhelmingly negative view of leadership from the perspective of the elite, why might Paul employ this topos in 1 Cor 9? This question becomes all the more pressing when the context is taken into consideration. Paul is trying to convince the Corinthian knowledgeable (aka "know-it-alls"), who are likely the social elite in the congregation,[37] to adopt the behavior of lowering themselves to consider the needs of the so-called weak. Though the knowledgeable are sometimes referred to as "strong" in light of the argument around food in Rom 14–15, here Paul refers to the faction only as those who think they have *gnōsis*. The know-it-alls have likely given the designation of "weak" to those who oppose their position. Since the issue of whether to consume idol food is a matter that the church has raised with Paul in their letter to him (see 7:1), Paul is likely using language that the letter has used to address the situation.

The dilemma of eating idol food includes social, financial, and theological ramifications. The knowledgeable are the ones who are invited to eat and drink in the local temples. Since most homes were too small to host a dinner party, the local temples offered dining halls for rent. All meals served at the local temple would have consisted of food sacrificed to the temple's deity.[38] Thus, the Corinthians are wondering whether it is acceptable for them to consume food that has been sacrificed to an idol. The knowledgeable have argued that there is no such thing as idols (8:4). Thus, it should not matter whether they consume food that has been dedicated to another god, because those gods are not real. The "weak," however, have concerns over eating such food. It is likely that, for them, there are still live questions about the efficacy of an idol's power (8:7–13). Paul fears that the

---

36. See also Hays, *First Corinthians*, 70–71.

37. Following the convincing argument of Gerd Theissen that the divisions of 1 Cor 8:1–11:1 and 11:17–34 are largely divisions between the "haves" and the "have-nots." See *The Social Setting of Pauline Christianity: Essays on Corinth*, ed. and trans. John H. Schütz (Philadelphia: Fortress, 1982), 121–44.

38. John Fotopoulos, *Food Offered to Idols in Roman Corinth: A Social-Rhetorical Reconsideration of 1 Corinthians 8:1–11:1*, WUNT 2.151 (Tübingen: Mohr Siebeck, 2003), 63–70.

theology of the knowledgeable will actually result in leading the weak back into a life of idolatry (8:10-13).

The matter is further complicated by the fact that the knowledgeable must maintain their social standing. Derek Newton observes, "Meals not only held 'religious' significance, but simultaneously were considered to act as markers of socio-economic class divisions, as opportunities to converse and build friendships, and as means of fulfilling socio-political obligations."[39] Refusing a dinner invitation would have social repercussions, since one could not afford to shame a business associate or benefactor who had gone to the expense of hosting the event. Paul is not completely unsympathetic with the precarious social position of the elite in the church. He agrees that the food itself does not actually pose a threat (8:8). This agreement accounts for his concession in 10:23-34 to consume whatever is sold in the market or offered in someone's home without asking questions. The litmus test for consumption has nothing to do with the food itself, but with whether consuming the food would potentially lead the "weak" to return to a life of idolatry. Thus, Paul ends this section by reframing the dilemma: "So, whether you eat or drink, or whatever you do, do all to the glory of God" (10:32). Paul's advice throughout 1 Cor 8:1-11:1 is directed toward the elite.

Who are the "weak"? The "weak" in this argument are likely those of lower classes who rarely, if ever, receive invitations to such banquets. They likely do not have to face the dilemma of whether to consume idol food in the grand banquet hall of a temple. Yet they know that their higher class "friends" are somehow participants in rites honoring another deity. Though Paul seems sympathetic to the theological rationale of the knowledgeable (8:1-6), he also reveals affinity for the arguments of the weak (10:19-21). In 10:20-21, he acknowledges that members of the congregation cannot partake of the cup of demons and the cup of the Lord. Though Paul certainly affirms that there is only one God and one Lord (8:6), like the weak, he acknowledges the existence of other spiritual forces. For this reason, he wants both sides to do all they can to remain faithful to a jealous Lord, who will not tolerate idolatry (10:1-22). In reality, both sides—the so-called knowledgeable and the so-called weak—are in danger of succumbing to their weakness.

How does Paul's rhetoric of slavery in 1 Cor 9:19-23 fit into his exhortation regarding idol food? Paul demonstrates through the scandalous rheto-

---

39. Derek Newton, "Food Offered to Idols in 1 Corinthians 8-10," *TynBul* 49 (1998): 181.

ric of being a slave to all what he sees as the responsibility of the so-called knowledgeable ones: to renounce their rights for the benefit of another's salvation. The so-called weak are in real peril of returning to a life of idolatry and, thus, being destroyed (8:11), and Paul blames the know-it-alls: "So by your knowledge those weak believers for whom Christ died are destroyed. But when you thus sin against members of your family, and wound their conscience when it is weak, you sin against Christ" (1 Cor 8:11-12). The knowledgeable must adapt their behavior in order to save the weak.

In 1 Cor 9:22, Paul gets to the heart of his illustration of adaptability. Unlike the knowledgeable, who act to protect their own interests even at the risk of the weak, Paul claims to become weak to win those who are weak. The references to Paul's "becoming" the other include *hōs*, "like." He became *like* a Jew or *like* one under the law or *like* one without law. In verse 22, however, the earliest manuscripts omit this term. Paul does not become *like* the weak; he *becomes* weak. This act of becoming, as noted above, is visibly manifested not only in Paul's manual labor, but also in his refusal to accept wages from the church. He is renouncing apostolic rights for financial support, which are visible in Peter's practice (9:5), supported by Scripture (9:8-13), obvious from common sense (9:7), and commanded by Jesus (9:14).[40] Paul marshals a vast array of evidence to show that he is purposely humbling himself by not taking what he is due. Since Paul's advice may have financial repercussions for the Corinthian elite, he demonstrates that his life models the advice that he is giving to the church. By working with his own hands, he has taken on a servile form of weakness for the benefit of others. Plus, his apostleship, as seen in 1 Cor 4:8-13, is not characterized by high status markers, but by poverty and homelessness.

Paul's voluntary self-lowering, a characteristic of the despised demagogue, is consistent with his understanding of the topsy-turvy effect of the cross. For those who prefer the benevolent patriarch model of leadership, the demagogue is detestable for renouncing his status and willingly lowering himself for the sake of the masses. This model of leadership seems like foolishness. In 1 Cor 1:18-25, Paul reminds the Corinthians of the scandal of the gospel. The word of the cross is foolishness to the sages of the world. God chose the foolish in order to shame the wise (1:27). The humiliation of the cross is evident in the portrait of Paul's apostleship as a slave to all. Paul

---

40. Paul's refusal to accept support (9:15-18) would contradict the Lord's command. See also David G. Horrell, *Solidarity and Difference: A Contemporary Reading of Paul's Ethics* (London: T&T Clark, 2005), 216-19.

is not judging his apostleship by the world's standards. He is not concerned that his leadership looks like foolishness to the elite. Instead, the word of the cross becomes the paradigm for Paul's leadership.

As noted at the beginning of this section, 1 Cor 9 is by no means the only time that Paul likens himself to a slave. It is the most prominent metaphor that Paul uses to depict his apostleship. In Philippians, he even jettisons the title "apostle" in the salutation to be referred to as a slave of Christ. Perhaps, Paul's earlier background as a persecutor always made him feel indebted to God's grace. Certainly, he does not shy away from the metaphor of service to describe one's life in Christ (e.g., Rom 6:12–23). Paul's life demonstrated that, even though he was a free man, his service to Christ made him willing to face any hardship for the sake of his mission. He was willing to become the least, and he encourages others who share a similar social status as himself to do the same. Importantly, while Paul commands all in the church to love one another and to bear one another's burdens, he never asks those who are already at the lowest end of the social and economic spectrum to lower themselves more. They have no status to relinquish. Rather, Paul's use of this metaphor indicates that he himself had status. The fact that he can encourage some in the church to follow his example suggests that members of these congregations also had status. The use of such a jarring metaphor to depict his leadership status might not have been the most "seeker-friendly" way to attract people into the church, but Paul seems uninterested in making the gospel more palatable to anyone. He will gladly look like a fool for Christ, and he will endure anything for the sake of this gospel—even imprisonment.

Paul in Chains

In contrast to his use of the slave metaphor to describe his ministry, when he had never been forced to be a slave in reality, Paul did know what it was like to be a prisoner for Christ. It is no secret that Paul's ministry frequently landed him in jail. Of the thirteen letters attributed to Paul in our canon, five seem to be written from prison: Philemon, Philippians, Ephesians, Colossians, and 2 Timothy. Even if Paul did not pen all these letters, there is no doubt that the apostle was quite familiar with jail. When considering Paul's ministry among and alongside the least, his jail time demonstrates that he is willing to take risks and relinquish his freedom for the sake of the gospel.

Paul's message frequently gets him into trouble with the locals. Not only do his letters make this claim, but Acts and the early church fathers also attest to Paul's imprisonments. According to 1 Clement, Paul was imprisoned seven times and suffered martyrdom (1 Clem. 5:6–7). In 2 Cor 11:23, he writes that he has "far more imprisonments" than his opponents, the so-called false apostles (2 Cor 11:23). This statement implies that when Paul is likely writing this letter (perhaps 55–56 CE), he has been in jail more often than Acts recounts by this point in Paul's story. According to Acts 16, Paul was imprisoned in Philippi and had a miraculous experience that resulted in the jailor's conversion. His incarcerations in Jerusalem, Caesarea, and Rome would date after the writing of 2 Corinthians. Since neither Paul's letters nor Acts give a comprehensive account of Paul's life and mission, it is hard to know how much of Paul's ministry is spent in jail. There is little reason, though, to doubt the story of his longer imprisonments at Caesarea and Rome in Acts. In each case, Paul spends two years there (Acts 24:27; 28:30). Considering that he has also done time in Jerusalem and Philippi and spent months as a prisoner on his voyage to Rome, prison has been a significant part of Paul's ministry. From jail, Paul awaits many trials before local governors, religious authorities, and even the emperor. In Philippians, as the ruling of the imperial court looms before him, Paul braces the church for the possibility of his death even as they pray for his deliverance (Phil 1:19–26; 2:17, 23–24). According to church tradition, Paul died in Rome, beheaded under the power of Nero.[41]

According to the biblical witness, Paul has spent years of his ministry in jail, but the descriptions of these incarcerations vary greatly, leaving one to wonder what Roman imprisonment was like. In his study about Paul's letters in light of Roman prison experiences, Richard Cassidy cautions that we know little about jails in the first-century Roman world. Reports about the Roman prison system are often anecdotal and focus on the treatment that a particular Roman ruler decreed for a specific enemy. Rome was not concerned to preserve a comprehensive description of its prison system. There was not a comprehensive "system" per se. In *Paul*

---

41. Paul's martyrdom is attested by the Acts of Paul; Ignatius, *To the Ephesians* 12:2; Polycarp, *To the Philippians* 9:1–2; Eusebius, *Ecclesiastical History* 2.25.4; Tertullian, *Antidote for the Scorpion's Sting* 15; *The Prescription Against Heretics* 36. The tradition of beheading stems from the Martyrdom of Paul (in the Acts of Paul); Eusebius, *Ecclesiastical History* 2.25.4; Tertullian, *Antidote for the Scorpion's Sting* 15:5–6.

Paul as the Least of These?

in Chains, Cassidy outlines three basic categories or grades of incarceration: prison, military custody, and free custody. These categories had varying degrees of severity with the category of "prison" lending itself to the most torturous of circumstances and "free custody" the least inhumane. Prisons often consisted of chains or confinement in a small space or both. Cassidy cites Diodorus Siculus's account of one prison where prisoners were crammed into a tiny room. The food rations were minimal and the quarters stank (*Library of History* 31.9.1-4).[42] Military custody could also employ chains, but the prisoner was supervised by military personnel. Treatment of the prisoner could vary greatly. Based on both the passion narratives and Paul's experiences, it would seem that beatings were a typical part of being arrested—especially if the prisoner was not expected to be a Roman citizen. In Acts 22:24, the tribune ordered that Paul be brought into the barracks and "examined by flogging." Paul, who had already been bound, asks, "Is it legal for you to flog a Roman citizen who is uncondemned?" (22:25). Yet in Acts's account of Paul's Roman imprisonment, he was guarded by a soldier (28:16), confined by a chain (28:20), but allowed to have visitors (28:23, 30-31). Nothing indicates that he was mistreated. The final category, free custody, did not typically entail chains. One might be detained under the supervision of magistrates or their households. Treatment here could vary from inhumane to relatively mild. Dio Cassius reports that Gallus's imprisonment under house arrest included just enough food to keep him from dying, but not enough food to have any strength (*Roman History* 58.3.5).[43]

Paul's prison experiences varied greatly. For instance, in Philippi, after being severely beaten, Paul and Silas were kept in the innermost cell, guarded by a jailor, and had their feet fastened in stocks (Acts 16:22-24). Stocks were not just a form of holding a prisoner, but an instrument of torture, since the feet and legs would have been stretched.[44] In contrast, in Caesarea, Felix ordered the centurion that Paul be kept in custody but have liberty to welcome friends who would attend to his needs (Acts 24:23). While under house arrest in Rome, however, he was restrained only by a

---

42. Richard J. Cassidy, *Paul in Chains: Roman Imprisonment and the Letters of St. Paul* (New York: Crossroad, 2001), 36-39.

43. Cassidy, *Paul in Chains*, 43.

44. Daniel G. Reid, "Prison, Prisoner," in *The Dictionary of Paul and His Letters*, ed. Gerald F. Hawthorne, Ralph P. Martin, and Daniel G. Reid (Downers Grove, IL: InterVarsity, 1993), 752.

light chain (28:20) and allowed to receive visitors (28:30).[45] In his transport to Rome, it appears that at times he had no chains or even the direct supervision of a guard, since he was granted some liberties to visit friends along the journey to receive care (Acts 27).

Prisons served as places to hold people awaiting trial. They were not considered the ultimate penalty for a crime, although, as noted above, some cells were designed to be more torturous than others.[46] Rome had other punishments readily available, like flogging, beheading, or crucifixion. In Acts, prison actually saves Paul's life (Acts 21–23). When the crowds from the temple want to kill him, the Roman soldiers sweep him away (Acts 21:30–34). While Rome is trying to sort out what kind of threat Paul might be, keeping Paul locked away prevents him from being murdered. The transport from Jerusalem to Caesarea to see Felix the governor included massive support: two hundred soldiers, seventy horsemen, and two hundred spearmen (23:23). Since Roman "justice" included bribery, Paul sat in jail for two years in Caesarea, while Felix waited for a bribe to release him.

Neither Paul's letters nor Acts portray prison as a detriment to his ministry. In Philippians, he talks about preaching the gospel to the imperial household (1:13; 4:22).[47] He is able to rejoice that his circumstances have allowed the gospel to go to places that he might not have otherwise reached. The author of Acts reports that, even in his role as prisoner, he preaches to Felix, Festus, and King Agrippa. King Agrippa jokes that Paul is trying to convert him (Acts 26:28). Acts ends with Paul proclaiming the gospel freely in the heart of the empire, even in his chains.

These incarcerations, though portrayed somewhat positively in the biblical witness, should not be romanticized. No one would argue that the life of the prisoner was glamorous. Prisoners were vulnerable, because they were largely considered expendable. Paul speaks of beatings, floggings, and starvation. There was no expectation that the jailor provide food, although, as noted by Cassidy, some might provide just enough food to keep the prisoner alive. Prisoners had to rely on the hospitality of friends, family, or strangers for food and clothing. According to Philippians, Epaphroditus has brought supplies to Paul (Phil 2:25). In Acts, Felix allows Paul some

---

45. For a discussion of the words used to describe Paul's chains, see Reid, "Prison, Prisoner," 752–54.

46. Reid, "Prison, Prisoner," 753.

47. Cassidy argues persuasively that Paul writes Philippians from jail in Rome (*Paul in Chains*, 124–210).

liberty in his Caesarean imprisonment to receive friends who tend to his needs (24:23). Similarly, in the narrative of the voyage to Rome, Paul is in military custody under the supervision of a centurion of the Augustan cohort, named Julius, who "treated Paul kindly, and gave him leave to go to his friends and be cared for" (Acts 27:3). Though Paul freely receives visitors while under house arrest in Rome, it is clear from Acts 28 that Paul is in prison at his own expense for at least two years (28:30).

Paul willingly faces these hardships because of his calling. His prison experiences shape his apostolic identity as a prisoner of Christ who longs to honor Christ with his body (Phil 1:20). He strives to follow Jesus not just in word but also in deed and encourages his churches to do the same (Phil 3:17). In Philippians, as he sits in prison and expects his next trial to result in death, he asks the Philippians to have the same mindset as Christ, who relinquished his status of being equal to God, to take on human form, even the form of a servant. Being a prisoner—relinquishing his own freedom for this gospel—was one way in which Paul demonstrated the mindset of Christ. The irony is that Saul the persecutor, who hunted down Christians to imprison them, likely died in Rome after a lengthy imprisonment for trying to convert people to follow Jesus. Paul did not have to die. Festus, Felix, and King Agrippa found the charges against him to be false, not worthy of capital punishment (see Acts 23:29; 25:25; 28:18). These rulers would be inclined to want to appease the Jews in Jerusalem (e.g., Acts 24:27; 25:9), but in Paul's case, they did not grant the wishes of the religious leaders. As a Roman citizen, the cards were stacked in Paul's favor. He could have downplayed the scandal of the gospel he was preaching. But he refused. He continued to proclaim the lordship of Jesus Christ, even in the heart of the Roman Empire.

Conclusion

Paul may be a giant of the Christian faith, but he saw himself as the least of the apostles, unworthy to be called an apostle because he had persecuted the church of God (1 Cor 15). The revelation of Jesus changed the direction of his mission from one who hunted and imprisoned believers to one who was willing to face hunger, starvation, beatings, and imprisonment for the sake of the gospel. It is true that Paul's letters contain boasts in his apostleship. Yet he is an apostle who boasts in his sufferings. His sufferings provide proof of the sincerity of his mission and the trustworthiness of his motives.

He did not see himself as high and mighty. He did see himself as called by God. Perhaps his temporary, but lengthy, incarcerations also helped inspire some of the metaphors that he used to describe his apostleship—for example, prisoner, slave, debtor, steward of God's mysteries. Perhaps he never felt worthy to be called by God to speak about Jesus when he had previously done everything in his power to end the Jesus movement. For all that he did to eradicate Christianity, after the revelation of Christ (Gal 1:12, 16), he tried to walk in the footsteps of Jesus. Christ had redeemed him from the dead. He owed his life and existence to God, and he never forgot that. He always felt indebted, a slave to Christ. For this reason, he went to foreign places with strange customs and made himself vulnerable. He tried to live a life worthy of the gospel by imitating Christ even unto death. Whenever we exalt Paul as a hero of the faith, we would do well to remember that Paul's story is really about God. God's grace can extend to all, and God's power can transform even a former persecutor to bring a message of life and hope to the world.

FURTHER READING

Cassidy, Richard J. *Paul in Chains: Roman Imprisonment and the Letters of St. Paul*. New York: Crossroad, 2001. Showing how Paul spends a significant amount of time in prison, Cassidy studies Roman imprisonment in the first-century world and reads Paul's prison letters through that lens.

Martin, Dale B. *Slavery as Salvation: The Metaphor of Slavery in Pauline Christianity*. New Haven: Yale University Press, 1990. Martin's study of the slavery metaphor in Paul's letters, with a particular focus on 1 Cor 9, includes a rich survey of vast amounts of ancient literature. Martin also includes a discussion of slavery and how it functions in the hierarchy of social status.

CHAPTER SEVEN

Good News for the Least of These

The view of the gospel with which my church typically operates—with which I typically operate—pales in comparison to Paul's understanding of the "good news." I have been an active church member my whole life; I am even married to a minister. But my encounters with the gospel in church settings, while powerful, tend to be limited. I would even venture to say—as a professor who trains future ministers—that many Christians operate with a gospel that just is not big enough.

Let me explain. I am not saying that we do not believe the gospel or that God has not somehow transformed our lives. It is just that we have a tendency to think that the gospel is about us—*all* about us. In the church of my youth, the gospel was equated with an individual's "eternal security." In other words, if you were to die tonight do you know where you would spend eternity? Once you prayed the "sinner's prayer," you were good, as though you had just purchased fire insurance. In the church of my adulthood, the gospel is often equated with humans trying to create the kingdom of God on earth—a noble goal, but one that frequently slips into the idolatry of relying on ourselves, or our government, rather than recognizing the power of the Spirit to work in the most unlikely places.

Whenever I read Paul's letters, I am reminded that the gospel is simply bigger. The gospel is not just about whether Jesus is "in your heart," though that can certainly be part of this good news. The gospel is not the passing of particular legislation, though that can be a result of God's work in the world. The gospel is about God—plain and simple. It is about a creator God who flatly refuses to abandon creation and will stop at nothing to bless creation. It is not only about a God who invests Godself in history, but also a God incarnate who takes on sin and death and wins. It is about a God who sees more in creation than its corruption. This God is able to take chaos and make shalom. With such a powerful and mysterious God at work in the world, we should expect the gospel to be bigger than our limited understandings of justice, goodness, or peace.

Paul taught me that. Paul taught me that "new creation" is indeed everything (Gal 5:16), that nothing can separate us from the love of God (Rom 8:31-39), that God is faithful and trustworthy (1 Cor 1:9; 10:13), and that God's promises are irrevocable (Rom 11:29). God's grace is also far-reaching. It knows no boundaries and shows no partiality (Rom 2:11). It is for the least and for the greatest, though the least are the ones most likely to perceive it as good news.

Paul also taught me that this new creation is costly. It comes only through the scandal of a Roman cross. It would be impossible to overstate how important the cross and resurrection are to Paul's theology. It is, after all, Paul's encounter with the resurrected Lord that changes everything about how he sees his world. Paul, however, never loses sight of the cross's scandal. I do not see how he could have either. He is a Jew traveling around the empire talking to non-Jews of every tribe, religion, and background and telling them that some poor Jewish man from a hillbilly town in a region of the empire that most of them care nothing about, nor will ever visit, was killed by the Romans for treason years ago, and the God of Israel—the Jewish God—raised that wandering peasant preacher from the dead. Somehow these non-Jewish people with their own gods and customs and virtues and values are supposed to stop and listen to this message and *believe* it. While we worry about making churches more seeker-friendly, Paul is working with a gospel that is simply a tough sell. Tyler Wigg Stevenson, in his book *Brand Jesus*, records the following scenario to try to capture for his audience in the American Bible Belt how fanatical this message must have sounded to the first-century world:

> What would we think if someone wrote to a church in modern America—Silicon Valley or Manhattan, say—with the wild claim that the messiah had arrived sometime in the mid-seventies; that he had been an undocumented Filipino migrant worker who spoke about the inbreaking kingdom of God; that, while working in Guam, he had been brought in by local ecclesiastical authority on trumped up civil charges; that the local governor had caved in to their demands and executed him for treason; and that his life and death

changed everything we thought we knew about God, the world, and ourselves.[1]

For us to grasp how this message is truly good news, we absolutely must recover its scandal. The more palatable we make the message, the more limitations we tend to place on God.

I am convinced that most of our misinterpretations of Paul's letters and the abuse that has been done in Paul's name are connected to the limitations that we place on the gospel. Anytime our reading of Scripture allows us to oppress a whole people, to limit God's activity, or to instill our own cultural hierarchies, is it really the gospel that we are preaching? Or worse, if we think that the gospel has nothing to do with our treatment of the poor, our adoption of cultural values, or our blindness to our own privilege, then we have severely limited the gospel. Too often our version of gospel only further reinstills the status quo. In Paul's gospel, though, the status quo is under attack by God. This chapter will attempt to sketch a vision of the gospel in Paul's theology and show how that gospel impacted Paul's mission and ministry.

What Is Paul's Gospel?

Perhaps we tend to operate with a gospel that is small because we cannot grasp the greatness of God's power and the fury—or, for many, the mere existence—of all the powers that oppose God. Paul, however, firmly links the gospel to God's power (Rom 1:16-17). For the apostle, life is at stake—not just the lives of individuals, but also the blessing of life abundant for the whole created order.

When Paul writes to the believers in Rome, a church that he did not establish, he begins his "good news" by spelling out the dire news. It is as though he does not think that anyone can comprehend the greatness of God's salvation without first realizing *why* it is that one needs to be saved. Though our twenty-first-century discussions of this letter, especially in denominations torn over issues of sexuality, get stuck on the so-called homosexual verses of Rom 1, our mere focus on any set of verses in chapter 1 only condemns us of sin all the more. The point of Rom 1 is to show

---

1. Tyler Wigg Stevenson gives credit to Gordon Zerbe for imagining this scenario (*Brand Jesus: Christianity in a Consumerist Age* [New York: Seabury, 2007], xv).

that *all* have sinned. If you are one of the lucky readers who can stand proud after reading the first chapter (which I find hard to believe with the condemnation of things like "gossip" or "deceit," not to mention "haughtiness" or "boastfulness"! [Rom 1:29–31]), then the opening lines of Rom 2 are designed to pull the rug out from under you: "Therefore you have no excuse, whoever you are, when you judge others; for in passing judgment on another you condemn yourself, because you, the judge, are doing the very same things" (Rom 2:1). Paul painstakingly lays out his case that *all* are guilty of "sin" (Rom 3:23). All are responsible to follow the revelation that they have—whether from creation that teaches humanity that it is not God (Rom 1:18–32) or the law that points out transgressions (see Rom 3:9–19; 4:15; Gal 3:19). And all fall short of the glory of God (Rom 3:23). One of my former students summarized the first three chapters of Romans, "Everyone sucks."

The good news is that God sees humanity—with all the wretchedness, weakness, insecurities, failures, and fears—and loves us and wants us anyway. While we were sinners and God's *enemies*, Christ died for us (Rom 5:8–10). This is powerful news. God sees more in us than we can possibly see in ourselves. God sees something worth redeeming. As amazing as this is, though, this is only *part* of the good news, because it has acknowledged only a portion of the bad news.

We have a limited view of the power of God's grace because we have a limited view of the power of sin. Sin is not restricted to our transgressions. Sure, trespasses are sins. We mess up. We constantly "miss the mark." But the sin situation is not about all the times that we fail to follow the rules. Paul's language for sin in Romans is daunting. Paul portrays sin as a superpower "in the world" (Rom 5:13). It rules people (5:21; 6:12). People can serve sin and be enslaved to sin (6:6, 17). Sin is something from which people need to be freed (6:18). Since the wages of sin is death (6:23), people have to die to be freed from sin's power (6:11). Beverly Roberts Gaventa speaks of Sin with a capital S, not only a cosmic force that causes people to trespass (aka, lowercase "sin"), but also an all-corrupting power that has distorted the goodness of God's creation.[2] It creeps through the world around us until everything is in its clutches. Sin is the cause of systemic evils, like racism, sexism, and the exploitation of the poor. Sin is what blinds people and desensitizes them to the injustices that occur in every-

---

2. Beverly Roberts Gaventa, *Our Mother Saint Paul* (Louisville: Westminster John Knox, 2007), 125–36.

day life. Sin is bigger than us and ensnares us even during those moments when we think we are being "good." Sin is the yeast that has worked its way through the dough, and no part of the dough can escape transformation. Sin has distorted our very image of goodness or justice. When we equate sin simply with human actions, we risk the idolatry of thinking that we can somehow control or defeat sin, as though we just need to buy the right self-help book or perform the right breathing exercises or reduce stress that might lead to sin. Paul's view of sin is not just disconcerting. It is self-defeating and downright overwhelming. There is no escape from sin.

Sin's power is far greater than ours, but it is also far greater than the sum of God's creation. *Nothing* in all creation can withstand the power of sin. To me, this is mind-boggling. Humans tend to have a puffed-up view of their own creative abilities and accomplishments—until an "act of nature" comes along that reminds us of our limitations. There is a lot of power, strength, and mystery in nonhuman creation. In Rom 8, Paul warns that sin has captured the whole of the created order. All creation longs for freedom from this superpower. All creation has suffered. All creation has been distorted from the goodness of Paradise. All creation longs to be restored and redeemed (Rom 8:20-23). Nothing has escaped sin's clutches.

Sin is an anti-God power that only God can defeat. God conquers sin by defeating sin's sidekick and greatest weapon: death. Like sin, the apostle treats death like a superpower. In 1 Cor 15:55, Paul even taunts death by quoting Hosea: "Where, O death, is your victory? Where, O death, is your sting?" Paul claims in Rom 5 that death came through sin and spread to *all* (5:12). Thus, like sin, death has exercised dominion since Adam's trespass (5:14, 17). In other words, where there is sin there is death, because "the wages of sin is death" (Rom 6:23).

God defeats sin and death by raising Jesus. As Paul words it in 1 Cor 15: "For since death came through a human being, the resurrection of the dead has also come through a human being; for as all die in Adam, so all will be made alive in Christ. But each in his own order: Christ the first fruits, then at his coming those who belong to Christ" (1 Cor 15:21-23). Without the resurrection, there is no hope because there is no victory over death (1 Cor 15:12-19). Without the resurrection, there is no sign that God has defeated this anti-God power. Paul does not think that Christ died by some accident (1 Cor 15:4). God willingly and knowingly handed Jesus over to the power of death to save the rest of creation from the superpowers of sin and death (Rom 4:25; 8:32). And God raised him from the dead. *God Godself took on death, at God's initiative, and won* (1 Cor 15:54-57). As a result of God's victory, people can be freed from the powers of sin and death (Rom 5:12–23).

How, though, can humanity participate in this victory? After all, these powers have already proven too great for us to bear. In short, humans place their trust in God to do for them what they cannot do for themselves. The term that Paul uses for this is *pistis*, which we often translate as "faith." It is misguided, however, to limit faith to a belief in a set of principles. Decades later when the early church is developing an understanding of orthodoxy, "faith" will come to be equated with sound teaching. At the time that Paul is writing Romans, what is considered sound teaching or doctrine is only at the beginning of formation. Here *pistis* is greater than a belief system. *Pistis* is an indication of loyalty and trust that is exhibited not merely in what one thinks, but how one acts. *Pistis* is just as all-encompassing as sin. *Pistis* leads to action. It is faith that causes believers to present themselves to the mercy of God rather than to remain in slavery to sin (Rom 5:12–14).

Placing trust in Christ's death and resurrection is central to this good news. Since Christ has been raised, death no longer has dominion over him (Rom 6:9b). Believers participate in that victory by being baptized "into Christ's death" (Rom 6:3). Paul's language to describe baptism in Rom 6 demonstrates that, for the apostle, the act of baptism embodies a cocrucifixion and coburial with Christ (Rom 6:4–9). Biblical scholars refer to this language as "union" or "participation" in Christ. The purpose of cocrucifixion with Christ is the hope of participation in his resurrection: "For if we have been united with him in a death like his, we will certainly be united with him in a resurrection like his" (Rom 6:5; see also 6:8). It is clear from the verb tenses in Rom 6:4–8 that the resurrection of believers is a future hope. Christ's resurrection is the firstfruits. It has already occurred. Believers live in the tension of having participated in Christ's death to sin, but awaiting resurrection.

Scholars refer to this tension as the "already/not yet," already God's kingdom has dawned through Christ, but it is not yet fully realized and will not be realized until Christ's return. Christ's life, death, and resurrection embody God's kingdom or, as Paul likes to refer to it, "new creation" (Gal 6:15; 2 Cor 5:17). Sin and all the effects of sin will not be fully eradicated until Christ comes again. Though God's ultimate victory over sin's power has been signaled in the resurrection of Jesus, the rest of creation is still suffering under sin's dominion. This is why in Rom 7 Paul can speak of knowing the good that needs to be done and wanting to do it, but still succumbing to sin. Though God has been victorious over sin, sin is still present in the world and remains a threat. Since only God has defeated sin, believers must have God's power to conquer sin. The presence of God's Holy Spirit is that power. The Spirit grants believers the ability to live in a way that is pleasing to God.

Participation in Christ's death entails the Spirit's work of transformation and renewal: "So if anyone is in Christ, there is a new creation: everything old has passed away; see, everything has become new!" (2 Cor 5:17). The power of sin to corrupt all creation is the reason this renewal is necessary. To use Paul's language, the world under the dominion of sin is "this present evil age" (Gal 1:4). The reign of the Spirit is the mark of God's victory over sin's power. The Spirit provides hope. For the Galatian church, Paul claims that the fruit or result of the Spirit's work is the presence of love, joy, peace, patience, kindness, generosity, faithfulness, gentleness, and self-control (Gal 5:22-23). In spite of our propensity to pick and choose which virtue among this list might be our spiritual gift, Paul is not trying to offer an exhaustive list here, nor is he giving us options. The fruit (singular) of the Spirit's work is all these things. The Spirit is so powerful that it can transform selfish people into creatures who exhibit some of the very characteristics of God. The Spirit is the marker of God's redemptive work, the sign of God's reign.

Life in the "already/not yet," this time between Christ's resurrection and second coming, is a war zone—a constant battle between the power of the Spirit and the desires of the flesh. If death is sin's greatest weapon, Paul uses "flesh" (*sarx*) to describe the force of sin at work in our bodies. On its own, the Greek word for flesh, *sarx*, simply means the physical material that makes up our bodies. It may refer to skin or to skin and muscles. Paul takes this term, though, and, in keeping with what he has done with sin and death, speaks of flesh as a force. It is the Spirit's nemesis. Flesh, according to Paul in Rom 8, is hostile to God. It is inimical to God's will. It weakens the holy, just, and good law of God (8:3). It leads to death (8:6). Flesh is nothing short of the corruption of God's good creation. To be clear, Paul does not think that the body is fundamentally evil. God, after all, created that body. Sin is so powerful that it has corrupted the goodness of God's creation. Flesh, too, must be redeemed from sin's power. Our bodies must be restored to the goodness of Eden. Paul insists on a bodily resurrection; our bodies will be redeemed from the effects of sin and transformed to reflect God's goodness (1 Cor 15:1-58). The presence of the Spirit's work in believers is a mark of that renewal, or sanctification, but the power of the flesh should not be underestimated. Sin's effects are still very much present in the world all around us. The whole of the created order does not yet experience the blessings of abundant life. Injustices permeate our world.

Paul stands within a Jewish tradition of expecting God to intervene in history and bring about God's justice. God has intervened through the cross. Paul also anticipates the Day of the Lord, a day of judgment. God's victory through the resurrection is often likened by Bible teachers to D-Day in World War II, the Battle of Normandy, the combat operation that marked the beginning of the end of the war. This battle marked a decisive victory, but the war kept on. D-Day is not the same as V-Day, or "Victory Day," when the battle is won and the war is over. Though Paul believes that God has won a decisive battle against sin and death on the cross, he is still awaiting the second coming of Christ, when God will redeem all creation from the power of sin and death. For Paul, the second coming is linked to judgment and to love. Romans, for instance, begins illustrating God's power for salvation by discussing the severity of God's impartial wrath. God's wrath toward all injustice stems from God's love of creation. The presence of injustice, after all, is the result of sin's dominion. All must be made right.

The result of God's rectification of creation is a restoration of the goodness of the created order. The prophetic witness longs for a time when predator will lie down with prey, death will not steal the young, and farmers will enjoy the fruit of their labor (Isa 65:18–25). Nations will beat their swords into plowshares, and war will be no more (Isa 2:4). It is a world of peace, or *shalom*. It is the blessing of abundant life that God has always desired for creation. It is not a replacement of the created order, but its renewal. The Spirit is at work even now making all things new. God does not abandon God's creation. God redeems it, because God wants nothing more than to bless it.

In short, Paul's gospel is cosmic in scope. It is bigger than we can possibly imagine. God's power for salvation is not limited to humanity, nor is it limited to a certain nation. God's power to save is not contingent upon human action either. God *is* rectifying the whole world, period. Yes, Paul anticipates judgment. Yes, Paul anticipates God's coming wrath. Yes, Paul calls on all the nations to place trust in God's salvation. But Paul does not think that God's saving acts are somehow on hold. This is an active God who is at work transforming, rectifying, redeeming, and blessing. Paul sees God at work among the most unlikely of peoples, and he is convinced that God will complete that work within his lifetime. The urgency of his mission stems from the clarity of this vision.

Paul's Revelation and the Urgency of His Mission

Vision itself is not such an objective concept. Let me explain. My red, long-haired dachshund, Hauerwas, like other dogs, has the same number of color receptors as a color-blind person: two. He cannot see red or any color variation that requires red (although you would never guess this by looking at the dog toy market!). Roughly speaking, we humans have three types of color sensitive cones—blue, green, and red. Some women possess a fourth color cone, but these rare tetrachromats may not be able to use that receptor, because our culture does not give them the vocabulary to articulate what they are seeing. Thus, they may not develop the skill to differentiate the colors. If they could use that fourth cone, they could see around ninety-nine million more color variations than the average person![3] Our world is designed to honor the sight experiences of the trichromat. Trichromats can see up to a million color variations and may even feel sorry for our "color-blind" friends who are limited to around ten thousand shades. While listening to a *RadioLab* podcast on color, however, I learned that humans—even the rare tetrachromats—are not that special when it comes to our multihued spectrum.[4]

While most humans have one more color receptor than our dogs, others in the animal kingdom can see colors that we cannot even imagine. Sparrows can see "ultraviolet," so creatively named because their color spectrum extends beyond "violet." In other words, they can see a world of color that we simply have no words to describe. Butterflies have five or six color receptors and can see colors beyond our dreams. The most impressive creature mentioned on the podcast, the creature with more color cones than any known living thing, is the mantis shrimp. This shrimp is receiving information from *sixteen* color receptors! Compared to our trichromatic world, the colorful world of the mantis shrimp must be amazing!

What do mantis shrimp and butterflies have to do with the gospel? Revelation is seeing the world as it really is, seeing what is actually there that was previously hidden to us because we simply did not have the abil-

---

3. A true tetrachromat can see ninety-nine million more shades than the average person. Fiona MacDonald, "Scientists Have Found a Woman Whose Eyes Have a Whole New Type of Colour Receptor," ScienceAlert, July 25, 2016, accessed August 29, 2018, www.sciencealert.com/scientists-have-found-a-woman-whose-eyes-have-a-whole-new-type-of-colour-receptor.

4. "Colors," *RadioLab*, WNYC Studios, May 21, 2012.

ity to see. Seeing itself is a gift from God. As Paul says, "God was pleased to reveal his Son to me, so that I might proclaim him among the nations" (Gal 1:15b–16a). When Paul has a revelation of the risen Christ, it changes the world as he knows it. He cannot un-see or un-know this experience. Paul is given a new pair of lenses that enable him to view the power of God redeeming, reclaiming, renewing, and rectifying the world all around him.

The power of those lenses cannot be overstated. Before this revelation, Paul was a zealous persecutor of God's church, an agent of its destruction (Gal 1:13: cf. 1 Cor 15:9). Acts portrays Saul as nothing more than a persecutor, ravaging the church and snatching away its members in chains (Acts 7:58; 8:1–3; and 9:1–2). He was intent on killing this Jesus movement, until encountering the resurrected Christ. To Paul's astonishment, God resurrected this Jewish, miracle-working hillbilly whose grass-root-like movement refused to die on that Roman cross. Seeing the risen Christ transforms Paul's perspective and causes him to rethink what he thought he knew about God and God's actions in the world. It is little wonder that Acts portrays this revelation as blinding, with something like scales falling off Paul's eyes (Acts 9:1–19; cf. 22:6–16; 26:12–18).

Paul sees that God has defeated death by raising Jesus. In Christ, Paul realizes the embodiment of life abundant. He sees the power of God's Spirit rippling through the universe, defeating sin's power at every turn. A war is raging in the world all around us, and God is winning. Paul sees this with clarity, but he also believes that sin has enslaved humanity and indeed the whole cosmos. He trusts that the God who raised Jesus from the dead, the God who revealed Jesus to him (Gal 1:12, 15–16), will also save *all* those who place their trust in him. God's *shalom* is being revealed, and that shalom is for all who trust in God. All can participate. God cares for all God's creation. This is good news. But Paul believes that time is running out. Christ will return soon to eradicate all injustice. Paul's mission is urgent. He is firmly convinced that this world is passing away (1 Cor 7:31). He sees glimpses of God's new creation, and it is glorious. But sin has enslaved and blinded others so they do not have eyes to see what is really happening. Paul longs to share his vision with anyone who will listen.

Even though the vision of the risen Christ comes with such clarity and transforms Paul's whole way of seeing the world and his whole life, the gospel is still enveloped in mystery. Mantis shrimp can see colors that we could never even imagine, but their brains are too small to process what they are seeing. Revelation is a gift from God, but revelation is still a mystery. We may catch a glimpse of God's kingdom, and at times, that glimpse is seen and *felt* with great clarity, but it remains a mystery to us how to recapture it. We do not own it. We do not control it. And yet God lets us participate in it. It defies our imaginations to describe it. Its beauty is beyond words. It captures us. It even enslaves us—not by the might of a forceful hand, but by its captivating love.

New Creation and the Witness of the Church

The gospel creates whole communities who, by the power of God's Holy Spirit, cultivate the "mind of Christ" in their midst. The church is called to embody the love that Christ demonstrated and look to the interests of others. It is not always easy to know how to embody that love, though.

As demonstrated in Paul's letter to the Galatians, the temptation can be to follow a set of rules or, in the Galatians' case, the law. While Paul affirms that the law is holy and just and good (Rom 7:12), following the law cannot actually bring life (Gal 3:19-21). The Galatians would do anything to advance in their faith. Grown men were even willing to be circumcised! Paul argues that the fruit of the Spirit rather than circumcision is the sign of new creation. Willingness to love sacrificially is certainly a sign of the Spirit's work. In Gal 5:13-14, Paul exhorts the Galatians to "become slaves to one another through love. For the whole law is summed up in a single commandment, 'You shall love your neighbor as yourself.'" Bearing one another's burdens is related to fulfilling the "law of Christ" (Gal 6:2). In fact, Paul here sounds a lot like Jesus, who came "not to abolish the law but to fulfill it" (Matt 5:17-20). The Galatians are tempted to place their trust in the law to lead to abundant life. Paul wants them to model Christ and follow the intent of the law. Like Jesus's teaching in the famous antitheses in the Sermon on the Mount (Matt 5:21-48), Paul is raising the stakes, not lowering them.

What would it look like to fulfill the law? One of my students once asked me this question in class, but he added a spin, "What would it look like to fulfill the law of speeding?" Of course, at this question, every student perked up. Apparently most in the room were guilty of breaking this law (the professor included). Obeying the law of speeding is not the same as fulfilling the law, though. Let me explain. The speeding laws are designed for safety. When my home state of Arkansas raised the speed limit on its interstates to 70 mph, I was elated. My husband and I lived out of state, and this would cut down our drive time to visit our family. On a family visit where we were talking about this new law with our state-trooper relatives, I heard the downside. There would be more fatalities when accidents occur. The speeders would only further increase their speed over 70 mph, and the roads were not designed for cars to go that fast. Plus, raising the speed limit did not remove the other variables—drunk drivers, deer crossing the road, the illegal tractor entering the roadway, and general driving stupidity. The speed limit was designed for the driver's safety, but a driver could obey this law and still be harmed by other variables. In short, *following the law did not guarantee life*. The speed limit was a guide. It could point out when people were driving unsafely, but it could not prevent them from doing so.

What would it look like to fulfill the law of speeding? To fulfill the law would require fulfilling the intention of the law. The law was designed to get people from point A to point B safely. In fact, all the traffic laws were designed for people's safety. Even if we all follow all the traffic laws all the time, there are still variables that are outside the laws' control—acts of nature, animal crossings, a driver's health, nightmarish traffic, etc. To fulfill these laws would be to create a way for a person to get from point A to point B safely 100 percent of the time. I have no idea what that looks like. It is hard to imagine how magnificent it would be to travel this way, but our culture's love of science fiction attempts a few examples. Perhaps we could use Portkeys or Apparate like the wizard world of Harry Potter, ask Scotty to beam us up like Captain Kirk in *Star Trek*, or fly around in Wonder Woman's invisible jet. Of course, even these systems have their flaws. The point is this: If you had access to a perfect teleportation system—a system that guarantees safe and efficient travel 100 percent of the time, who would want to go back to the way things were?

To turn back to the biblical text, the law was a guide to help Israel be a nation where each person had what was needed for abundant life. The intention of the law was a just, fair, and equitable society that would be a light to the nations. The law was indeed holy, just, and good (Rom 7:12). The commandments, however, could not create or guarantee abundant life for all (Gal 3:21). Though people were called to love their neighbors as themselves, the law could not produce a people who loved sacrificially. The law could only point out where people were failing to demonstrate that love. Weakened by the flesh (Rom 8:3), the law was impotent in its struggle against sin. Christ, however, in his victory over sin and death, fulfills the intention of the law through his sacrificial love for all. "To fulfill the law of Christ" (Gal 6:2) is to love as Christ has loved—sacrificially for the sake of another.

Good News for the Least of These

The church is called to embody Christ's love in our world, to love our neighbors as ourselves, to be beacons of God's light, and to embody the kind of abundant life that God wants for all creation. The church is called to be "new creation" in the midst of the "present evil age." New creation is the abundant, Spirit-filled life of God's kingdom. New creation is the restoration of the created order. It is a place where sin has been defeated and the corruption of sin has been eradicated. It is beyond a restoration of paradise; it is the blessed life that God always wanted for creation.

God's Spirit transforms the believers into people who have the ability to *love*. Paul has a high view of the church's calling because he operates with an extraordinary view of God's power. Believers cannot become "new" on their own, nor can they somehow work hard enough to usher in God's kingdom. These are acts of God. The transformative power of God's Spirit creates a community of individuals who are "in Christ." They become Christ's body in the world. In Rom 15:7–13, Paul shares a vision of what this eschatological community looks like. Using the voices of the Prophets, the Writings, and the Law, Paul envisions a church of every tribe and nation praising God together. What might be boundaries to the outside world are not barriers in the church. The "least" in the larger society are not considered inferior or dispensable in the church. Rather, the church is called to be a place that honors the diversity of God's creation and welcomes all in its midst. In Paul's perspective, the church who walks by the Spirit in the midst of this "present evil age" (Gal 1:4) will truly be a light to the world.

What Is at Stake? A Lesson from First Church Corinth

Jesus's actions on the cross—his sacrificial love for all—embodies what it means to live a life worthy of the gospel (Phil 1:27). It seems only fitting to conclude a book on Paul and the "least of these" by appealing to a passage in which the apostle accuses the Corinthians of failing to remember Jesus when they fail to include the least at the table. In 1 Cor 11:17–34, we have instructions regarding the Lord's Supper. It is the only place in all Paul's letters that mentions the Eucharist. If the Corinthians had not been abusing the table, we would not know that Paul's gentile churches were engaging in a ritual that remembers and proclaims the night of Jesus's death.

Before reciting Jesus's breaking of the bread and drinking of the cup, though, Paul describes a bit of the scene at the Corinthian table as he has heard it, presumably from Chloe's people (1 Cor 1:11). In 1 Cor 11:17–22, it is apparent that there are divisions among the believers whenever they are performing the ritual. Some have food and drink, and others go hungry. This is not like any church potluck I have ever experienced. Then again, the culture in which I grew up was very different from that of Roman Corinth. My parents entertained guests often. Rather than place all the food on the table, since our table was neither large enough to hold all the food nor all the guests, it was our tradition to serve "buffet style" from the kitchen. As members of the host family, we knew to honor our guests by letting them go through the line first. This is what our Southern culture expected from us—to serve the best food to our guests. The church potluck was no different. The dishes were set out in an appealing line-up on fold-up tables that had been bleached down and covered with worn tablecloths. All were welcome, and people typically ate too much—especially the men, who made quite the show of having too much dessert to choose from. The small church of my childhood could not fathom a church gathering where some would sit hungry.

This could not be further from Corinthian culture. Roman hospitality was designed to showcase social distinctions and to remind all of their place in society. The Roman writer Juvenal pokes fun at Roman table etiquette. The host serves the choicest foods to the most important guests, adequate food to the guests who are important, but not as influential as the top tier, and cheap scraps of food to everyone else (e.g., a lobster garnished with asparagus versus a crab and half an egg; *Satires* 5.80–91). As Pliny the Younger notes, every guest at a dinner party was graded: "The best dishes were set in front of himself and a select few, and cheap scraps of food before the rest of the company. He had even put the wine into tiny little flasks, divided into three categories, not with the idea of giving his guests the opportunity of choosing, but to make it impossible for them to refuse what they were given. One lot was intended for himself and for us, another for his lesser friends (all his friends are graded), and the third for his and our freemen."[5] Some made the A list, some the B list, and some were considered lucky that they were on the premises. To make matters worse, even the seats in the dining room were graded. The dining room was called a "triclinium," because there were three couches: one for the host and the most important guests, one for the lesser guests, and one for the least of the company.

As if the dining-room etiquette were not offensive enough, the sheer challenge of the gathering space further complicated the church's meeting.

---

5. *Letters* 2.6 (Radice, LCL).

In the closing of Rom 16 where Paul sends greetings from some in Corinth to the churches in Rome, he mentions Gaius, who can host the whole Corinthian church in his home (Rom 16:23). Given that Paul uses the qualifier "whole," it is possible that the whole assembly does not gather each and every time.[6] Nonetheless, Gaius has a house. This fact alone means he is not among those "who have nothing" (1 Cor 11:22). The odds of his dining room being large enough to cram in the whole church are slim to none. Most large dining rooms could hold only nine diners.[7] Yet First Church Corinth has far more than nine people. We cannot know with certainty how many people are part of the church. From the evidence in Acts 18, Rom 16, and the Corinthian correspondence, at least sixteen individuals are affiliated with this community, and some of these are heads of households. Paul explicitly mentions the household of Stephanus (1 Cor 1:16). Since households included a large number of people, from blood relatives to servants, and since many in the church appear to be married (e.g., 1 Cor 7:1-7), the church could have as many as fifty to one hundred people. Some would even estimate more. Clearly, the invitation list has exceeded the space available at the venue.

With only a handful of diners able to eat in the dining room, this meant that others had to cram into the spaces available. The most obvious choice of space would be the atrium, a courtyard surrounded by a colonnade. The atrium would be open to the elements. There would be a small pool in the middle to collect rainwater and to help reflect light into the surrounding rooms. This would not be an ideal place to dine.

The space is not the only dilemma. According to 1 Cor 11, folks are arriving at different times. With the average laborer working from sunup to sundown, there are real limits on how early a church gathering could start. Whenever the workers arrive, though, they find that some have already been there long enough to be full and drunk (1 Cor 11:21). Even if they are among the fortunate ones who come earlier, they might be among the "have-nots" who get to witness the food being delivered from the kitchen to those leisurely reclining in the triclinium. There would be no expectation in Roman culture that the host provide for those in the courtyard whatever was served in the triclinium. Furthermore, those reclining in the triclinium are most likely of the same social class as Gaius. They have

---

6. Jerome Murphy-O'Connor, *St. Paul's Corinth* (Collegeville, MN: Liturgical, 2002), 183.

7. Murphy-O'Connor, *St. Paul's Corinth*, 180.

the ability to arrive early and to start their happy hour because they most likely do not work with their own hands for a living. Based on how Paul describes his manual labor (1 Cor 9:6; cf. 4:12), some in the church find this work demeaning.[8] They are part of a social class that is not expected to get their hands dirty. Gerd Theissen has famously argued that the social stratification of the Corinthian church is at the root of many of the church's issues.[9] In 1 Cor 11:17-22, there are divisions between the "haves" and the "have-nots." Some have plenty, and some have nothing. Some have homes to eat in before they come, and others arrive late, presumably because they have had to work all day.

Nothing in Corinthian culture would teach these disparate classes of people to love each other. Their social norms are designed to maintain the hegemonic structures that preserve the power and privilege of a select few. As discussed in chapter 1, those who are of elevated social status, though not many, might be attracted to the church because it is a place in their society where they can be influential figures, benefactors, to a small group of people. This would bring them some honor. Of course, it would be easier to claim the title of benefactor if Paul, the founder of the community, would take money from these patrons, which he flatly refuses to do (1 Cor 9:1-27). Receiving their money would place him in a situation where he could not correct their behavior. Given that some of their behavior is wreaking havoc in the church (e.g., 1 Cor 4:9-13; 5:1-13; 6:1-11; 8:1-11:1), he does not need to be indebted to them. The differences among these classes of people are real, and Paul expects the Corinthians not just to tolerate one another, but also to love each other.

The enactment of cultural norms in the assembly prompts strong language from Paul. For the apostle, a table where some are drunk and sated while others go hungry is not the Lord's Table at all (11:20-21). Paul likens the Corinthians' behavior to despising God's church and humiliating those who have nothing (11:22). The rich are treated with honor, and the rest are not even given the dignity of receiving food and drink. This is a meal like

---

8. See Ronald F. Hock, *The Social Context of Paul's Ministry: Tentmaking and Apostleship* (Philadelphia: Fortress, 1980); also Hock, "Paul's Tentmaking and the Problem of His Social Class," *JBL* 97 (1978): 555-64; cf. Todd D. Still, "Did Paul Loathe Manual Labor? Revisiting the Work of Ronald F. Hock on the Apostle's Tentmaking and Social Class," *JBL* 125 (2006): 781-95.

9. Gerd Theissen, *The Social Setting of Pauline Christianity: Essays on Corinth*, ed. and trans. John H. Schütz (Philadelphia: Fortress, 1982).

any other meal in their culture. The only difference is that they do appear to be going through the motions of celebrating the bread and cup of the Lord in the midst of this selfish potluck. This church thinks that it is celebrating the Eucharist. However, the way in which they are going about it demonstrates that they are not remembering Jesus.

To correct their behavior, Paul rehearses the tradition as he passed it on to them (11:23–26). He reminds them of the night when Christ was handed over (*paradidōmi*) for their trespasses. Though our English translations often interpret *paradidōmi* as "betrayed," a reference to the Judas tradition, Paul does not cite the Judas tradition elsewhere. He does, however, use this same verb in Romans to refer to Jesus's death. In Rom 4:25, Paul writes that Jesus is handed over to death for our trespasses, and in Rom 8:32, he makes it explicit that God is the one handing Jesus over.[10] Richard Hays notes the connection between the language that Paul uses to describe Jesus and the language used in the Septuagint to depict the suffering servant.[11]

> Isa 53:6 LXX: "And the Lord gave him up (*paradidōmi*) for our sins."
> Isa 53:12b LXX: "and he bore the sins of many, and on account of their iniquities he was handed over (*paradidōmi*)."

In other words, Paul's use of the language coincides with the prophetic witness of one who willingly submitted to God's will, who gave himself up for the sake of others. Remembering Jesus's death is more than breaking bread and drinking from the cup; it is remembering and enacting Jesus's actions. The charge—"Do this in remembrance of me"—is not about going through the motions of a ritual. Christ's body and blood were sacrificed "for you" (1 Cor 11:24). To echo Paul's words in Romans, Jesus was handed over to death for our trespasses. In 1 Cor 11:26, Paul says, "as often as you eat this bread and drink the cup, you proclaim the Lord's death until he comes." Merely consuming the elements does not distinguish this meal from any other. The church is called to remember Jesus's actions of willingly giving himself up for our sins by being willing to love as Christ has loved—beginning with the person sitting beside them in the assembly.

---

10. For an excellent discussion of *paradidōmi* (handed over), see Gaventa, *Our Mother Saint Paul*, 113–23.

11. Richard B. Hays, *First Corinthians*, IBC (Louisville: Westminster John Knox, 1997), 198.

Enacting the table rightly demands corporate responsibility. Though examining oneself is certainly part of the ritual (1 Cor 11:28), it can be tempting to be focused on one's own feelings and forget how one's behaviors in the community affect others. Paul calls the church to "discern the body" in 1 Cor 11:29. Remembering Jesus's body in the Eucharist is linked to remembering others who comprise the "body of Christ." Getting the Corinthians to have the mindset of Christ has been a constant refrain in this letter since the beginning (see 1 Cor 1:10-2:16). This is by no means the first time in 1 Corinthians that Paul has had to teach those who have status to consider the needs of others. In 1 Cor 8, he says the actions of the "know-it-alls" are destroying their brother or sister for whom Christ died (1 Cor 8:11). Now, here at a feast that is supposed to enact Christ's love even unto death, the Corinthians' table etiquette has only reinstilled their culture's way of honoring those of high status and excluding the poor. Paul offers some very practical advice: "When you come together to eat, wait for one another. If you are hungry, eat at home" (1 Cor 11:33b-34a). Another way to translate these instructions is: welcome one another. In other words, do not simply wait for someone to walk in the door so that you can start eating. Honor those who have come in after a long day's work as you would honor a guest. Show hospitality to the "have-nots" who must arrive later but who are nonetheless a vital part of this body. Give those who would not ever be invited to a banquet a seat of honor. Not only are all welcome here, but *it is not the Lord's banquet without them.*

The implications of Paul's instructions are unsettling: If all are not welcome at this table, then it is not really the Lord's Table at all. If the believers' actions exclude a brother or sister for whom Christ died, then the church is not remembering Jesus's death. If only those of the same socioeconomic status are gathered around the table, then this practice looks nothing like the sacrificial love of Christ, who relinquished his status for all—even for the least.

At the heart of Paul's ethical instructions for the Lord's Table is the christological paradigm visible in the hymn (Phil 2:5-11). Christ, though having equality with God, made himself nothing, taking the very form of a servant. Christ willingly relinquished his rights and status for those who were unworthy. In Romans, Paul even calls humanity "enemies" of God (Rom 5:10). The christological paradigm of self-lowering (Phil 2:5-11) is central to Paul's view of the gospel. This model includes service and solidarity with the "least of these," in whose form the Son of God chooses to reside (Phil 2:7).

The Philippian hymn is divided into two parts: Christ's humiliation and God's exaltation of Jesus. The poem illustrates Jesus's refusal to exploit his status and emphasizes his humility. Multiple clauses and qualifiers highlight this humiliation: Jesus "emptied himself, taking the form of a slave, being born in human likeness. And being found in human form, he humbled himself and became obedient to the point of death—even death on a cross." Thus, Jesus suffers humiliation in the form of his life *and* in the form of his death. In similar fashion, in the second half of the hymn, God's "super-exaltation" of Jesus is also exaggerated to emphasize the greatness of his name and the worthiness of his worship by all (Phil 2:9-11). God "gave him the name that is above every name, so that at the name of Jesus every knee should bend, in heaven and on earth and under the earth, and every tongue should confess that Jesus Christ is Lord, to the glory of God the Father" (Phil 2:9b-11).

The hymn illustrates the instructions in the verses that precede it. In Phil 2:3-4, the apostle charges the church: "Do nothing from selfish ambition or conceit, but in humility regard others as better than yourselves. Let each of you look not to your own interests, but to the interests of others." The nations have no concept of charity or love purely for the sake of another. Christ's example is more than a paradigm to emulate. Paul wants them to "have the same mind" as Christ (Phil 2:5). Richard Hays calls this a "conversion of the imagination."[12]

Christ's willingness to relinquish his status for the sake of the world's salvation becomes the filter through which Paul sees his world. It is the reason that Paul willingly suffers mistreatment, abuse, and danger for the sake of carrying out his gospel mission. This cruciform paradigm is also at the heart of his instructions to the churches. For example, before he corrects the problems in First Church Corinth, Paul reminds the Corinthians of the topsy-turvy nature of the gospel (1 Cor 1:18-2:16). God, in God's wisdom, chose the foolish things of the world, in order to demonstrate God's power. The scandal of the cross is the very wisdom of God, but this will never make sense by the world's standards. This willingness to allow the cross to shape one's mindset and behavior is to have the "mind of Christ" (1 Cor 2:16).

For churches who are reading Paul's letters today—especially as we seek to remember Jesus's death—Paul's admonitions challenge us. I wonder what Paul would think of our twenty-first-century churches. Who is

---

12. Hays, *First Corinthians*, 11.

absent around our tables? Whom have we excluded from the table? What "gospel" is being proclaimed by our Lord's Supper practices? Is the Lord's sacrificial love visible in our table etiquette? Or are we, like the believers two thousand years ago, still allowing our cultural norms to dictate the depths of our love toward one another? How have we relinquished power and privilege to welcome, as an honored guest, the least and most vulnerable in our society? From Paul's perspective, if we are failing to do these things, we are just going through the motions. We might be verbalizing Jesus's words and partaking of the bread and cup, but, if we are not loving and welcoming to all, it is not really the Lord's death that we remember and proclaim. Therefore, it cannot really be the Lord's Supper.

Conclusion

The gospel that Paul preaches obliterates any distinctions used in our culture to foster hierarchy, privilege, and power. As good as this news is, it creates scandal, disrupts the status quo, and demands allegiance from all who place their trust in it. I can imagine that many, if not most, of those who hear Paul preaching think that he is crazy. His insistence that this world is passing away (1 Cor 7:31) might be akin to Chicken Little running around declaring that the sky is falling. A few people somehow get past the "foolishness" of a Jewish peasant being killed on a Roman cross (1 Cor 1:18–25) and, by the grace of God, see what Paul sees, a resurrected Lord who beckons them to follow. Though Peter's sermon on the day of Pentecost is met with thousands of converts (Acts 2:41), Paul's work seems to yield converts in the dozens. When he does have more success, he finds himself at the center of murder plots, brought before government officials, beaten, imprisoned, stoned, or kicked out of town. We have no idea how this treatment may have affected the enthusiasm of those initial curious followers. Based on his letters, though, these congregations are not huge churches scattered throughout the empire. They are churches with people who are struggling with what it means to live in faithfulness to a jealous God, the God of Israel, the God of a people from a foreign land. This gospel makes demands on them. It is not enough for them to believe that God is actively at work rectifying the world, now they must embody Christ's love in the world.

Having the mind of Christ looks like standing in solidarity with the least, considering the needs of others, and willingly relinquishing one's own status for the sake of another's well-being. This mindset does not engage in self-promotion or seek selfish interests. It seeks to love others as Christ has loved us. The famous "love chapter" of 1 Cor 13 is not about weddings; it is about how believers are called to love. The whole of the Christian witness is based on this countercultural *agapē* love. It is love with expectation of nothing in return. In Roman culture, it is perhaps the least noble of the kinds of love.[13] It is love linked to the pity you might have for a beggar rather than the familial love (*philia*) that causes you to risk life and limb for the security of your household or the passionate love you might share with a lover (*erōs*). *Agapē* is love that you give away freely even when you have everything to lose and nothing to gain. Loving like Christ has loved looks like a crazy kind of love that keeps no records of wrongs nor insists on its own way. It is patient, kind, enduring, resilient, and hopeful. It is a love that honors the least among us and humbles the proud. It is a kind of love that simply does not make sense in our culture. It is the love that God has shown for us in Jesus and the kind of love that God's Spirit enables us to embody in our world, especially to the "least of these."

FURTHER READING

Gorman, Michael J. *Becoming the Gospel: Paul, Participation, and Mission.* Grand Rapids: Eerdmans, 2015. *Becoming the Gospel* is the third in a trilogy, building on the arguments of *Cruciformity: Paul's Narrative Spirituality of the Cross* and *Inhabiting the Cruciform God: Kenosis, Justification, and Theosis in Paul's Narrative Soteriology.* In *Becoming the Gospel,* Gorman combines missiology and hermeneutics in his quest to read Paul's letters missionally.

Gaventa, Beverly Roberts. *When in Romans: An Invitation to Linger with the Gospel according to Paul.* Grand Rapids: Baker, 2016. In this series of lectures, Gaventa provides a grand scope of the larger themes of Romans. This book provides an accessible way to engage deep theological concepts.

---

13. Sarah Ruden, *Paul among the People: The Apostle Reinterpreted and Reimagined in His Own Time* (New York: Pantheon, 2010), 171–72.

Bibliography

Aarlandson, James M. *Women, Class, and Society in Early Christianity*. Peabody, MA: Hendrickson, 1997.
Aasgaard, Reidar. "Children in Antiquity and Early Christianity: Research History and Central Issues." *Familia* 33 (2006): 23-46.
———. "Like a Child: Paul's Rhetorical Uses of Childhood." Pages 249-77 in *The Child in the Bible*. Edited by Marcia J. Bunge. Grand Rapids: Eerdmans, 2008.
———. "*My Beloved Brothers and Sisters!*" *Christian Siblingship in Paul*. JSNTSup 265. Early Christianity in Context 2. London: T&T Clark, 2004.
———. "Paul as a Child: Children and Childhood in the Letters of the Apostle." *JBL* 126 (2007): 129-59.
Allmen, Daniel von. *La Famille de Dieu: la symbolique familiale dans le paulinisme*. Fribourg: Éditions Universitaires. Göttingen: Vandenhoeck & Ruprecht, 1981.
Anderson, Herbert, and Susan B. W. Johnson. *Regarding Children*. Louisville: Westminster John Knox, 1994.
Armstrong, David. "All Things to All Men: Philodemus' Model of Therapy and the Audience of *De Morte*." Pages 15-54 in *Philodemus and the New Testament World*. Edited by John T. Fitzgerald, Dirk Obbink, and Glenn S. Holland. Leiden: Brill, 2004.
Atkins, Margaret, and Robin Osborne. *Poverty in the Roman World*. Cambridge: Cambridge University Press, 2006.
Bakke, O. M. *Childhood in Early Christian Traditions*. Translated by Brian P. McNeil. Minneapolis: Fortress, 2005.
Balla, Peter. *The Child-Parent Relationship in the New Testament and Its Environment*. WUNT 135. Tübingen: Mohr Siebeck, 2003.
Barclay, John M. G. "Jesus and Paul." Pages 492-503 in *Dictionary of Paul and His Letters*. Edited by Gerald F. Hawthorne, Ralph P. Martin, and Daniel G. Reid. Downers Grove, IL: InterVarsity, 1993.
———. *Paul and the Gift*. Grand Rapids: Eerdmans, 2015.

———. "Paul, Philemon, and the Dilemma of Christian Slave Ownership." *NTS* 37 (1991): 161–86.

———. "Paul's Story: Theology as Testimony." Pages 133–56 in *Narrative Dynamics in Paul: A Critical Assessment*. Edited by Bruce W. Longenecker. Louisville: Westminster John Knox, 2002.

———. "Poverty in Pauline Studies: A Response to Steven Friesen." *JSNT* 26 (2004): 363–66.

Barnett, Paul. *Paul: Missionary of Jesus*. Grand Rapids: Eerdmans, 2008.

Barrett, C. K. "Jesus and the Word." Pages 213–23 in *Jesus and the Word, and Other Essays*. Edinburgh: T&T Clark, 1995.

———. *The First Epistle to the Corinthians*. Black's New Testament Commentary. Peabody, MA: Hendrickson, 1996.

Bartchy, S. S. Mallon. *Chrēsai: First-Century Slavery and the Interpretation of 1 Corinthians 7:21*. SBLDS. Missoula, MT: Scholars, 1973.

Betz, H. D. *Galatians*. Hermeneia. Philadelphia: Fortress, 1979.

Blank, Josef. *Paulus und Jesus: Eine theologische Grundlegung*. SANT 18. Munich: Kösel-Verlag, 1968.

Blomberg, Craig. *Neither Poverty nor Riches: A Biblical Theology of Possessions*. New Studies in Biblical Theology. Downers Grove, IL: InterVarsity, 2000.

Blount, Brian. *Invasion of the Dead: Preaching Resurrection*. Louisville: Westminster John Knox, 2014.

———, ed. *True to Our Native Land: An African American New Testament Commentary*. Minneapolis: Fortress, 2007.

Bockmuehl, Markus. "1 Thessalonians 2:14–16 and the Church in Jerusalem." *TynBul* 52 (2001): 1–31.

———. "Simon Peter and Bethsaida." Pages 55–91 in *The Missions of James, Peter and Paul: Tensions in Early Christianity*. Edited by Bruce D. Chilton and Craig A. Evans. NovTSup 115. Leiden: Brill, 2005.

Boer, Martinus C. de. *Galatians*. NTL. Louisville: Westminster John Knox, 2011.

———. "Paul and Apocalyptic Eschatology." Pages 345–83 in *The Origins of Apocalypticism in Judaism and Christianity*, vol. 1 of *The Encyclopedia of Apcalypticism*. Edited by John J. Collins. New York: Continuum, 1998.

Borg, Marcus J. "An Appreciative Disagreement." Pages 227–43 in *Jesus & the Restoration of Israel: A Critical Assessment of N. T. Wright's Jesus and the Victory of God*. Edited by Carey C. Newman. Downers Grove, IL: InterVarsity, 1999.

Böttrich, Christfried. "Petrus und Paulus in Antiochen (Gal 2,11–21)." *BTZ* 19 (2002): 224–39.

Boyarin, Daniel. *A Radical Jew: Paul and the Politics of Identity*. Berkeley: University of California Press, 1994.

———. *Border Lines: The Partition of Judaeo-Christianity*. Philadelphia: University of Pennsylvania Press, 2004.

Bradley, Keith R. *Discovering the Roman Family: Studies in Roman Social History*. New York: Oxford University Press, 1991.
Braxton, Brad R. *No Longer Slaves: Galatians and African American Experience*. Collegeville, MN: Liturgical, 2002.
Bruce, F. F. *1 and 2 Corinthians*. Grand Rapids: Eerdmans, 1971.
———. *Paul and Jesus*. London: SPCK, 1974.
Brueggemann, Walter. *The Land: Place as Gift, Promise, and Challenge in Biblical Faith*. Philadelphia: Fortress, 1977.
Buckland, W. W. *The Roman Law of Slavery*. Cambridge: Cambridge University Press, 1908.
Bultmann, Rudolf. "Jesus and Paul." Pages 183-201 in *Existence and Faith*. London: Hodder & Stoughton, 1961.
———. *Jesus and the Word*. London: Nicholson & Watson, 1935.
———. "The Significance of the Historical Jesus for the Theology of Paul." Pages 220-46 in *Faith and Understanding*. New York: Harper & Row, 1966.
Bunge, Marcia J., ed. *The Child in the Bible*. Grand Rapids: Eerdmans, 2008.
———, ed. *The Child in Christian Thought*. Grand Rapids: Eerdmans, 2001.
———. "The Child, Religion, and the Academy: Developing Robust Theological and Religious Understandings of Childhood." *JR* 86 (2006): 549-79.
Burge, Gary M. "Land." Pages 570-75 in *The New Interpreter's Dictionary of the Bible*. Nashville: Abingdon, 2008.
Burke, Trevor J. *Family Matters: A Socio-Historical Study of Kinship Metaphors in 1 Thessalonians*. JSNTSup 247. London: T&T Clark International/Continuum, 2003.
———. "Paul's Role as 'Father' to His Corinthian 'Children' in Socio-Historical Context (1 Corinthians 4:14-21)." Pages 95-113 in *Paul and the Corinthians: Studies on a Community in Conflict: Essays in Honour of Margaret Thrall*. Edited by Trevor J. Burke and J. Keith Elliott. Leiden: Brill, 2003.
Byrne, Brendan. *Romans*. SP. Collegeville, MN: Liturgical, 2007.
Byrskog, Samuel. "A New Perspective on the Jesus Tradition: Reflections on James D. G. Dunn's *Jesus Remembered*." *JSNT* 26 (2004): 459-71.
Caird, George B. *Principalities and Powers: A Study in Pauline Theology*. Oxford: Clarendon, 1956.
Campbell, Barth. "Flesh and Spirit in 1 Cor 5:5: An Exercise in Rhetorical Criticism of the New Testament." *JETS* 36 (1993): 331-42.
Campbell, Douglas A. *Framing Paul: An Epistolary Biography*. Grand Rapids: Eerdmans, 2014.
Campbell, Ken M. *Marriage and Family in the Biblical World*. Downers Grove, IL: InterVarsity, 2003.
Carter, Warren. *Matthew and the Margins: A Sociopolitical and Religious Reading*. Sheffield: Sheffield Academic, 2000.
Cassidy, Richard J. *Paul in Chains: Roman Imprisonment and the Letters of St. Paul*. New York: Crossroad, 2001.

Castelli, Elisabeth A. *Imitating Paul: A Discourse of Power*. Louisville: Westminster John Knox, 1991.

Catchpole, David. "Q's Thesis and Paul's Antithesis." Pages 347-66 in *Forschungen zum Neuen Testament und seiner Umwelt: Festschrift für Albert Fuchs*. Edited by C. Niemand. Linzer Philosophisch-Theologische Beiträge 7. Frankfurt: Peter Lang, 2002.

Cherry, David, ed. *The Roman World: A Sourcebook*. Oxford: Wiley Blackwell, 2001.

Chilton, Bruce. "Jesus and the Repentance of E. P. Sanders." *TynBul* 39 (1988): 1-18.

Chilton, Bruce D., and Craig A. Evans. *The Missions of James, Peter and Paul: Tensions in Early Christianity*. NovTSup 115. Leiden: Brill, 2005.

Chow, J. "Patronage in Roman Corinth." Pages 104-25 in *Paul and Empire: Religion and Power in Roman Imperial Society*. Edited by R. A. Horsley. Harrisburg: Trinity, 1997.

Clarke, Anthony. *Secular and Christian Leadership in Corinth: A Socio-Historical and Exegetical Study of 1 Corinthians 1-6*. Leiden: Brill, 1993.

Cohen, Shaye J. D., ed. *The Jewish Family in Antiquity*. BJS 289. Atlanta: Scholars Press, 1993.

Cohick, Lynn. *Women in the World of the Earliest Christians: Illuminating Ancient Ways of Life*. Grand Rapids: Baker Academic, 2009.

Collins, Adela Yarbro. "The Function of 'Excommunication' in Paul." *HTR* 73 (1980): 251-63.

Connolly, Joy. "Mastering Corruption: Constructions of Identity in Roman Oratory." Pages 130-51 in *Women and Slaves in Greco-Roman Culture: Differential Equations*. Edited by Sandra R. Joshel and Sheila Murnaghan. London: Routledge, 1998.

Conzelmann, Hans. *First Corinthians*. Hermeneia. Philadelphia: Fortress, 1975.

Cousar, Charles B. *Galatians*. IBC. Louisville: Westminster John Knox, 1982.

———. *The Theology of the Cross: The Death of Jesus in the Pauline Letters*. OBT. Minneapolis: Fortress, 1990.

Couture, Pamela. *Seeing Children, Seeing God: A Practical Theology of Children and Poverty*. Nashville: Abingdon, 2000.

Cox, Cheryl Anne. *Household Interests: Property, Marriage Strategies, and Family Dynamics in Ancient Athens*. Princeton: Princeton University Press, 1998.

Cranfield, C. E. B. *The Epistle to the Romans*. ICC. 2 vols. Edinburgh: T&T Clark, 1975-79.

Crossan, John Dominic, and Jonathan L. Reed. *In Search of Paul: How Jesus's Apostle Opposed Rome's Empire with God's Kingdom; A New Vision of Paul's Words and World*. San Francisco: HarperSanFrancisco, 2004.

Davies, W. D. *The Gospel and the Land: Early Christianity and Jewish Territorial Doctrine*. Berkeley: University of California Press, 1974.

Davies, W. D., and Dale C. Allison. *A Critical and Exegetical Commentary on the Gospel according to Saint Matthew*. ICC. 3 vols. Edinburgh: T&T Clark, 1988-97.

Dawn, Marva. *Is It a Lost Cause? Having the Heart of God for the Church's Children.* Grand Rapids: Eerdmans, 1997.
Deissmann, A. *Paul: A Study in Social and Religious History.* New York: Hodder and Stoughton, 1926.
Demand, Nancy. *Birth, Death, and Motherhood in Classical Greece.* Baltimore: Johns Hopkins University Press, 1994.
DeVries, Dawn. "Toward a Theology of Childhood." *Int* 55 (2001): 161-73.
Dixon, Suzanne, ed. *Childhood, Class and Kin in the Roman World.* London: Routledge, 2001.
———. *The Roman Family.* Ancient Society and History. Baltimore: Johns Hopkins University Press, 1992.
———. *The Roman Mother.* Norman: Oklahoma University Press, 1988.
Downs, David. *Alms: Charity, Reward, and Atonement in Early Christianity.* Waco: Baylor University Press, 2016.
———. *The Offering of the Gentiles: Paul's Collection for Jerusalem in Its Chronological, Cultural, and Cultic Contexts.* WUNT 2.248. Tübingen: Mohr Siebeck, 2008.
Dungan, David L. *The Sayings of Jesus in the Churches of Paul: The Use of the Synoptic Tradition in the Regulation of Early Church Life.* Philadelphia: Fortress, 1971.
Dunn, James D. G. *Jesus, Paul, and the Law: Studies in Mark and Galatians.* Louisville: Westminster John Knox, 1990.
———. "Jesus Tradition in Paul." Pages 155-78 in *Studying the Historical Jesus: Evaluations of the State of Current Research.* Edited by Bruce Chilton and Craig A. Evans. NTTS 19. Leiden: Brill, 1994.
———. "Paul's Knowledge of the Jesus Tradition: The Evidence of Romans." Pages 193-207 in *Christus bezeugen: Festschrift für Wolfgang Trillig zum 65. Geburtstag.* Edited by Karl Kertelge, Taugott Holtz, and Claus-Peter März. Freiburg: Herder, 1990.
———. "Prolegomena to a Theology of Paul." *NTS* 40 (1994): 407-32.
———. *The Theology of Paul the Apostle.* Grand Rapids: Eerdmans, 1998.
———. *The Theology of Paul's Letter to the Galatians.* New Testament Theology. Cambridge: Cambridge University Press, 1993.
Eastman, Susan. *Rediscovering Paul's Mother Tongue.* Grand Rapids: Eerdmans, 2007.
Ellis, E. Earle, and Erich Grässner, eds. *Jesus und Paulus: Festschrift für Werner Georg Kümmel zum 70. Geburstag.* Göttingen: Vandenhoeck & Ruprecht, 1975.
Epp, Eldon. *Junia: The First Woman Apostle.* Minneapolis: Fortress, 2005.
Fauconnier, Gilles, and Mark Turner. *The Way We Think: Conceptual Blending and the Mind's Hidden Complexities.* New York: Basic, 2002.
Felder, Cain Hope, ed. *Stony the Road We Trod: African American Biblical Interpretation.* Minneapolis: Fortress Press, 1991.
Finley, M. I. *Ancient Slavery and Modern Ideology.* New York: Viking, 1980.
Fotopoulos, John. *Food Offered to Idols in Roman Corinth: A Social-Rhetorical Reconsideration of 1 Corinthians 8:1-11:1.* WUNT 2.151. Tübingen: Mohr Siebeck, 2003.

Fowl, Stephen. *Ephesians: A Commentary*. NTL. Louisville: Westminster John Knox, 2012.

Francis, J. "As Babes in Christ—Some Proposals Regarding 1 Corinthians 3:1-3." *JSNT* 7 (1980): 41-60.

Fraser, J. W. *Jesus & Paul: Paul as Interpreter of Jesus from Harnack to Kümmel*. Abingdon: Marcham, 1974.

Frederickson, David E. "Paul, Hardships, and Suffering." Pages 172-97 in *Paul in the Greco-Roman World*. Edited by J. Paul Sampley. Harrisburg: Trinity Press International, 2003.

Friesen, Steven J. "Poverty in Pauline Studies: Beyond the So-Called New Consensus." *JSNT* 26 (2004): 323-61.

Friesen, Steven J., and Walter Scheidel. "The Size of the Economy and the Distribution of Income in the Roman Empire." *JRS* 99 (2009): 61-91.

Furnish, Victor Paul. *Jesus according to Paul*. Understanding Jesus Today. Cambridge: Cambridge University Press, 1993.

———. "The Jesus-Paul Debate: From Baur to Bultmann." Pages 17-50 in *Paul and Jesus: Collected Essays*. Edited by A. J. M. Wedderburn. JSNTSup 37. Sheffield: Sheffield Academic, 1989.

Gardner, Jane, and Thomas Weidemann. *The Roman Household: A Sourcebook*. Routledge Sourcebooks for the Ancient World. New York: Routledge, 1991.

Garland, David E. *1 Corinthians*. BECNT. Grand Rapids: Baker Academic, 2003.

Gaventa, Beverly Roberts, ed. *Apocalyptic Paul: Cosmos and Anthropos in Romans 5-8*. Waco: Baylor University Press, 2013.

———. *Our Mother Saint Paul*. Louisville: Westminster John Knox, 2007.

———. *When in Romans: An Invitation to Linger with the Gospel according to Paul*. Grand Rapids: Baker, 2016.

Gench, Francis Taylor. *Encountering God in Tyrannical Texts: Reflections on Paul, Women, and the Authority of Scripture*. Louisville: Westminster John Knox, 2015.

Gerber, Christine. *Paulus und seine 'Kinder': Studien zur Beziehungsmetaphorik des paulinischen Briefe*. BZNW 136. Berlin: Walter de Gruyter, 2005.

Gerhardsson, Birger. "The Secret Transmission of the Unwritten Jesus Tradition." *NTS* 51 (2005): 1-18.

Gil'adi, Avner. *Infants, Parents, and Wet Nurses*. Leiden: Brill, 1999.

Gillman, Florence M. *Women Who Knew Paul*. Zacchaeus Studies: New Testament. Collegeville, MN: Liturgical, 1992.

Golden, Mark. *Children and Childhood in Classical Athens*. Ancient Society and History. Baltimore: Johns Hopkins University Press, 1990.

Gonzalez, Justo. *Faith and Wealth: A History of Early Christian Ideas on the Origin, Significance, and Use of Money*. Eugene, OR: Wipf & Stock, 2002.

Gorman, Michael J. *Apostle of the Crucified Lord: A Theological Introduction to Paul and His Letters*. 2nd ed. Grand Rapids: Eerdmans, 2017.

———. *Becoming the Gospel: Paul, Participation, and Mission*. Grand Rapids: Eerdmans, 2015.

Glad, Clarence E. *Paul and Philodemus: Adaptability in Epicurean and Early Christian Psychagogy*. Leiden: Brill, 1995.

Glancy, Jennifer A. *Slavery in Early Christianity*. Oxford: Oxford University Press, 2002.

Green, Joel B. "Good News to Whom? Jesus and the 'Poor' in the Gospel of Luke." Pages 59–74 in *Jesus of Nazareth: Lord and Christ*. Edited by Joel B. Green and Max Turner. Carlisle: Paternoster, 1994.

Grenz, Stanley J., with Denise Muir Kjesbo. *Women in the Church: A Biblical Theology of Women in Ministry*. Downers Grove, IL: InterVarsity, 1995.

Gundry-Volf, Judith. "The Least and the Greatest: Children in the New Testament." Pages 29–60 in *The Child in Christian Thought*. Edited by Marcia J. Bunge. Grand Rapids: Eerdmans, 2001.

Hagner, Donald A. *Matthew 14–28*. WBC 33A. Word: Dallas, 1995.

Harlow, Mary, and Lena Larsson Lovén. *Families in the Roman and Late Antique World*. London: Bloomsbury Academic, 2012.

Harrill, J. Albert. "Paul and Slavery." Pages 301–45 in *Paul in the Greco-Roman World*. Edited by J. Paul Sampley. Rev. and enl. ed. London: Bloomsbury T&T Clark, 2016.

———. *Slaves in the New Testament: Literary, Social, and Moral Dimensions*. Minneapolis: Fortress, 2006.

———. *The Manumission of Slaves in Early Christianity*. HUT 32. Tübingen: Mohr Siebeck, 1995.

Harrington, Wilfrid. *Jesus and Paul: Signs of Contradiction*. Wilmington, DE: Michael Glazier, 1987.

Havener, Ivan. "A Curse for Salvation—1 Corinthians 5:1–5." Pages 334–44 in *Sin, Salvation, and the Spirit*. Edited by Daniel Durken. Collegeville, MN: Liturgical, 1979.

Hays, Richard B. *First Corinthians*. IBC. Louisville: Westminster John Knox, 1997.

Hellerman, Joseph H. *The Ancient Church as Family*. Minneapolis: Fortress, 2001.

Hengel, Martin. *Between Jesus and Paul*. Translated by John Bowden. Minneapolis: Fortress, 1983.

———. *Property and Riches in the Early Church*. Philadelphia: Fortress, 1974.

Henten, Jan Willem van, and Athalya Brenner, eds. *Families and Family Relations in Early Judaisms and Early Christianities: Texts and Fictions*. Studies in Theology and Religion 2. Leiden: Deo, 2000.

Herzog, Kristin. *Children and Our Global Future: Theological and Social Challenges*. Cleveland: Pilgrim, 2005.

Hock, Ronald F. "Paul and Greco-Roman Education." Pages 198–227 in *Paul in the Greco-Roman World: A Handbook*. Edited by J. Paul Sampley. Harrisburg, PA: Trinity Press International, 2003.

———. "Paul's Tentmaking and the Problem of His Social Class." *JBL* 97 (1978): 555–64.

———. *The Social Context of Paul's Ministry: Tentmaking and Apostleship*. Philadelphia: Fortress, 1980.

Holmberg, Bengt. *Paul and Power*. Lund: CWK Gleerup, 1978.

Hooker, Morna. "Hard Sayings: 1 Cor 3:2." *Theology* 69 (1966): 19–22.

Hoppe, Leslie J. *There Shall Be No Poor among You: Poverty in the Bible*. Nashville: Abingdon, 2004.

Horrell, David G. *Solidarity and Difference: A Contemporary Reading of Paul's Ethics*. London: T&T Clark, 2005.

Horsley, Richard, ed. *Paul and Empire: Religion and Power in Roman Imperial Society*. Harrisburg: Trinity, 1997.

Hurd, John C. "Paul Ahead of His Time: 1 Thess 2:13–16." Pages 21–36 in *Anti-Judaism in Early Christianity: Paul and the Gospels*. Edited by Peter Richardson and David Granskou. Vol. 1 of *Studies in Christianity and Judaism*. Waterloo: Wilfrid Laurier University Press, 1986.

Jensen, David H. *Graced Vulnerability: A Theology of Childhood*. Cleveland: Pilgrim, 2005.

Johnson, Matthew V., James A. Noel, and Demetrius K. Williams, eds. *Onesimus Our Brother: Reading Religion, Race, and Culture in Philemon*. Minneapolis: Fortress Press, 2012.

Joshel, Sandra R. *Slavery in the Roman World*. Cambridge Introduction to Roman Civilization. Cambridge: Cambridge University Press, 2010.

Joshel, Sandra R., and Sheila Murnaghan. *Women and Slaves in Greco-Roman Culture: Differential Equations*. London: Routledge, 1998.

Jülicher, Adolf. *Paulus und Jesus*. Religionsgeschichtliche Volksbücher für die deutsche christliche Gegenwart 1.14. Tübingen: Mohr, 1907.

Jüngel, Eberhard. *Paulus und Jesus: Eine Untersuchung zur Präzisierung der Frage nach dem Ursprung der Christologie*. HUT 2. Tübingen: Mohr Siebeck, 1964.

Kahl, Brigitte. *Galatians Re-Imagined: Reading with the Eyes of the Vanquished*. Minneapolis: Fortress, 2010.

Käsemann, Ernst. *Commentary on Romans*. Grand Rapids: Eerdmans, 1980.

Keck, Leander E. "The Poor among the Saints in the New Testament." *ZNW* 56 (1965): 100–129.

Keener, Craig. *Paul, Women & Wives: Marriage and Women's Ministry in the Letters of Paul*. Peabody, MA: Hendrickson, 1992.

Kennedy, George. *The Art of Persuasion in Greece*. Princeton: Princeton University Press, 1963.

Kertzer, David I., and Richard P. Saller. *The Family in Italy from Antiquity to the Present*. New Haven: Yale University Press, 1991.

Kidd, R. M. *Wealth and Beneficence in the Pastoral Epistles*. SBLD 122. Missoula: Scholars Press, 1990.

Kirk, J. R. Daniel. *Jesus Have I Loved, but Paul? A Narrative Approach to the Problem of Pauline Christianity*. Grand Rapids: Baker, 2011.

Klausner, Joseph. *From Jesus to Paul*. Translated by W. F. Stinespring. New York: Macmillan, 1943.

Knox, John. *Chapters in a Life of Paul*. London: SCM, 1950.

Kraemer, Ross Shepard, and Mary Rose D'Angelo. *Women & Christian Origins*. Oxford: Oxford University Press, 1999.

Lacey, W. K. *The Family in Classical Greece*. London: Thames & Hudson, 1968.

Lakoff, George, and Mark Johnson. *Metaphors We Live By*. Chicago: University of Chicago Press, 1980.

———. *Philosophy in the Flesh*. New York: Basic, 1999.

Lewis, Lloyd A. "An African American Appraisal of the Philemon-Paul-Onesimus Triangle." Pages 232–46 in *Stony the Road We Trod: African American Biblical Interpretation*. Edited by Cain Hope Felder. Minneapolis: Fortress, 1991.

———. "Philemon." Pages 437–43 in *True to Our Native Land: An African American New Testament Commentary*. Edited by Brian K. Blount. Philadelphia: Fortress, 2007.

Longenecker, Bruce. "Exploring the Economic Middle: A Revised Economy Scale for the Study of Early Urban Christianity." *JSNT* 31 (2009): 243–78.

———. *Remember the Poor: Paul, Poverty, and the Greco-Roman World*. Grand Rapids: Eerdmans, 2010.

———. "Socio-Economic Profiling of the First Urban Christians." Pages 36–59 in *After the First Urban Christians: The Social-Scientific Study of Pauline Christianity Twenty-Five Years Later*. Edited by Todd D. Still and David G. Horrell. London: T&T Clark, 2009.

———. *The Triumph of Abraham's God: Transformation and Identity in Galatians*. Edinburgh: T&T Clark, 1998.

Lyons, George. *Pauline Autobiography: Toward a New Understanding*. Dissertation Series. Atlanta: Society of Biblical Literature, 1985.

MacDonald, Margaret Y. *The Power of Children: The Construction of Christian Families in the Greco-Roman World*. Waco: Baylor University Press, 2014.

Marshall, Kathleen, and Paul Parvis. *Honouring Children: The Human Rights of the Child in Christian Perspective*. Edinburgh: Saint Andrews Press, 2004.

Martin, Clarice J. "The *Haustafeln* (Household Codes)." Pages 206–31 in *Stony the Road We Trod: African American Biblical Interpretation*. Edited by Cain Hope Felder. Minneapolis: Fortress Press, 1991.

Martin, Dale B. *The Corinthian Body*. New Haven: Yale University Press, 1995.

———. *Slavery as Salvation: The Metaphor of Slavery in Pauline Christianity*. New Haven: Yale University Press, 1990.

———. "Slave Families and Slaves in Families." Pages 207–30 in *Early Christian Families in Context: An Interdisciplinary Dialogue*. Edited by David Balch and Carolyn Osiek. Grand Rapids: Eerdmans, 2003.

BIBLIOGRAPHY

Marty, Martin E. *The Mystery of the Child*. Grand Rapids: Eerdmans, 2007.
Martyn, Dorothy W. "The Child and Adam: A Parable of the Two Ages." Pages 317-33 in *Apocalyptic and the New Testament: Essays in Honor of J. Louis Martyn*. Edited by Joel Marcus and Marion L. Soards. JSNTSup 24. Sheffield: Sheffield Academic Press, 1989.
Martyn, J. Louis. *Galatians*. AYB 33A. Doubleday: New York, 1997.
———. *Theological Issues in the Letters of Paul*. Nashville: Abingdon, 1997.
Meeks, Wayne A. *The First Urban Christians: The Social World of the Apostle Paul*. New Haven: Yale University Press, 1983.
———. "The Image of the Androgyne: Some Uses of a Symbol in Earliest Christianity." *History of Religions* 13 (1974): 165-208.
Meggitt, Justin J. *Paul, Poverty and Survival*. Studies of the New Testament and Its World. Edinburgh: T&T Clark, 1998.
Meier, John P. *A Marginal Jew*. 3 vols. New York: Doubleday, 1991-2001.
Mercer, Joyce Ann. *Welcoming Children: A Practical Theology of Childhood*. St. Louis: Chalice, 2005.
Miller-McLemore, Bonnie. *Let the Children Come: Reimagining Childhood from a Christian Perspective*. San Francisco: Jossey-Bass, 2004.
Moltmann, Jürgen. "Child and Childhood as Metaphors of Hope." *Theology Today* 56 (2000): 592-603.
Moxnes, Halvor, ed. *Constructing Early Christian Families: Family as Social Reality and Metaphor*. London: Routledge, 1997.
Müller, Peter. *In der Mitte der Gemeinde: Kinder im Neuen Testament*. Neukirchen-Vlyun: Neukirchener Verlag, 1992.
Murphy-O'Connor, Jerome. *Jesus and Paul: Parallel Lives*. Collegeville, MN: Liturgical, 2007.
———. *St. Paul's Corinth*. Collegeville, MN: Liturgical, 2002.
Nathan, Geoffrey S. *The Family in Late Antiquity: The Rise of Christianity and the Endurance of Tradition*. London: Routledge, 2000.
Neils, Jenifer, and John H. Oakley. *Coming of Age in Ancient Greece: Images of Childhood from the Classical Past*. New Haven: Yale University Press, 2003.
Newton, Derek. *Deity and Diet: The Dilemma of Sacrificial Food at Corinth*. Sheffield: Sheffield Academic, 1998.
———. "Food Offered to Idols in 1 Corinthians 8-10." *TynBul* 49 (1998): 179-82.
Nickle, K. F. *The Collection: A Study of Paul's Strategy*. London: SCM, 1966.
Oakes, Peter. "Constructing Poverty Scales for Graeco-Roman Society: A Response to Steven Friesen's 'Poverty in Pauline Studies.'" *JSNT* 26 (2004): 367-71.
Odell-Scott, D. W. "Let the Women Speak in Church: An Egalitarian Interpretation of 1 Cor 14:33b-36." *BTB* (1983): 90-93.
Osiek, Carolyn, and David Balch. *Families in the New Testament World*. Louisville: Westminster John Knox, 1997.

Osiek, Carolyn, and Margaret Y. MacDonald. *A Woman's Place: House Churches in Earliest Christianity*. Minneapolis: Fortress, 2006.
Parkin, Tim, and Arthur Pomeroy. *Roman Social History: A Sourcebook*. New York: Routledge, 2007.
Patterson, Cynthia B. *The Family in Greek History*. Cambridge: Humanities Research Centre, 1997.
Patterson, O. *Slavery and Social Death: A Comparative Study*. Cambridge: Harvard University Press, 1982.
Petersen, Norman. *Rediscovering Paul: Philemon and the Sociology of Paul's Narrative World*. Philadelphia: Fortress, 1985.
Polaski, Sandra Hack. *Paul and the Discourse of Power*. Sheffield: Sheffield Academic, 1999.
Potter, D. S., and D. J. Mattingly. *Life, Death, and Entertainment in the Roman Empire*. Ann Arbor: University of Michigan Press, 1999.
Rawson, Beryl. *Children and Childhood in Roman Italy*. Oxford: Oxford University Press, 2003.
———, ed. *Marriage, Divorce, and Children in Ancient Rome*. Canberra: Humanities Research Centre. Oxford: Clarendon, 1991.
———, ed. *The Family in Ancient Rome: New Perspectives*. London: Croom Helm, 1986.
Reeves, Rodney. *Spirituality according to Paul: Imitating the Apostle of Christ*. Downers Grove, IL: InterVarsity, 2011.
Richards, E. Randolph. *Paul and First-Century Letter Writing*. Downers Grove, IL: InterVarsity, 2004.
——— and Brandon J. O'Brien. *Paul Behaving Badly: Was the Apostle a Racist, Chauvinist Jerk?* Downers Grove, IL: InterVarsity, 2016.
Richardson, Peter, and John C. Hurd. *From Jesus to Paul: Studies in Honour of Francis Wright Beare*. Waterloo: Wilfrid Laurier University Press, 1984.
Ridderbos, Herman. *Paul and Jesus: Origin and General Character of Paul's Preaching of Christ*. Philadelphia: Presbyterian and Reformed, 1958.
Robbins, Vernon K. *The Tapestry of Early Christian Discourse: Rhetoric, Society and Ideology*. London: Routledge, 1996.
Ruden, Sarah. *Paul among the People: The Apostle Reinterpreted and Reimagined in His Own Time*. New York: Pantheon, 2010.
Rupprecht, A. A. "Slave, Slavery." Pages 881–82 in *Dictionary of Paul and His Letters*. Edited by Gerald F. Hawthorne, Ralph P. Martin, and Daniel G. Reid. Downers Grove, IL: InterVarsity, 1993.
Saller, Richard. *Patriarchy, Property and Death in the Roman Family*. Cambridge: Cambridge University Press, 1994.
Sanders, E. P. *Paul: A Very Short Introduction*. Oxford: Oxford University Press, 2001.
———. *Paul, the Law, and the Jewish People*. Philadelphia: Fortress, 1983.
Sandnes, Karl Olav. *A New Family: Conversion and Ecclesiology in the Early Church with*

Cross-Cultural Comparisons. Studies in the Intercultural History of Christianity 91. Bern: Peter Lang, 1994.

Schäfer, Klaus. *Gemeinde als "Bruderschaft": Ein Beitrag zum Kirchenverständnis des Paulus.* Europäische Hochschulschriften 23.333. Frankfurt am Main: Peter Lang, 1989.

Schmidt, T. T. "Riches and Poverty." Pages 826-27 in *Dictionary of Paul and His Letters.* Edited by Gerald F. Hawthorne, Ralph P. Martin, and Daniel G. Reid. Downers Grove, IL: InterVarsity, 1993.

Scott, James M. *Adoption as Sons of God: An Exegetical Investigation into the Background of ΥΙΟΘΕΣΙΑ in the Pauline Corpus.* WUNT 2.48. Tübingen: Mohr Siebeck, 1992.

Seccombe, David. "Was There Organized Charity in Jerusalem before the Christians?" *JTS* 29 (1978): 140-43.

Smith, Abraham. "Paul and African American Biblical Interpretation." Pages 31-42 in *True to Our Native Land: An African American New Testament Commentary.* Edited by Brian K. Blount. Minneapolis: Fortress Press, 2007.

Smith, Mitzi J. "Ephesians." Pages 348-62 in *True to Our Native Land: An African American New Testament Commentary.* Edited by Brian K. Blount. Minneapolis: Fortress Press, 2007.

———. "Slavery in the Early Church." Pages 11-22 in *True to Our Native Land: An African American New Testament Commentary.* Edited by Brian K. Blount. Minneapolis: Fortress Press, 2007.

———. "Utility, Fraternity, and Reconciliation: Ancient Slavery as a Context for the Return of Onesimus." Pages 47-58 in *Onesimus Our Brother: Reading Religion, Race, and Culture in Philemon.* Edited by Matthew V. Johnson, James A. Noel, and Demetrius K. Williams. Minneapolis: Fortress Press, 2012.

Soulen, R. Kendall. *The God of Israel and Christian Theology.* Minneapolis: Fortress, 1996.

Stambaugh, J., and David Balch. *The Social World of the First Christians.* Philadelphia: Fortress, 1986.

Stevenson, Tyler Wigg. *Brand Jesus: Christianity in a Consumerist Age.* New York: Seabury, 2007.

Still, Todd D. "Did Paul Loathe Manual Labor? Revisiting the Work of Ronald F. Hock on the Apostle's Tentmaking and Social Class." *JBL* 125 (2006): 781-95.

———, ed. *Jesus and Paul Reconnected: Fresh Pathways into an Old Debate.* Grand Rapids: Eerdmans, 2007.

Still, Todd D., and David G. Horrell. *After the First Urban Christians: The Social-Scientific Study of Pauline Christianity Twenty-Five Years Later.* New York: T&T Clark, 2009.

Strange, William A. *Children in the Early Church: Children in the Ancient World, the New Testament and the Early Church.* Carlisle: Paternoster, 1996.

Tamez, Elsa. *Struggles for Power in Early Christianity.* Translated by Gloria Kinsler. Maryknoll, NY: Orbis, 2007.

Theissen, Gerd. *The Social Setting of Pauline Christianity*. Edited and translated by John J. Schütz. Studies of the New Testament and Its World. Edinburgh: T&T Clark, 1982.

Thiselton, Anthony C. *The First Epistle to the Corinthians*. NIGTC. Grand Rapids: Eerdmans, 2000.

Thompson, Michael B. *The New Perspective on Paul*. Grove Biblical Series 26. Cambridge: Grove, 2002.

Tiffany, Frederick C., and Sharon H. Ringe. *Biblical Interpretation: A Roadmap*. Nashville: Abingdon, 1996.

Wall, John. "Childhood Studies, Hermeneutics, and Theological Ethics." *JR* 86 (2006): 523-48.

Watson, Francis. *Paul and the Hermeneutics of Faith*. London: T&T Clark, 2004.

Weaver, Paul. "Reconstructing Lower Class Roman Families." Pages 101-14 in *Childhood, Class, and Kin in the Roman World*. Edited by Suzanne Dixon. London: Routledge, 2001.

Wedderburn, A. J. M., ed. *Paul and Jesus: Collected Essays*. JSNTSup 37. Sheffield: JSOT Press, 1989.

Wenham, David. *Paul: Follower of Jesus or Founder of Christianity?* Grand Rapids: Eerdmans, 1995.

Westermann, L. *The Slave Systems of the Greek and Roman Antiquity*. Philadelphia: American Philosophical Society, 1955.

Wheeler, Sondra. *Wealth as Peril and Obligation: The New Testament on Possessions*. Grand Rapids: Eerdmans, 1995.

White, John L. "God's Paternity as Root Metaphor in Paul's Conception of Community." *Forum* 8 (1992): 271-95.

White, L. Michael, and O. Larry Yarbrough. *The Social World of the First Christians: Essays in Honor of Wayne Meeks*. Minneapolis: Fortress, 1995.

Wiedemann, Thomas. *Adults and Children in the Roman Empire*. New Haven: Yale University Press, 1989.

Williams, Demetrius K. "'No Longer as a Slave': Reading the Interpretation History of Paul's Epistle to Philemon." Pages 11-46 in *Onesimus Our Brother: Reading Religion, Race, and Culture in Philemon*. Edited by Matthew V. Johnson, James A. Noel, and Demetrius K. Williams. Minneapolis: Fortress Press, 2012.

———. "The Bible and Models of Liberation in the African American Experience." Pages 33-59 in *Yet with a Steady Beat: Contemporary U.S. Afrocentric Biblical Interpretation*. Edited by Randall C. Bailey. Atlanta: Society of Biblical Literature, 2003.

Winter, Bruce. *After Paul Left Corinth: The Influence of Secular Ethics and Social Change*. Grand Rapids: Eerdmans, 2001.

———. *Roman Wives, Roman Widows: The Appearance of New Women and the Pauline Communities*. Grand Rapids: Eerdmans, 2003.

BIBLIOGRAPHY

———. *Seek the Welfare of the City: Christians as Benefactors and Citizens.* Grand Rapids: Eerdmans, 1994.
Wordelman, Amy. "Everyday Life: Women in the Period of the New Testament." Pages 482-88 in *The Women's Bible Commentary*. Expd. ed. Edited by Carol A. Newsom and Sharon H. Rindge. Louisville: Westminister John Knox, 1998.
Wire, Antoinette Clark, *The Corinthian Women Prophets: A Reconstruction through Paul's Rhetoric*. Minneapolis: Fortress, 1990.
Wrede, William. *Paul*. London: P. Green, 1907.
Yarbrough, O. Larry. "Parents and Children in the Letters of Paul." Pages 126-41 in *The Social World of the First Christians: Essays in Honor of Wayne Meeks*. Edited by L. Michael White and O. Larry Yarbrough. Minneapolis: Fortress, 1995.

Index of Authors

Aasgaard, Reidar, 110n8, 120n44
Aristotle, 111, 138
Armstrong, David, 137n15
Artemidorus of Daldis, 117, 136

Balch, David L., 118n36, 126
Barclay, John M. G., 4n7, 116n25
Boer, Martinus de, 91
Bradley, Keith, 120n45, 121n47
Brueggemann, Walter, 99
Byrne, Brendan, 103n28

Campbell, Barth, 122n49
Cassidy, Richard, 148, 149, 150n47, 152
Chow, J., 140n24
Cicero, 38, 138
Clarke, Andrew D., 77n32, 140n24
Collins, John J., 113n20, 122n49
Connolly, Joy, 138n19
Conzelmann, Hans, 109n3

Davies, W. D., 97-98, 102
Deissmann, Adolf, 140n27
Dio Cassius, 77, 89, 149
Dio Chrysostom, 79-80
Diodorus Siculus, 149
Dixon, Suzanne, 77, 133n3
Downs, David, 1n1, 30n36, 31, 33
Dunn, James, 92

Ellis, E. Earle, 124n54
Euphorion, 106

Fotopoulos, John, 144n38
Fowl, Stephen, 79-80
Francis, J., 122
Frank, Richard I., 77n32
Friedman, Norman, 110
Friesen, Steven, 17-18, 19, 116n25

Garland, David, 108
Gaventa, Beverly Roberts, 105, 106, 120n45, 126, 156, 169n10, 173
Gench, Francis Taylor, 55, 83, 85
Glad, Clarence E., 137n15
Glancy, Jennifer A., 40n30, 50, 136n9
Gorman, Michael J., 173

Hagner, Donald, 2
Hanson, Ann, 74n28, 118
Harrill, J. Albert, 38, 50, 143
Hays, Richard, 61, 122n49, 143, 169, 171
Hock, Ronald F., 23n22, 140, 168n8
Hooker, Morna, 120
Horrell, David G., 33, 146n40
Hugo, Victor, 35

Ignatius, 125

189

INDEX OF AUTHORS

Johnson, Mark, 110
Josephus, 112
Joshell, Sandra R., 50
Juvenal, 166

Kahl, Brigette, 88, 90, 91, 94, 107
Keener, Craig, 73
Kennedy, George, 137n16
Kirk, J. R. Daniel, 7n13
Kittay, Eva Fedder, 110
Klijn, A. F. J., 104n29

Lakoff, George, 110
Lewis, Lloyd A., 42–43, 50
Livy, 88
Longenecker, Bruce W., 1n1, 5, 17–18, 19, 23, 26, 29–30, 33, 116n25

MacDonald, Margaret, 74, 80, 86, 118n36, 119n43
Martin, Clarice J., 83n41, 86
Martin, Dale B., 37, 38, 51, 131n2, 135, 136, 137, 139, 140, 143, 152
Martyn, J. Louis, 88n2, 93n11, 94n12, 107
Meeks, Wayne, 5n10, 16–17, 33, 135
Meggitt, Justin J., 5n10, 14, 15, 17, 21, 30n36, 33, 116n25
Morley, Neville, 12n1, 14

Newton, Derek, 145

Oakes, Peter, 116n25
Osborne, Robin, 12n1
Osiek, Carolyn, 74, 80, 86, 118n36, 119n43, 126

Patterson, Orlando, 36
Philo, 111, 112, 113, 137, 138, 139
Pliny, 116

Pliny the Younger, 166
Plutarch, 79, 81, 89, 138, 143
Polybius, 88, 89, 138

Rawson, Beryl, 117n30, 118n37, 126, 133n3
Reid, Daniel G., 149n44
Ringe, Sharon, 52
Ruden, Sarah, 7n13, 44, 59, 61–62, 86
Rufus, Musonius, 80
Rupprecht, A. A., 37n15

Scheidel, Walter, 14
Schmidt, T. E., 4
Seneca, 72
Severian, 104
Smith, Mitzi J., 36, 42n35
Soranus, 118
Sosthenes, 22
Soulen, R. Kendall, 85, 100, 105
Stevenson, Tyler Wigg, 154–55
Still, Todd D., 4n7, 23n22, 33, 141–42, 168n8
Strabo, 89
Strange, W. A., 126–27

Tamez, Elsa, 72, 86
Theissen, Gerd, 25, 116n25, 124, 144n37, 168
Thiselton, Anthony C., 66–67, 134n5, 143n34

Wiedemann, Thomas, 111n11, 112n16, 117n33, 124n55, 133n3
Williams, Demetrius K., 41n32
Winter, Bruce, 23, 24, 25, 60, 136n8, 142
Wire, Antoinette, 67
Wrede, William, 3

Yarbrough, Larry O., 111n10

Index of Subjects

abandonment, 117n30, 118n36
Abraham, 34, 93, 94–96
Abrahamic promise, 98, 99, 101, 106
abundance, 28, 50, 95, 99, 106, 160, 162
abuse, 83
acts of mercy, 2, 30
adaptability, 139, 146
adelphoi, 2
adultery, 61, 118
Agabus, 27
agapē, 82, 173
agricultural metaphor, 102
Agrippa, 150
almsgiving, 30n36, 31
"already/not yet," 158, 159
American dream, 39
Andronicus, 40
apostleship, 129–30, 134, 140, 142, 146, 147, 151–52
Apphia, 22, 41, 42
Aquila, 21, 142
Archippus, 22, 41, 42
assets, 37
Augustus, 77
authority, 72, 76, 80, 119, 129

baptismal confession, 35, 45
baptismal formula, 42n34, 48, 56, 67, 84
Baptist Faith and Message Statement, 63, 64
barbarians, 88–92
Barnabas, 28
barrenness, 114
bearing one another's burdens, 26, 30, 31, 32, 48, 147, 163
beatings, 128, 150
benefactors, 168
benevolent patriarch, 137, 138, 143, 146
"Biblical Womanhood," 53–55
bivocational minister, 141
blessing, 28
body of Christ, 170
bribery, 150
brotherhood, 41, 44, 48–49

Caesar, Julius, 38
canon, 8, 20
capital punishment, 130
caricature, 71, 87
Celts, 88–92
charity, 26, 29
children, 15, 76–77, 111n10

191

INDEX OF SUBJECTS

children of God, 106
Chloe, 22, 57, 81, 165
Christology, 1
church
   high view of, 83
   leadership of, 54, 64
   as least of these, 108–27
   mission of, 2, 74
   witness of, 163–65
church potluck, 166
circumcision, 45, 91, 93, 94, 105
citizenship, 38, 39
collection, 27, 29
colors, 161
community, 43, 83
congruity, 4, 5
consensus, 17, 27, 33, 79, 116
consummation, 100
contradiction, 66
conversion, 131, 172
Corinth, 19–20, 22, 25, 59, 60, 61, 75, 124, 165–72
corporate responsibility, 170
cosmos, 80, 97, 102, 105, 106, 162
Council on Biblical Manhood and Womanhood, 53–55
countercultural, 62, 82, 173
covenant, 100
coworkers, 64–65, 84
creation, 100, 153, 156
Crispus, 21, 22
critical scholarship, 9
cross, 154
cruelty, 39–40
cultural norms, 168

daily life, 115–19
Danvers Statement of Biblical Manhood and Womanhood, 53–55, 56
Day of the Lord, 160
death, 36, 117, 130, 148, 152, 157, 162
debt, 27, 41, 42

decency, 59, 71
demagogue, 137–39
demons, 145
diets, 94, 101
dignity, 62–63
dining rooms, 166–67
disease, 15
diversity, 85
divine judgment, 113–14, 120, 121, 123, 160
division, 125
doctrine, 158
domination, 90
dreams, 117, 136
drunkenness, 26

ecclesiology, 1
education, 119
ektrōma, 132–33
elderly, 112
elite, 13, 18, 62, 141, 144, 145
emotions, 70, 138
employment, 15
entitlement, 59
Epaphroditus, 150–51
Ephesus, 71–74
equality, 42n34, 44, 56, 57, 59, 62, 84
Erastus, 20, 21
erōs, 42, 173
eschatological blessing, 103
eschatology, 1, 143n34
ethics, 1, 11
Euodia, 54, 64
evangelicals, 6

faith, 158
fall, 54
false teachers, 73–74
family, 74–75, 78
famine, 24n25
Felix, 149, 150
feminism, 53

Index of Subjects

Festus, 150
First Church Corinth, 20, 22, 25, 59, 60, 61, 75, 124, 165-72
flattery, 139, 140, 141
flesh, 122, 159, 164
food, 14-15, 24n25, 120, 150
foolishness, 90-91, 108, 110, 115, 124
freedom, 37, 43-44, 49
fruit of the Spirit, 105, 122, 159
fulfillment, 100, 163-64

Gaius, 21, 116n25, 125, 167
Galatians, 87-107
Gallus, 149
Gauls, 88-92
gender, 56, 59, 62-63, 84
generosity, 27-28, 31
gentiles, 10, 29, 84, 93, 96
gnōsis, 144
God
   faithfulness of, 95-96
   grace of, 27, 154
   power of, 134, 152, 155
goodness, 157
gospel
   defection from, 92
   as food, 120
   as "good news," 153-73
   preaching of, 55, 150
   and slavery, 34-35
   and social upheaval, 43, 44, 48
government, 153
gratitude, 72

Hagar, 93
hair, 61
hate, 7-8
"haves" and "have-nots," 59, 61, 124, 144n37, 167, 170
head-covering, 55-63
Hellenistic Jewish literature, 104
hermeneutical dilemma, 54

history, 13
Holy Spirit
   fruit of, 105, 122, 159
   life in, 101-2
   outpouring of, 84
   transformation of, 165
homelessness, 128, 146
homes, 21
homosexuality, 7-8, 53, 155
honor, 59, 62
hope, 105
hospitality, 2, 22, 25-26, 91-92, 128, 166-67, 170
hosts, 21
household, 39, 55, 60, 63
household codes, 54, 70, 75, 78-79, 83
housing, 15
human dignity, 62-63
humiliation, 25, 32, 129, 146, 168, 171
humility, 126, 129, 142, 171
hunger, 26
husband-wife relationship, 78
hymn, 170-71

identity, 81, 87, 99
idle, 24-25
idolatry, 153, 157
idol food, 58-59, 144-46
immaturity, 124
imprisonment, 128, 147-51
"in Christ," 98, 102, 122, 165
indebtedness, 27, 41, 42
infants, 108-27, 133
inheritance, 39, 96-97, 102, 103, 106, 120
injustice, 160, 162
innocence, 112, 115
interpolation, 66
interpretation, 101, 120
irrationality, 115

James, 3, 29

193

INDEX OF SUBJECTS

Jerusalem offering, 26–28, 29
Jesus Christ
   being "in," 98, 102, 122, 165
   body of, 170
   generosity of, 27–28
   humiliation of, 171
   imitation of, 32
   love of, 29, 81–83, 164–65, 173
   mind of, 172
   portrait of, 2
   resurrection of, 157, 158, 162
   sacrifice of, 32
jewelry, 71–72
Jews, 91
John, 29
Judaism, 30, 94
Judas tradition, 169
judgment, 113–14, 120, 121, 123, 160
Julia, 64
Julius, 151
Junia, 54, 64–65
Junian Latin, 38
Junias, 64–65
justice, 150, 157
justification, 2–3, 85

kingdom of God, 1, 81, 83, 101, 102, 114–15, 153
knowledgeable, 144–45, 146

labor, 23, 25, 140–42, 168
land, 96–100
law, 29, 94, 95, 130, 163–64
leadership, 64, 137, 144, 146
Les Misérables, 35, 49
liberal Protestants, 6
limitations, 157
logos, 111–12, 115, 126
Lord's Table, 32, 58, 165, 168–70, 172
love, 32, 78–83, 91–92, 165, 173
Lydia, 22, 60, 64, 74, 81

male-female dichotomy, 85
manna, 28
manual labor, 140–42
manumission, 36, 37–38, 44, 48
manuscripts, 65–66
marginal note, 66
marriage, 39, 44, 48, 54, 60, 75, 76, 77, 81
martyrdom, 148
Mary, 64
maturity, 125–26
mercy, acts of, 2, 30
metaphor, 102, 108, 110, 123–24, 129, 132
middling groups, 13–14, 16, 19, 20
miscarriage, 132–33
modern slavery, 37
modesty, 59, 71
Moses, 123–24
mourning, 117
mutualism, 30
mutuality, 76
mystery, 161–63

naming, 119
neighbor, 30
nēpioi, 111n10, 112, 116
Nereus's sister, 64
Nero, 148
new creation, 85, 97, 101, 105, 154, 158, 163–65
Nympha, 21, 22, 54, 60, 64, 74

offering, to Jerusalem, 26–28
Onesimus, 22, 40, 41–44, 48, 49
oppression, 83
otherness, 90
over-realized eschatology, 143n43

paidagōgoi, 109, 119, 120, 126
paidia, 111n10
paradidōmi, 169

Index of Subjects

parent-child relationship, 76–77
parousia, 75, 79
Pastoral Epistles, 70
paterfamilias, 119, 121, 129
patronage system, 23–25, 38, 72, 142
Paul
   congregations of, 16–19
   gospel of, 155–60
   vs. James, 3
   as least of these, 128–52
   as persecutor, 130–34
   personality of, 7, 8
   portraits of, 2–3
   on poverty, 16–32
   in prison, 147–51
   reputation of, 9
   on slavery, 7–8, 40–52, 78, 134–47
   as tentmaker, 140, 141
   on women, 9, 52–86
Pausanius, 89
peace, 160
peculium, 37
persecution, 130–34, 162
Peter, 29
Philemon, 8, 21–22, 41–44, 48, 49
philia, 82, 173
Philippian hymn, 170–71
Phoebe, 22, 54, 64
physical violence, 39
pistis, 158
pneumatikos, 108–9, 121, 122
pneumatology, 1
poor
   Paul on, 16–28
   remembering of, 10, 28–32
   in Roman world, 12–16
   spiritualization of, 4–5
porneia, 76
poverty, 146
power, 137
pregnancy, 114
Prisca, 21, 22, 54, 60, 64, 142

prison, 128, 147–51
privilege, 73
progeny, 96, 98, 101
progressive Protestants, 6
promises, 96–97
prophecy, 65
proslavery, 9, 34
prosperity, 99, 100
prosperity gospel, 31
prostitution, 39, 58, 60, 61, 76
Protestants, 2, 3, 6
psychikos, 108–9
public assembly, 79, 94
purity standards, 40n30

rape, 39
reciprocity, 28, 30
reconciliation, 47, 85, 142
redemption, 105
renewal, 159
reputation, 70–71
respect, 59
responsibility, 28
resurrection, 154, 157, 159
revelation, 161–62
revolution, 49
rituals, 119
Roman culture, 166–67, 173
Rome, 15, 19–20

sacrificial love, 78–83
Sarah, 93, 95
sarkinoi, 109, 121
sarx, 159
security, 99
selfishness, 173
self-lowering, 170
service, 28, 134
servitude, 129, 130, 137
sexual abstinence, 67
sexual immorality, 76
sexuality, 155

INDEX OF SUBJECTS

shalom, 160, 162
shame, 59, 61, 67, 70
sickness, 15
Silas, 149
silence, 63-69, 73
sin, 156-57, 159-60, 164
singleness, 75, 76
"slave of Christ," 136
slavery
    cruelty of, 39-40
    Paul on, 7-8, 40-52, 78, 134-47
    in Roman world, 15, 35-40
    women in, 62
social death, 36
social status, 17, 20, 25-26, 38, 42, 72, 136, 141
social upheaval, 42, 44, 48
solidarity, 172
soteriology, 1
Southern Baptists, 52, 63
sovereignty, 100
spiritual forces, 145
starvation, 150
Stephanus, 20, 22, 167
Stephen, 131
stereotypes, 70, 87, 89
stillbirth, 132-33
submission, 63-65, 73, 78-83
subsistence level, 13, 19, 23, 26, 30, 71
sufferings, 151-52
Syntyche, 54, 64
systematic theology, 1, 7

taxation, 36
teachable, 73
teachers, 92-94
tetrachromat, 161n3
tithes, 16
Titus, 28
torture, 40
traditions, 9
training, 119
transformation, 159
translations, 45-46, 132
"triclinium," 166-67
Tryphaena, 64
Tryphosa, 64

United Methodists, 53
unity, 84, 85, 141
untimely birth, 132-33
Urbanus, 40

veiling, 55-63, 67
versatility, 135, 139
victory, 157-58, 160
violence, 39
virgins, 77
vulnerable, 113, 115, 116, 119, 120, 124, 126

weakness, 133, 143-46
wealth, 4, 17
wisdom, 91, 122
witness, of the church, 163-65
women
    and eschatological community, 83-85
    in leadership, 84
    in ministry, 7-8
    and Pauline mission, 9, 52-86
    role of, in family, 74-75
    as vulnerable, 15
work, 23, 25, 140-42
world, 102
World War II, 160

Index of Citations from Scripture and Other Ancient Sources

Old Testament

Genesis
2:24	82
12:1–3	96
12:3	96, 98, 101
12:7	96
13:15	96
15:1–6	96
15:6	96
15:17	96
17:7	96
17:8–9	100
18:18	96, 101
22:18	96
24:35	34

Exodus
3:8	100
3:17	100
13:5	100
16:18	28
32:13	134

Leviticus
19:18	30
20:24	100
25:2	100n24
25:42	134n6
25:55	134n6
27:30–33	100n24

Numbers
11:11	134
12:7	134
12:12	132
13:27	100
14:24	134
34:1–12	99

Deuteronomy
3:24	134
9:27	134
11:24	99
14:22	100n24
26:9–15	100n24
32	124
32:1–43	123
32:5	123
32:6	123
32:10	123
32:11	123
32:13	123
32:13–14	123
32:15	123
32:18	123
32:19–20	123
32:21	124
32:23–26	123
32:26–27	123
32:28–29	123
32:36	123, 134
32:39	123
32:43	123

Joshua
1:1	134
5:14	134

1 Samuel
1:11	134
3:9	134

1 Kings
8:22–40	134
11:13	134

Job
3:16	132

Ecclesiastes
6:3	132

Isaiah
2:4	160
11:6–8	104, 116
53:6	169
53:12	169
65	105, 115

INDEX OF CITATIONS

65:17-25	104, 105
65:18-25	160
65:20	115
65:23	105, 115
65:25	115

Joel

3:1-5	84

NEW TESTAMENT

Matthew

5:3-11	1
5:17-20	163
5:21-48	163
10:40	2
10:41	2
10:42	2
11:2-6	1
11:5	1
24:19	114
25	1, 2
25:31-46	2, 12
25:40	2
28:19-20	2

Mark

3:17	114

Luke

4:17-21	1
4:18-19	1
6:20-23	1
7:18-23	1
9:51	27
21:23	114

Acts

2:17-18	84
2:41	172
7:58	162
7:58-8:3	131
8:1-3	162
9:1-2	162
9:1-12	131
9:1-19	162
9:4-5	131
9:26	131
14	127
14:4	8
14:19	8
16	22, 64, 148
16:14-15	60, 74
16:22-24	149
16:37	130
17:6-9	23
18	22, 167
18:1-27	21
18:2	80
18:2-3	64
18:3	10, 140n26
18:8	21, 22
18:17	22
19:21	27
20:34	10
20:35	10
21-23	150
21:7-8	27
21:7-14	27
21:13	27
21:39	130
22:3	130
22:4-5	131
22:6-16	162
22:7-8	131
22:25	149
22:25-29	130
23:23	150
23:29	151
24:23	149, 151
24:27	148, 151
25:9	151
25:25	151
26:10-12	131
26:12-18	162
26:14-15	131
26:28	150
27	150
27:3	151
28	127, 151
28:16	149
28:18	151
28:20	149
28:23	149
28:28	150
28:30	148, 150, 151
29:30-31	149

Romans

1	155
1:1	129, 134
1:14	91, 129
1:16-17	27, 155
1:18	121
1:18-32	156
1:29-31	156
2:1	156
2:11	154
3:9-19	156
3:23	156
4	95
4:1-25	95
4:3	95
4:9-12	95
4:11	95
4:11-12	95
4:13	102
4:13-25	95
4:15	156
4:16	95
4:16-17	95
4:17	95
4:19	95
4:24	95
4:25	95, 157, 169
5	157
5:8-10	156
5:10	170

Index of Citations

5:12	157	13:1–7	80, 97	2:6–16	122
5:12–14	158	13:8–10	30n33	2:14	109
5:12–21	102, 105	14–15	144	2:16	109, 171
5:12–23	158	15:1–13	35	3	109, 110, 119, 120, 121, 123, 124, 125, 126
5:13	156	15:7–13	26, 83, 85, 165	3:1	11, 108, 112, 125
5:14	157	15:10	124	3:1–2	129, 133
5:17	157	15:25–27	10, 28	3:1–3	108n1
5:21	156	15:26	28	3:2	119, 120, 120n46, 126
6:3	158	15:26–27	27	3:3	108, 109, 121, 125
6:4–8	158	15:31	27	3:5	129, 134
6:4–9	158	16	20, 40, 84	3:6	129
6:5	158	16:1–2	22, 54, 64	3:10–15	121
6:6	156	16:1–16	86	3:11	121
6:8	158	16:3–4	60, 64	3:13	109, 121, 124
6:9	158	16:3–5	21, 54	3:13–15	124, 125, 143n34
6:11	156	16:6	64	3:15	121
6:12	156	16:7	54, 64, 65	3:17	121
6:12–23	147	16:12	67	3:23	122, 124
6:17	156	16:13	64	4:1	125, 136
6:18	156	16:15	64	4:1–2	129, 134
6:23	156, 157	16:23	20, 21, 60, 116, 125, 167	4:4–5	121, 121n48
7	158			4:5	143n34
7:5–6	110n3			4:5–7	142
7:6	102	**1 Corinthians**		4:6	143n34
7:12	98, 163, 164	1:1	22, 129, 134	4:8	143
7:16	98	1:7	143n34	4:8–12	142
7:18	110n3	1:7–8	78, 121	4:8–13	146
7:25	110n3, 129, 134	1:9	154	4:9	129, 134, 142
8	105, 122, 157, 159	1:10	122	4:9–13	168
8:1–17	110n3	1:10–2:16	170	4:10	129, 142, 143n34
8:2	102	1:11	57, 165		
8:3	159, 164	1:14	21, 22	4:11	12, 129, 142
8:5–8	109	1:16	167	4:11–13	8
8:6	159	1:17–34	58	4:12	10, 129, 140n26, 142, 168
8:8	122	1:18–25	146, 172	4:13	129, 142, 144
8:13	122	1:18–2:16	91, 91n7, 108, 171	4:14	120, 121
8:20–23	157	1:26	20	4:14–15	126
8:31–39	154	1:27	119, 146	4:15	120, 126
8:32	157, 169	1:30	27, 122	4:20	120
10:19	124	2:3	143	4:20–21	121
11:13	129, 134	2:6	109, 143n34	4:21	120, 121, 126
11:29	98, 154				
12:19	124				

199

INDEX OF CITATIONS

5	125
5–7	40n30
5:1–5	109n3
5:1–13	43, 168
5:5	109, 109n3, 121n48, 122, 122n49
6:1–11	58, 168
6:9	120, 121
6:9–11	122
6:11	121
6:12	66
6:12–20	43, 58, 60
6:15–16	76
6:19	76
6:19–20	62
7	45, 48, 55, 60, 69, 75, 76, 77, 79, 86
7:1	57, 79, 144
7:1–6	60, 67
7:1–7	167
7:2	76
7:2–4	76
7:3	76
7:4	76
7:5	76
7:6	75
7:7	76
7:8–9	46
7:10	5, 46, 75
7:11	47
7:12	5, 76
7:13	47
7:15	47
7:17	46
7:17–24	10, 45, 135
7:18–19	46
7:20	46
7:20–24	40, 44
7:21	45, 46, 47, 78
7:21–23	46, 78, 136
7:23	47, 78
7:24	46
7:25	5, 76
7:25–38	69
7:25–40	76
7:28	46
7:29	69, 121, 143n34
7:29–31	47
7:31	76, 77, 121, 143n34, 172
7:32	46
7:34	69, 76
7:35	76
7:36	76
7:36–38	46
7:40	76
8	170
8:1	57
8:1–6	143n34, 145
8:1–11	145
8:1–13	58, 125, 135
8:1–11:1	58, 144n37, 168
8:4	144
8:6	145
8:7–13	144
8:8	145
8:10–13	145
8:11	146, 170
8:11–12	146
9	140, 141, 144, 147
9:1	140
9:1–2	129, 134
9:1–27	124, 140, 168
9:5	146
9:6	168
9:7	146
9:8–13	146
9:10–23	136
9:14	5, 141, 146
9:15–18	146n40
9:18	141
9:19	129, 134, 140
9:19–23	134, 143, 145
9:22	139, 146
10:1–22	125, 145
10:5	121
10:11	121, 143n34
10:13	154
10:19–21	145
10:20–21	145
10:22	124
10:23	66
10:23–34	145
11	69, 167
11:2–16	55, 56, 58, 59, 61, 62, 64, 65, 71, 86
11:3	57
11:5	59, 66, 68, 69
11:5–6	61
11:6	59
11:10	56
11:11	57
11:12	57
11:17–22	25, 116, 165, 168
11:17–34	32, 35, 58, 61, 125, 144n37, 165
11:20–21	168
11:22	25, 26, 32, 167, 168
11:23	5, 6
11:23–26	25, 169
11:24	169
11:26	143n34, 169
11:28	170
11:29	170
11:33	25
11:33–34	170
12:1	57
12:12–13	67, 122
12:13	35, 48, 56
13	82, 173
13:11	111n10, 112, 112n14
14	68
14:20	111n10, 112
14:28	65
14:30	65
14:31	65
14:32	65, 68

14:33-36	86	8-9	32	**Galatians**	
14:34	66	8:1	27	1:1	129, 134
14:34-35	53, 63, 64, 65, 66, 67, 68	8:1-9:15	10	1:1-9	92, 93
		8:4	28	1:2	88
14:35	64, 68	8:6	28	1:4	34, 83, 105, 159, 165
14:36	66	8:7	28		
14:37	65	8:9	4, 27	1:6-9	90, 92, 93n11
14:40	65	8:10-15	28	1:10	129, 134
15	129, 133, 151, 157	8:13-14	28	1:11-17	93, 131
15:1	65	8:15	28	1:12	129, 132, 151, 162
15:1-58	159	8:19	28	1:13	131, 162
15:4	157	8:20	28	1:15-16	162
15:5-7	132	8:24	28	1:16	129, 132, 151
15:8	129, 132	9:1	28	1:18-24	93
15:8-11	131	9:5	28	1:23	131
15:9	129, 130, 131, 133, 134, 162	9:6-12	31	2	28
		9:6-16	31	2:1-10	93
15:10	131	9:8	31	2:10	4, 5, 10, 29, 30
15:12-19	157	9:8-15	27	2:15	130
15:21-23	157	9:10	31	2:16	122
15:54-57	157	9:12	28, 32	3	96, 98
15:55	157	9:13	28, 32	3:1	88, 90, 91
16:1	57	10:10	143	3:1-5	93
16:1-4	10, 22	11:7	141	3:2	91
16:2	28	11:16-30	143	3:2-5	94
16:3	28	11:19	129	3:5	91
16:15	20, 22	11:22	130	3:6	95
16:15-16	22	11:22-33	142	3:6-29	95
16:16	22	11:23	129, 134, 148	3:6-4:7	95
16:19	21, 64	11:23-25	142	3:8	94, 95, 96, 98, 101
16:22	121, 143n34	11:23-27	8	3:14	94, 101
		11:23-30	129	3:16	96, 98
2 Corinthians		11:25-27	128	3:17	95, 96
1:1	129, 134	11:26	143	3:17-18	98
3:1	123	11:27	12, 142	3:18	94, 95
3:6	129, 134	11:29-30	129	3:19	156
3:17	56	12:7-10	143	3:19-21	163
4:5	129, 134	12:10	8, 129	3:19-29	95
4:7-10	8	12:11	129	3:21	95, 96, 102, 164
5:17	105, 158, 159	12:12	129, 134	3:22	102
6:4	129, 134	16:1	28	3:26	96
6:4-10	8	16:17	22	3:28	35, 42, 42n34, 48, 84, 92
7:31	162				

INDEX OF CITATIONS

3:29	102	5:6	83	1:23	129, 134
4	96, 98	5:11–20	80	1:25	129, 134
4:7	96	5:21	81	3:18–4:1	79
4:12–15	31	5:21–33	86	4:15	21, 54, 60, 64, 74
4:14	92	5:22	81		
4:15	30, 92	5:22–32	63	**1 Thessalonians**	
4:16	92	5:24	82	1:10	121
4:17	93	5:25	82	2:2	142
4:21–5:1	93	5:25–27	79	2:6	129, 134
4:21–5:2	95	5:25–33	82	2:7	129, 133
4:28	87, 96	5:26–27	82	2:9	10, 129, 140n26
5	122	5:29	82	2:17	129, 133
5:7–12	93	5:31	82	4:9–12	20
5:12	92	6:9	82, 83	4:10–12	142
5:13	110n3, 134	6:10–20	80	4:11–12	23
5:13–14	163			4:12	24
5:14	29, 30	**Philippians**		5:19	84
5:16	122, 154	1:1	129, 134		
5:16–21	122	1:13	150	**2 Thessalonians**	
5:19	110n3	1:19–26	148	3:6–12	20
5:21	102	1:20	151	3:6–13	142
5:22	102	1:27	165	3:6–15	24
5:22–23	159	2:1–11	122, 122n51	3:8	10
5:24	110n3, 122	2:3–4	171		
6:2	30, 163, 164	2:5	171	**1 Timothy**	
6:8	102	2:5–11	11, 25, 82, 129, 170	1:1	129, 134
6:9	102	2:7	34, 170	1:12–17	131
6:9–10	30	2:9–11	171	1:13	131
6:12–14	93	2:17	148	2	53, 69
6:13	95	2:23–24	148	2:1–2	80
6:15	95, 105, 158	2:25	129, 151	2:1–15	79
		3:4–6	130	2:2	73
Ephesians		3:4–17	131	2:7	129, 134
1:1	129, 134	3:6	131	2:8	71
1:19–23	80	3:7–11	132	2:8–15	86
2:2	80	3:17	151	2:9	71
2:6	80	4:2–3	54, 64	2:9–3:15	63
3:7	129, 134	4:13–19	31	2:11	73
4:27	80	4:14–18	4	2:11–12	64, 65, 68, 73, 74
5	78	4:22	150	2:12	72
5:1–2	81			2:14–15	71n24
5:2	81	**Colossians**		3:2	80
5:5	81	1:1	129, 134	3:3	64

Index of Citations

3:4	71
3:4–5	80
3:5	71
3:7	80
3:12	71
5	72
5:1–16	79
5:3–16	86
5:5	70
5:9	70
5:9–15	70
5:13	71, 73
5:14	69
5:16	69
6:1–2	79
6:3–10	73
6:17–19	31, 73, 79

2 Timothy

1:1	129, 134
1:11	129, 134
3:6–7	73
4:19	21

Titus

1:1	129, 134
2:1–3:8	79
2:3	70
2:5	70, 80
2:8	80
3:1	80

Philemon

9	42
9–10	41
11	22, 41
12	42
13	41
16	41
17	43
17–19	43
19	42, 43
21–22	42, 43

22	22, 41

James

1:27	3, 12

1 Peter

2:18–3:7	79

2 Peter

3:16	7

Deuterocanonical Works

Wisdom of Solomon

12:21	103n28
18:6	103n28

Sirach

42:9–14	70
44:21	103

2 Maccabees

2:17–18	103n28

3 Maccabees

3:12	113
3:27	113

Old Testament Pseudepigrapha

2 Baruch

10:10	114
10:13–16	114
14:1–19	103
14:7	103
14:19	103
22:13	103
25:4	104
28:1	115
30:1	104

32:2–4	103
32:7	104
32:9	104
33:9	114n22
44:12–14	104
51:3	104
57:1–3	104

1 Enoch

5:7	103
5:7b	103
5:7–10	103
99	114
99:5	114

4 Ezra

6:55	103
6:55–59	103
7:9	104

Jubilees

19:21	103
22:14	103
32:19	103

Psalms of Solomon

12:6	103n28

Testament of Judah

23:3	113

Sibylline Oracles

2	113n20
2:190–95	113
2:196–214	113
2:214–20	113
2:297–99	113n21
2:298	114n23
3	104
3:268	113n19
3:482	114n23
3:619–23	104

3:669–771	104
3:701–30	104
3:767–95	104
3:780	104
3:784	104
3:787–95	104
3:788–95	115
13:8	112n17

DEAD SEA SCROLLS

4QapGen

21:8–14	103n28

ANCIENT JEWISH SOURCES

Josephus

Jewish Antiquities

1.352	113n18
2.307	113n18
2.465	113n18
2.496	113n18
3.201	113n18
6.138	113n18
6.262	113n18
9.231	113n18
12.172	112
13.345	113n18
14.480	113n18

Philo

Against Flaccus

62	113
68	113n18

Allegorical Interpretation

1.94	112
2.53	111
2.64	111

3.210	111n10

On the Cherubim

63	112

On the Life of Joseph

33–34	139
34	137
34–36	138
35	138
67	139

On the Life of Moses

1.155	103

Who Is the Heir?

73	112n15

APOSTOLIC FATHERS

1 Clement

5:6–7	148

CLASSICAL AND CHRISTIAN WRITINGS

Aristotle

Nicomachean Ethics

1163b12–15	25n27
1385a35–1385b3	25

Poetics

4.1292a	138
1457b	110n6

Rhetoric

2.2.8	72
3.10.2	111n9
3.10.4	110n6
3.10.6	111n9

Cicero

Eighth Philippic

32	38

On Duties

1.47–48	25n27

On Friendship

95	138

On Old Age

10.33	116

Demosthenes

4 Philippic

10.44	138

Dinarchus

Demosthenes

1.31	138
4	138

Dio Cassius

Roman History

12.2	89
39.45.7	89
46.55.5	89
54.16	77
58.3.5	149

Diodorus Siculus

Library of History

5.32.1	88
9.4	138
31.9.1–4	149

Eusebius

Ecclesiastical History

2.25.4	148n41

Index of Citations

Ignatius

To the Ephesians
12:2 — 148n41

To the Trallians
5:1 — 125

Isocrates

To Demonicus
29 — 25n27, 72

Julian

Oration 1 [Panegyric in Honor of Constantius] 89

Juvenal

Satires
5.80–91 — 166

Livy
39.6.3 — 88

Lucian

Zeuxis or Antiochus
8–12 — 89

Pausanius

Description of Greece
10.21.6 — 89
10.22.3–4 — 89

Pliny

Natural History
7.1 — 117n27

Pliny the Younger

Letters
2.6 — 166n5

Plutarch

Advice to Bride and Groom, Moralia
142e — 81

Camillus
28.3 — 89

Comparison of Romulus with Theseus
2 — 138

Pyrrhus
26.6 — 89

Polybius
1.6.5 — 88
2.21.1–3 — 89

History
3.80 — 138
15.21 — 138

Polycarp

To the Philippians
9:1–2 — 148n41

Quintilian

Institutes of Oratory
11.1.3 — 138
11.1.14 — 138

Seneca

Letters
81.27 — 25n27

On Benefits
1.4.2 — 72
2.22.1 — 25n27, 72
2.24.2 — 25n27, 72
2.25.3 — 25n27
4.20.2 — 25n27
4.24.2 — 25n27

Strabo

Geography
4.4.2 — 89

Tertullian

Antidote for the Scorpion's Sting
15 — 148n41
15:5–6 — 148n41

The Prescription against Heretics
36 — 148n41

Shepherd of Hermas

Mandates
2.1.1 — 111n13

Similitudes
9.29.1 — 112n14

www.ingramcontent.com/pod-product-compliance
Lightning Source LLC
Chambersburg PA
CBHW021809220426
43662CB00006B/243